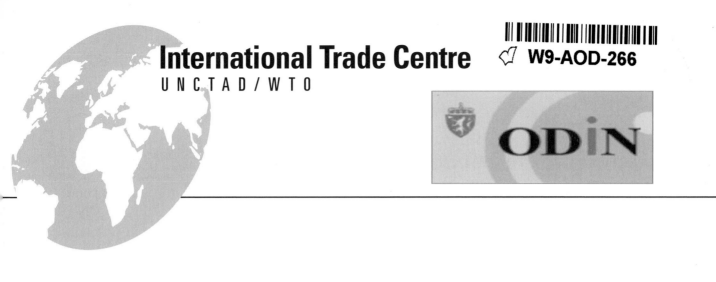

International Trade Centre
UNCTAD / WTO

W9-AOD-266

ODiN

Converting LDC Export Opportunities into Business

A strategic response

Geneva 2001

HF
1417.5
.C6
2001

ABSTRACT FOR TRADE INFORMATION SERVICES

2001

03 000
CON

INTERNATIONAL TRADE CENTRE UNCTAD/WTO
Converting LDC Export Opportunities into Business: A Strategic Response
Geneva: ITC/ODIN, 2001. xvi, 165 p.

Publication largely based on research and discussion papers prepared for the Business Sector Round Table held during the Third United Nations Conference on the Least Developed Countries (Brussels, 14-20 May 2001) – draws lessons from successful entrepreneurs in LDCs and describes how to turn opportunities into effective business; reviews possibilities in 13 trade sectors of major potential for LDCs and looks at measures that can facilitate the creation of an enabling environment, including the range of trade support services that can help exporters improve their performance and increase their market competitiveness.

Subject descriptors: **Least developed countries, Export promotion, Export potential, Trade policy, Cotton, Fish products, Wood products, Fruits, Vegetables, Spices, Oilseed products, Medicinal plants, Coffee, Cut flowers, Tourism, Business services.**

English, French

ITC, Palais des Nations, 1211 Geneva 10, Switzerland

Digital image on the cover: © PhotoDisc, Inc.

ITC/P99.E/DTCC/01-IX

ISBN 92-9137-197-1
United Nations Sales No. E.01.III.T.8

Foreword

Preparations were well under way for the Third United Nations Conference on the Least Developed Countries (UNLDC III) when conference officials, seeking to integrate a business dimension, asked the International Trade Centre (ITC) to organize an appropriate round table in parallel to UNLDC III.

ITC staff saw a unique chance to bring trade opportunities to the attention of a highly visible forum whose participants could consider how to exploit them for export success, sustainable development and poverty reduction in LDCs. Similarly, the Government of Norway saw an opportunity to advance the substantive preparations for UNLDC III, in line with its own private-sector development strategy, by hosting a Private-Sector Symposium in Oslo in January 2001 and by announcing on that occasion a substantial contribution for the ITC Business Sector Round Table (BSRT).

An enabling environment for business and investment is a precondition for the development of the private sector in LDCs. As this book underlines, the 'enabling environment' is a broad concept encompassing good governance, transparent public administration, functioning regulations and judicial systems, and adequate physical, social and institutional infrastructure. If LDCs and their peoples are to benefit from globalization, they must be empowered to utilize their capacities fully. This means that LDCs must reshape their domestic legal and institutional structure in order to ensure an enabling environment for enterprises. Developed countries must also change their approach to development cooperation and trade in order to obtain a more balanced partnership and a more equitable sharing of opportunities. It is in the common interest of all to do so.

An effective dialogue between government, private sector and civil society is necessary to foster an enabling environment for development. The Business Sector Round Table on 16 May 2001 proved to be an excellent opportunity for bringing key players from the public and private sectors together in order to facilitate public-private partnerships.

During the Round Table it became clear that a new generation of LDC exporter is coming to the fore, business leaders characterized by an entrepreneurial daring to venture into new fields and by dedication to quality and customer satisfaction. Models of perseverance and long-term commitment to their businesses, this new generation believes in its workers and gives attention to building their skills and sharing the fruits of success with them. It is keenly sensitive to social goals and to the importance of strategic partnerships and networking. Some 20 LDC entrepreneurs/exporters participated in the event. They were joined by other business persons and senior trade officials from LDCs, and by representatives of multilateral agencies and donor governments. In all, over 250 individuals participated or attended.

The initiative has already borne fruit. A Haitian entrepreneur met a Burundi business leader at the Round Table and started an immediate collaboration. Within one month he went on an exploratory mission to Burundi, with ITC support, to investigate possible business linkages. The Round Table, reports the Association of Benin Processors and Exporters of Cashew Nuts, was also the catalyst for immediate contacts and technical discussions with cashew exporters in LDCs (such as Burkina Faso and Senegal) and developing countries. These contacts, and meetings held later, have led to a project proposal for regional action by eight countries in favour of cashew export promotion.

For LDC exporters and for LDC and other officials working on trade development, the Government of Norway and ITC earnestly hope that this publication, too, will prove to be a useful guide and permanent source of inspiration. We are grateful to UNCTAD for the opportunity to organize the Round Table on the occasion of UNLDC III.

J. Denis Bélisle
Executive Director
International Trade Centre

Anne Kristin Sydnes
Minister of International Development
Government of Norway

About this book

ITC conceived the Business Sector Round Table for the Third United Nations Conference on the Least Developed Countries (14-20 May 2001) as an opportunity for analysing and revealing export potential in LDCs as a whole, focusing on sectors of particular importance to these countries and highlighting constraints as well as opportunities. Selected LDC exporters would tell their stories, demonstrating how they were able to overcome often formidable constraints and 'make it' in the highly competitive international environment. Export strategy processes underway in LDCs would be considered along with the enabling circumstances needed to replicate these exceptional export successes on a much wider scale. Finally, it was decided that a book, prepared for wide distribution in LDCs, would document the discussion and experience and serve as a road map for export development over the ensuing years. This was the initial vision which has now culminated in this publication.

At the Round Table, three main issues were posed for discussion. The first was: 'What realistic export opportunities are there for LDCs?' The two other issues were explored in more depth during an e-discussion, opened to a wider audience: 'How can successful exporters become less the exception and more the rule in LDCs?' and 'How can exports make the difference in reducing poverty?'

This book is based largely on research conducted for the Round Table. It notes the opportunities for LDCs in current markets (chapter 1). It draws lessons from successful entrepreneurs and describes a framework for turning opportunities into business (chapter 2). It reviews the possibilities in 13 trade sectors of major potential for LDCs (chapter 3). It looks at the measures that can encourage the creation of an enabling environment (chapter 4), including the range of trade support services that can help exporters to do better (chapter 5).

Research carried out for the Round Table is presented on a special web page (*http://www.intracen.org/bsrt/*), as are the conclusions of the event. The web page is continually updated.

The papers prepared for the event, with supplementary research, were rearranged and edited for this book. The volume also draws on contributions from the e-discussion. The book is intended to offer practical advice to strategy-makers on how to create an enabling environment for their own entrepreneurs on the basis of the experience of successful business leaders in LDCs.

Acknowledgements

The Government of Norway, ITC's partner in the Business Sector Round Table, gave generous financial support for the event and this publication. The cooperation of Knut Langeland, Counsellor, Permanent Mission of Norway to the United Nations Office at Geneva, was much appreciated.

The contributions of the following are acknowledged:

- *Martin V. Dagata,* for overall leadership and guidance from concept to the event and book preparation; *Ashish Shah*, for day-to-day management and coordination; *Peter Walters*, for spearheading pre-event research; *Bertil Byskov, Micaela Maftei* and their colleagues, for the product profiles; *Friedrich von Kirchbach* and *Jean-Michel Pasteels*, for background papers on LDC export opportunities; and *Doreen Conrad*, for assistance on the profiles of the services sectors.

- *Anant Vijay*, for identifying the LDC success stories and directing the preparation of the write-ups; *Imamo Ben Mohamed, Roberto Cordon, Christophe Casillas, Alex Corpuz, Francesco Geoffroy* and *Lilia Naas Hachem* for providing assistance.

- *Sunil Sinha,* for the research material for the Round Table, including the essence of the export opportunities framework. He and *Thierry Noyelle* provided ideas for the structure of the event and the interpretation of its proceedings.

- *Hendrik Roelofsen, Sabine Meitzel, Jean-François Bourque, Carlo Cattani, Karin Fock, Shyam Gujadhur, Hema Menon* and *Philip Williams* for their various contributions to the publication.

- *Peter Hulm,* for bringing the copy together and contributing text; *Leni Sutcliffe* for copy editing; *Isabel Droste Montgomery* and *Carmelita Endaya* for copy preparation; and *Françoise Kurdziel*, for designing and managing the BSRT web page.

Contents

CHAPTER 3

Export performance and prospects of LDCs: the sectoral opportunities

CHAPTER 4
Building an enabling environment   88

CHAPTER 5
Support services for export development in LDCs   111

APPENDICES

Boxes

Figures

Note

The following abbreviations are used:

ACP	African, Caribbean and Pacific (Group of States)
BSRT	Business Sector Round Table
CDI	Centre for the Development of Industry (European Commission)
EU	European Union
FAO	Food and Agriculture Organization of the United Nations
FDI	Foreign direct investment
FOB	Free on board
GATS	General Agreement on Trade in Services
GATT	General Agreement on Tariffs and Trade
GDP	Gross domestic product
GSP	Generalized System of Preferences
HACCP	Hazard analysis critical control points
IMF	International Monetary Fund
ISO	International Organization for Standardization
ITC	International Trade Centre UNCTAD/WTO
JITAP	Joint ITC/UNCTAD/WTO Integrated Technical Assistance Programme in Selected Least-Developed and Other African Countries
LDC(s)	Least developed country(ies)
MFA	Multifibre Arrangement
NGO(s)	Non-governmental organization(s)
ODA	Official development assistance
PRSP	Poverty Reduction Strategy Paper
PSD	Private-sector development
SME(s)	Small and medium-sized enterprise(s)
SQAM	Standardization, quality assurance, accreditation and metrology
TPO(s)	Trade promotion organization(s)
TSI(s)	Trade support institution(s)
UNCTAD	United Nations Conference on Trade and Development
UNDP	United Nations Development Programme
UNIDO	United Nations Industrial Development Organization
USAID	United States Agency for International Development
WTO	World Trade Organization

Measures

ha	Hectare
km	Kilometre
lb	Pound
m^2	Square metre
m^3	Cubic metre
sq. ft	Square foot

Box 1
LDCs: who they are

'Least developed countries' (LDCs) are officially designated as such on review by the United Nations Economic and Social Council. The criteria used as the basis for the designation include: low income (that is, a per capita gross domestic product – GDP – of under US\$ 800 for countries joining the list now); low levels of human development (a combined health, nutrition and education index); and economic vulnerability (a composite index based on indicators of instability, inadequate diversification and the handicap of small size). LDCs are home to 10.4% of the world's population.

The average per capita GDP in LDCs was US\$ 287 in 1998, compared with US\$ 27,402 in developed countries and US\$ 1,260 in all developing countries. People in LDCs can expect to live for only 51 years, and only one in four births is attended by trained health personnel. One child in 10 dies before his or her first birthday, and half the population is classified as illiterate.

The 49 LDCs are: Afghanistan, Angola, Bangladesh, Benin, Bhutan, Burkina Faso, Burundi, Cambodia, Cape Verde, Central African Republic, Chad, Comoros, Democratic Republic of the Congo, Djibouti, Equatorial Guinea, Eritrea, Ethiopia, Gambia, Guinea, Guinea-Bissau, Haiti, Kiribati, Lao People's Democratic Republic, Lesotho, Liberia, Madagascar, Malawi, Maldives, Mali, Mauritania, Mozambique, Myanmar, Nepal, Niger, Rwanda, Samoa, Sao Tome and Principe, Senegal, Sierra Leone, Solomon Islands, Somalia, Sudan, Togo, Tuvalu, Uganda, United Republic of Tanzania, Vanuatu, Yemen and Zambia.

Sources: *UNCTAD, The Least Developed Countries 2000 Report (United Nations Sales No. E.00.II.D.21); World Trade Organization.*

Chapter 1

World trade trends: challenges and opportunities for LDCs

The Third United Nations Conference on the Least Developed Countries, held in Brussels from 14 to 20 May 2001, focused the world's attention on the economic and social plight of LDCs,[1] the world's poorest 49 countries in terms of indicators such as GDP per head of population.

In the Programme of Action for the Least Developed Countries for the Decade 2001-2010 adopted at the Conference,[2] the international community recognized that the growth and development prospects of LDCs have suffered in the previous decade from declining financial resources (including a drop in development assistance), a heavy and unsustainable debt burden, falling or volatile commodity prices, complex trade barriers, lack of economic and export diversification or market access for key LDC products, and problems within the LDCs themselves. Now with a marginal share in world trade (0.54% in 2000), as the Programme of Action notes, LDCs (with the exception of oil producers) saw their share in world trade decline significantly in 2000.

Nevertheless, international trade *is* important for LDCs, and much more than many realize. It matters in both developmental and business terms. The import and the export trade provide a large proportion of the jobs available. In all, merchandise trade (imports and exports) make up 40% of GDP.

One of the seven commitments made in the Programme of Action is to enhance the role of trade in development. Trade will continue to be the LDC's mainstay for generating resources for growth and development, complementing development assistance and private capital flows in these countries. 'The share of trade in GDP remains relatively high in most LDCs compared with other developing countries,' the Programme of Action points out. And the actions to be taken range from capacity building of individuals and institutions to fostering regional trading arrangements and promoting the services trade of LDCs, whether in tourism, transport or back-office operations.

---

1   See box 1 for an explanatory note on LDCs.
2   *Programme of Action for the Least Developed Countries for the Decade 2001-2010* (United Nations General Assembly, A/CONF.191/11, 8 June 2001), hereinafter referred to as Programme of Action for LDCs or Programme of Action.

Box 2

United Nations Programme of Action for the Least Developed Countries for the Decade 2001-2010

Adopted by the Third United Nations Conference on the Least Developed Countries in Brussels on 20 May 2001

'1.   The least developed countries (LDCs) represent the poorest and weakest segment of the international community. The economic and social development of these countries represents a major challenge for LDCs themselves, as well as for their development partners. Extreme poverty, the structural weakness of their economies and the lack of capacities related to growth and development, often compounded by geographical handicaps, hamper efforts by these countries to improve effectively the quality of life of their peoples. These countries are characterized by their exposure to a series of vulnerabilities and constraints such as limited human, institutional and productive capacity; acute susceptibility to external economic shocks, natural and man-made disasters and communicable diseases; limited access to education, health and other social services and to natural resources; poor infrastructure; and lack of access to information and communication technologies. In the context of these vulnerabilities and constraints, needed international support has been inadequate. More commitment to provide increased and more effective international support for LDCs is required to overcome these conditions. To be effective, sustainable development strategies concerning LDCs should seek to address these vulnerabilities, taking into account the special needs, problems and potentials of each country...

2.   Ten years after the adoption of the Paris Programme of Action by the Second United Nations Conference on LDCs in 1990, the objectives and goals set therein have not been achieved. LDCs are being bypassed by the process of globalization, leading to their further marginalization... Declining availability of financial resources, domestic and external, including ODA, a heavy and unsustainable debt burden, falling or volatile commodity prices, complex trade barriers, lack of economic and export diversification and market access for key products which LDCs benefit from, as well as supply-side constraints, have seriously affected the growth and development prospects of LDCs.'

– Taken from the introduction to the Programme of Action for the Least Developed Countries.

The picture changes close up

In fact, close up, the gloomy overall picture of LDCs often changes for the better, sometimes quite radically, when individual regions, countries, sectors, industries and companies are looked at.

LDCs have penetrated several high-growth markets...

For example, though primarily boosted by oil exports, LDC trade is now recovering from the slump that lasted into the first part of the 1990s. In addition, manufactures rather than commodities now account for more than half of non-fuel exports from LDCs. What does this mean for the exporter and strategy-maker seeking to increase an LDC's presence on the international market?

Thirteen key export sectors

Analysing the statistics available, ITC has drawn a number of conclusions for LDCs seeking to improve their competitive position:

❑ Thirteen export sectors[3] have been important to LDCs, and are likely to continue to play a key role in their export trade in the future.

❑ Several LDCs derive more than half of their foreign exchange earnings from the export of services, though official statistics are distorted by financial transfers.

❑ LDCs have penetrated several high-growth markets and far-sighted entrepreneurs have built highly competitive companies and industries.[4]

Petroleum and gemstones are also important for a number of LDCs. Furthermore, these countries are gradually moving their products up the value chain in the leather sector.

Petroleum. The petroleum sector accounts for 25% of total exports from LDCs and, as a group, LDCs are net exporters of crude oil, led by Angola and Yemen. Nevertheless, a number of new actors are appearing on the oil scene, such as Equatorial Guinea and the Sudan. Among the other significant oil-exporting countries is the Democratic Republic of the Congo, with exports worth US$ 110 million in 1999. Oil exploration has been particularly intense in Niger over recent years, especially near Lake Chad and close to the Libyan border.

LDCs export mainly unrefined petroleum. Non-crude oil products make up only 5% of total exports in the petroleum sector, reflecting a lack of refining capacity and competitiveness. Hence, the oil-exporting LDCs are net importers of refined products.

Precious stones. Precious stones account for more than US$ 2 billion worth of exports, with raw diamonds making up the bulk of these exports. The real trade value is probably much higher than that estimated from trade statistics in the light of unrecorded trade. In terms of income generation, this is a key sector for countries like Angola, the Democratic Republic of the Congo, Liberia and Sierra Leone. However, the peculiarities of the market make it difficult to predict future opportunities in the sector, though India has demonstrated the benefits of taking a strategic approach to export development, particularly of gems and semi-precious stones.

Business achievers in adversity

..and many LDC businesses are making tremendous efforts, pushing forward against the current.

Thus, the overall disappointing trade performance of LDCs as a group should not overshadow the tremendous effort put in by members of the business community in these countries to move ahead, pushing forward against the current. Without these efforts, the situation would be far worse. One can say that successful firms and countries have been achievers in adversity. They show that there are tangible opportunities for countries and sectors despite very difficult overall conditions. For strategy-makers, the lesson of these entrepreneurs' success is that LDCs can take concrete steps to establish an enabling environment for business that promotes development and poverty reduction.

---

3   Cotton fabrics, textiles and clothing, tourism, fish products, business-related services, coffee, cotton and fibres, wood and wood products, oilseed products, fruits and nuts, vegetables, spices, cut flowers and foliage, and medicinal plants (see chapter 3).

4   A number of LDC entrepreneurial 'success stories' can be found in the boxes throughout this book and in appendix I. Contact information is also provided in the appendix.

LDCs and world trade in the 1990s

First, however, it is necessary to sketch some of the developments in world trade with which LDCs have had to contend, if only to point out the opportunities these have also presented for some entrepreneurs and industries in these countries.

Exports growing faster than production, with a big jump in LDCs

'For LDCs as a whole the growth of real per capita GDP...jumped significantly ...in 1995...the most sustained improvement in the terms of trade of the LDCs since the early 1980s...
– *UNCTAD, The Least Developed Countries 2000 Report*

LDC trade may be small on the international scale, but it certainly matters for development.

The non-oil exporting African LDCs today finance about half their imports through foreign trade.

During the 1990s, world production of goods by volume rose at about 2% yearly, while global exports of goods expanded at 6.5% a year. The annual rate of growth in the value of international trade in commercial services was also around 6% (in real terms). By the end of the 1990s, world exports of goods were worth over US$ 5,500 billion and exports of commercial services had climbed to over US$ 1,300 billion.

Merchandise exports from LDCs rose to US$ 34 billion in 2000. This was a jump of 27% from US$ 26.7 billion in 1999.

The increasing share in world trade achieved by LDCs stands in stark contrast to the declining trend they followed in the early and mid-1990s. The share they attained in 2000 (0.54%) was the highest in 15 years. Since merchandise trade (imports included) accounts for 40% of their GDP, a large proportion of employment in LDCs is directly or indirectly related to trade. LDC trade may be small on the international scale, but it certainly matters for business and development strategists. However, as figure 1 clearly shows, the turnaround in the LDC trade has not been enjoyed by the non-oil-exporting African countries.

It might seem surprising that the African LDCs, even when Angola is excluded, increased their export-to-import ratio from their low levels in the 1980s. Most LDCs have a trade deficit. Yet, since 1993, financing of imports by exports has significantly improved. In 2000 the ratio reached 80% (compared to 60% for African LDCs some 20 years ago) if oil exporters are included. Estimates by the

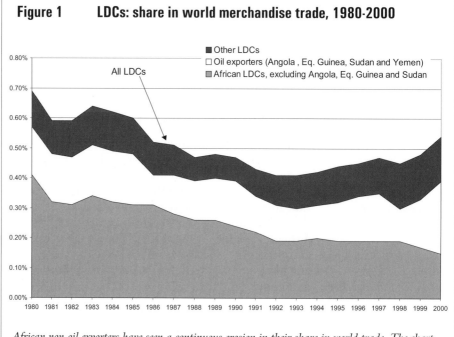

Figure 1   LDCs: share in world merchandise trade, 1980-2000

African non-oil exporters have seen a continuous erosion in their share in world trade. The chart points up the contrast between non-oil exporters and those that sell fossil fuels.

Sources: WTO Statistics Division and FAO for Eritrea.

World Trade Organization (WTO) reveal that the African LDCs have to some extent managed to reduce their imports in proportion to their exports. The non-oil-exporting African LDCs finance about half their imports through exports, a slow climb from the lows of 40% in the early 1980s.

Marked regional variations

There are marked regional variations in the impact of globalization on trade. Above-average growth in the value of merchandise trade is being recorded in Latin America and Asia (particularly by the Asian tigers). Below-average growth is found in Africa, the Middle East and Western Europe (including the European Union).

A relatively small number of countries account for a large proportion of world trade.

Moreover, a comparatively small number of countries continue to account for a large proportion of global trade. Among the leading 24 and 25 exporters of goods and of services (which in both instances hold about 83% of world trade), the industrialized countries predominate, as expected. It should be noted, however, that the newly industrialized countries/areas, such as the Republic of Korea, Mexico, Taiwan Province (China), Malaysia and Thailand, have made impressive progress in developing their export capacity in manufactures.

LDCs specialize in sectors where world trade is not dynamic

Bangladesh and Cambodia, both strong exporters of textiles and garments, did well. Senegal, Haiti and Lesotho also improved their trade position in this sector.

Only three of the 30 leading export sectors in LDCs – men's clothing, women's clothing and other apparel – saw an increase in world demand above the average growth of world trade for all goods in value terms (an estimated 2.7%), as figure 2 indicates. However, Bangladesh and Cambodia, strong in the textiles and garments sector, achieved major gains. Senegal, Haiti and Lesotho also improved their trade performance over the 1995-2000 period in the same sector.

Table 1	Trade performance of LDC garment exporters, 1999							
	BANGLADESH		**CAMBODIA**		**MYANMAR**		**HAITI**	
	Value	Rank	Value	Rank	Value	Rank	Value	Rank
Export value, 1999 (US$ million)	3,027	17	947	37	361	56	268	60
Annual export growth (1995-1999)	16%	46	136%	4	64%	8	74%	6
Per capita exports, 1999 (US$/inhabitant)	24.9	66	92.2	39	7.9	90	36.6	59
Number of major products	17	63	10	85	15	66	4	110
Number of major markets	4	43	2	87	3	66	1	127

Position 1 in the ranking corresponds to the best performer among 130 exporting countries.

ITC compared and ranked the trade performance of 184 countries in 14 different sectors in 1999. LDCs are not systematically at the bottom of the rankings. Cambodia, for instance, was the 37th largest exporter of garments out of 130 countries worldwide, with exports of close to US$ 1 billion. Myanmar and Haiti were among the 10 fastest growing garment exporters, and their exports were not negligible, at more than US$ 250 million each.

Information on every LDC, with export performance profiles, is available from the ITC website at www.intracen.org.

Figure 2   LDCs: export profile

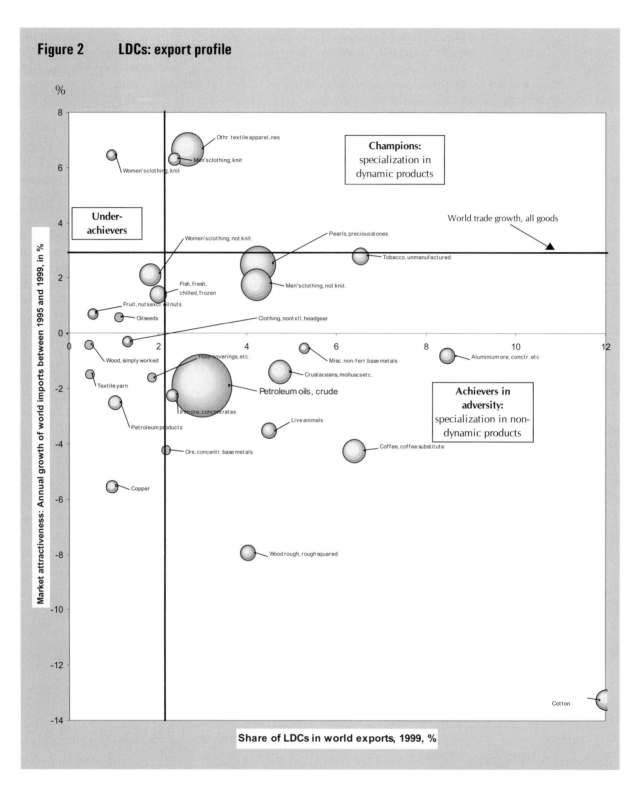

Source: ITC calculations based on COMTRADE statistics.

Note: The size of the circles corresponds to export values in LDCs in 1999.

'The terms-of-trade of the
LDCs worsened in 1998 and
1999 with a drop in
commodity prices whose
breadth and depth has
not been seen since the
early 1980s.'
– *UNCTAD, The Least
Developed Countries 2000
Report*

In general, however, LDC exports have been highly dependent on commodity prices, of which the deterioration has been dramatic during the second half of the 1990s. In 2000 the trade situation for many LDCs worsened, as the prices of non-oil primary commodities remained low when the prices of oil products went up. Since the oil price shocks occurred in the context of a historic 10.5% growth in the volume of world trade over 1999, this indicates that most non-oil-producing LDCs saw their share in world trade decline significantly in 2000.

But manufactures are playing a growing part in exports

Nevertheless, a number of LDCs are escaping the traditional reliance on commodity trade to earn foreign currency. In Africa, for example, the 1999 export value of manufactures was higher than earnings from food exports or from non-food commodities. Even before the oil price boom, according to ITC estimates, manufactures were the largest group of products in exports by value (though they have now been overtaken by fuels). In the second half of the 1990s, for non-African LDCs, exports of manufactures increased by more than half to over US$ 7 billion.

Globalization and liberalization

Most commentators would argue that there are both 'old' and 'new' forces driving globalization forward, even if self-reinforcing cumulative effects on both demand and supply have no doubt been important in pushing both output and trade. The second half of the twentieth century witnessed sustained progress in reducing man-made barriers to trade through multilateral, regional and unilateral liberalization. Between industrial countries, the first two liberalization impulses have been particularly important, notably the GATT/WTO-orchestrated multilaterally negotiated reductions of non-tariff and tariff barriers.

For developing countries, unilateral liberalization has been important

Unilateral liberalization has been more important than multilateral or regional agreements in lowering trade barriers in developing countries.

For developing countries a large number of regional integration schemes have been established. To varying degrees, these have played a role in lowering barriers, albeit a limited one. More important has been the influence of *unilateral* trade liberalization programmes, often instituted as part of the conditional lending arrangements of the International Monetary Fund (IMF) and the World Bank.

Declining 'natural' barriers

The traditional sources of trade generation have been reinforced by declining 'natural' barriers. Containerization and the increased scale of international trade have reduced the unit costs of international transport. Increasingly, however, a major impetus to international commercial contact and coordination of international production has been given by the communications revolution. Telecommunications improvements and electronic communications have dramatically reduced the difficulties and costs of transactions at great distance and across time zones.

International fragmentation of industrial processes

These technological changes, combined with the changing social, economic and political environment for foreign investment and inter-country commercial engagement, have increased international fragmentation of industrial processes. The reduction of capital controls, increased integration of capital markets and changed attitudes to foreign direct investment (FDI) have fostered multinational enterprises, and these transnational corporations, with wider market horizons, have helped to spread technologies and product innovation.

Market access and the Uruguay Round

The Agreements resulting from the Uruguay Round (concluded in 1994 after eight years of negotiations) went into effect in 1995. Developing and least developed countries have been given varying periods of transition for implementing these Agreements.

'Most important is compliance with, and implementation by, the developed market economies, both in letter and in spirit, of the various WTO market access provisions for the LDCs to have an even playing ground to compete internationally.'
– Akmal Hossain, a trade consultant from Bangladesh, in the ITC e-Discussion

The average applied tariff rates in developed countries for many manufactured goods will be very low indeed. Nevertheless, protection will continue to be high in a few sensitive product areas such as textiles and clothing, where trade is significant and imports are responsive to price changes.

In addition, substantial tariffs will remain in many industrial countries, providing a loading against imports from developing countries. This makes it more difficult for them to develop downstream processing.

The Uruguay Round will also have a major impact on the incidence of non-tariff measures, reducing their use over agreed phase-in periods. For developed countries, the two outstanding features will be the reduction in the use of non-tariff measures in agriculture, principally through tariffication or elimination of prohibited measures, and the reduced application of export restraints on textiles and clothing. The phase-out of the import-quota-driven Multifibre Arrangement (MFA) and the gradual integration of the textiles and clothing sector into WTO is being effected over a 10-year period.

Agricultural gains

Overall, the Agreement on Agriculture was undoubtedly one of the main achievements of the Uruguay Round. The Agreement brought the agricultural sector under more transparent rules and set the stage for future progressive liberalization of trade in the sector. The Agreement provided for the elimination or tariffication of non-tariff measures, the full binding of the new tariffs by developed and developing countries and phased tariff reductions, and cuts in the level of domestic support measures as well as in export subsidies and the volume of subsidized exports. It also produced substantial tariff cuts for a wide variety of fruit, vegetable and tropical products, which stand to benefit LDCs.

The main products exempted from tariffication were rice and, for developing countries, some staple foods. Further, import licensing is still widely used as a sanitary and phytosanitary measure. Many countries also chose to introduce tariff quotas for a number of products and some developing countries regard the prohibition of the use of variable levies not as an absolute ban but rather as an admonition not to exceed bound levels.

The Agreement's shortcomings included setting tariffs at high levels, thus reducing the potential benefits from tariffication. Moreover, the level of domestic support and even export subsidies remained high for some products. Further liberalization of this sector will benefit LDC exporters.

Regional integration and trade opportunities

For trade in many goods and services, the best prospects lie in supplying neighbouring countries. Such countries may well have formed natural trading zones before the advent of the colonial powers and/or historical divisions into countries. Moreover, differences in climatic conditions, factor endowment and natural resources may give rise to trade in goods and services that may not be possible with more distant international markets.

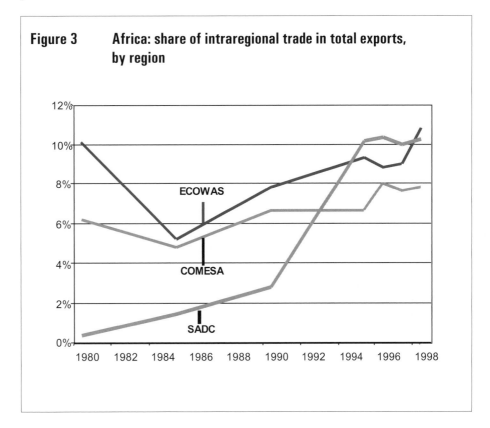

Figure 3   Africa: share of intraregional trade in total exports, by region

This chart shows the evolution of intraregional trade as a percentage of total exports for three African subregions: the Economic Community of West African States (ECOWAS), Common Market for Eastern and Southern Africa (COMESA, consisting mainly of East African countries) and Southern African Development Community (SADC). All three regions follow a clear upward trend. COMESA's intraregional trade has grown twice as fast as trade with third countries. After the end of the anti-apartheid boycott of South Africa, intraregional SADC exports have evolved rapidly. Inclusive of the non-recorded trade among neighbouring countries, this share is significantly higher.

The number of regional trade agreements (RTAs) has risen rapidly in recent years. The extent to which RTAs overlap has also increased, although there are significant variations in product coverage and rules of origin. On the whole, the newer agreements tend to have deeper coverage, extending beyond the exchange of tariff concessions into areas of domestic policies; a number of agreements now also cover the services sector. Around 250 agreements are now in force, including 170 notified to GATT/WTO.

Although developed countries may reduce tariff and non-tariff barriers, the greatest barriers to trade will remain between developing countries.

Trade within effective RTAs has generally been growing much faster than trade with non-members. An analysis of seven regional groupings (APEC, the European Union, NAFTA, ASEAN, CEFTA, MERCOSUR and the Andean Community)[5] shows that, on average, imports from other members increased at 7% a year in the period 1990-1998, while imports from non-members increased at 5.5%.

For LDCs the important RTAs are COMESA and SADC in Africa, the fledgling SAFTA[6] in South Asia and APEC. Though progress has been made in some products and in trade facilitation in general, these RTAs have yet to show their full potential as drivers of trade and economic integration between the countries concerned.

> Trade within regions covered by regional trade agreements has been growing faster than trade with non-members.

Plurilateral agreements and other arrangements

More significant for LDCs has been the evolution of plurilateral agreements, such as the Cotonou Agreement, replacing the Lomé Convention, which offers preferential access (often duty- and quota-free) to the EU market for African, Caribbean and Pacific (ACP) countries. As a consequence of the Uruguay Round, the ACP States' preferential access to the EU market has been reduced. However, many studies have shown that the ACP countries have benefited from preferential access only with regard to a few products. This situation is not expected to change much as a result of the EU Trade Ministers' decision in February 2001 to give the world's LDCs free access to EU markets for all products other than weapons by the year 2009.

Canada, Japan, the Republic of Korea, New Zealand and Norway have also announced significant measures to improve market access for LDCs. And for the African LDCs, the African Growth and Opportunities Act (AGOA), signed into law in the United States in 2000, offers duty- and quota-free access to the American market, although it is too recent for its impact to be evaluated.

Agenda for more negotiations

The WTO Agreements have established a built-in agenda for further negotiations to improve market access in certain areas, e.g. agriculture and services. Developing countries have argued that a further reduction in tariff protection and production subsidies in the agricultural sector, for example, would result in substantial increases in imports into Western Europe, Japan, the Middle East, North Africa and India. LDCs have the opportunity to benefit from this growth.

In the case of services, the extension of WTO disciplines to a wider range of services sectors is planned, thus broadening the scope of the General Agreement on Trade in Services (GATS). This should accelerate the already rapid growth in the trade in services.

Beyond the built-in agenda, there are likely to be a range of both traditional and new issues affecting market access that will enter into future multilateral and regional trade negotiations. Further liberalization of the trade in manufactures could be achieved by cutting average tariffs and reducing tariff escalation.

---

5   APEC: Asia-Pacific Economic Cooperation forum (not an RTA); NAFTA: North American Free Trade Agreement; ASEAN: Association of South-East Asian Nations; CEFTA: Central European Free Trade Agreement; MERCOSUR: Southern Common Market.
6   COMESA: Common Market for Eastern and Southern Africa; SADC: Southern African Development Community; SAFTA: South Asian Free Trade Area.

Erosion of privileges?

An issue of concern to many developing countries, however, is that further multilateral liberalization and negotiation of reciprocal regional arrangements will erode even further any tariff preferences they have under the Generalized System of Preferences (GSP). However, it should be recognized that the benefits to developing countries of preferences are limited and often highly constrained, and that most-favoured-nation (MFN) liberalization erodes intra-industrial-country preferences (in Europe and North America) and creates large opportunities for displacement by developing countries of exports from the industrialized world.

In general, preferences have already been pretty well eroded by the combination of MFN liberalization and regional developments. MFN has to be the only answer in the longer term and the concern is with competitiveness during the transition.

Against this, however, one must place the concern of many developing countries that improved market access from the lowering of traditional trade policy barriers merely induces defensive responses. Recent decades have already witnessed a growth in the use of contingent protection measures (e.g. anti-dumping measures) in both developed and developing countries. In addition there is a concern that the use of standards (product, environmental and labour standards) might feature increasingly in multilateral and regional trade negotiations and serve to restrict market access.

Implications for exports from LDCs

The period set for special and differential treatment for LDCs under the Uruguay Round is now running out.

LDCs are likely to confront major new challenges in international trade policies as the transition periods given to them for the implementation of the WTO Agreements come to an end. The major challenges concern preshipment inspection, intellectual property rights (IPRs) and trade-related investment measures (TRIMs). As regards IPRs, LDCs may wish to discuss their lack of access to IPR protection systems and how to protect their trademarks, knowledge systems, and indigenous plants and other raw materials from unfair exploitation by foreign companies.

The financial services sector

The absence of an efficient financial services sector is itself a major impediment to the growth of the private sector and trade in many LDCs.

The expansion of WTO rules and disciplines to various services sectors represents both an opportunity and a threat. Liberalization, particularly of financial services, has been viewed with concern by LDCs. Many still have highly protected financial markets, with State ownership of inefficient commercial banks. They fear that, in an open market, domestic institutions will be unable to compete with foreign banks, leading to their collapse.

While these concerns are not to be minimized, the absence of an efficient financial services sector is itself a major impediment to the growth of the private sector and trade in many LDCs. There are thus benefits to be obtained to offset the adverse consequences of liberalization. Moreover, provided systems are put in place for the mutual recognition of professional qualifications, LDCs could gain substantially from the broadening of GATS.

The question of standards

The rise in standards and certification requirements in developed markets reflects customer concerns with health, safety and the environment, as well as with the ethical issues of the use of child and forced labour. For LDCs, these requirements represent formidable challenges. They lack SQAM (standardization, quality assurance, accreditation and metrology) systems and are therefore unable to meet international standards. They also do not have access to cost-effective systems of certification. The investment required is well beyond the means of most, if not all, LDCs.

These are issues that will no doubt form the subject of intense negotiations during the next round of multilateral trade negotiations. Whatever the outcome, compliance with international standards and certification to these standards will be required of LDC exporters, if for no other reason than to meet the growing demand of consumers in developed countries. In these circumstances, compliance can be a source of competitive advantage to LDC exporters, though they will need to obtain assistance to implement SQAM systems.

Environment-related barriers will get higher

Contrary to the widely held view that non-tariff barriers work against the more advanced exporting countries, particularly automobile manufacturers, a recent study carried out by ITC, using the United Nations COMTRADE database and UNCTAD's database on trade barriers, found that LDCs have been significantly more affected than other developing nations by environment-related trade barriers (ETBs). Though only half of LDC exports consist of products that could be affected by ETBs, 40% of these products are

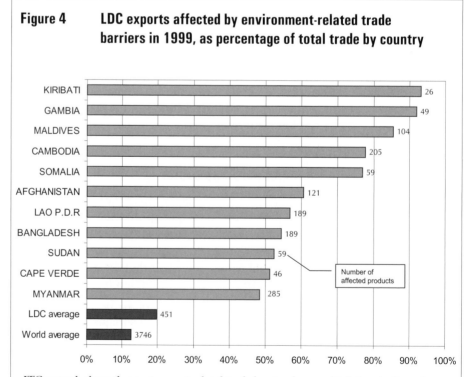

Figure 4   LDC exports affected by environment-related trade barriers in 1999, as percentage of total trade by country

ITC research shows that environment-related trade barriers have multiplied and affect a large part of world trade. Significantly, LDCs are the group most seriously hit by these barriers.

Source: *ITC estimates on the basis of primary data from: United Nations Statistics Division, COMTRADE database; and UNCTAD, database on trade barriers.*

directly subject to such controls, compared to less than 20% for developing, transition and developed countries. ETB protection peaked for food items and for plants, bulbs and cut flowers. At least 90% of world trade in these products was subject to ETBs in 1999. The total value of international trade directly affected by ETBs amounts to US$ 679 billion – 13% of world trade.

In the future, LDCs may face even tougher hurdles as a result of growing environmental concerns worldwide. This is especially the case for agricultural products, which are among the products most exported by LDCs. The high cost for exporters of complying with such trade barriers means that the impact could be critical.

The premium on international competitiveness

'Before exporting, you have to produce, and produce well.'
– *Nancy Abeiderrahmane, camel milk entrepreneur from Mauritania, in the ITC e-Discussion*

Improved market access is likely to be accompanied by further loss of preferential access. This will place greater premium on international competitiveness. The size and/or locational advantages of some emerging exporters (such as China and Mexico) could lead to the perception that size and first-mover advantages will exclude later entrants and reinforce the agglomeration or concentration of international production and exporting activity. There is a suggestion that LDCs will not be able to benefit from the ladder-of-development effect because of their small size and distance from international markets, and because they are not first movers. Some fear that, in practice, they have no absolute factor cost advantages over their more successful developing country competitors.

Relative, not absolute, costs are the key

There is, however, considerable evidence that relative (not absolute) factor supplies and factor costs play a major role in explaining the shares and the broad commodity patterns of trade obtained by individual countries. Indeed, the fragmentation of international production means that there is even more scope for specialization in specific processes or components that require particular input mixes. The increasing refinement of product chains raises opportunities for matching the production (input) requirements of particular stages or processes of production with appropriate supplies available globally.

Add value to exports to overcome the obstacles

Moreover, there are various opportunities for LDCs to exploit the increasing fragmentation of markets, for example by adopting niche market strategies for discrete market segments. This would help to mitigate the disadvantages of location, size and entering markets after the first movers.

The key to success lies in converting comparative advantages into competitive advantages and overcoming constraints to exporting by establishing an enabling environment for export development.

Chapter 2

Lessons from LDC business successes: an export opportunities framework

What kind of opportunity is available to LDCs for increasing the value of their exports? The work of the International Trade Centre (ITC) with developing and transition economies, and in particular with LDCs, has highlighted several possibilities for countries to do better in international trade. The sectoral profiles presented in chapter 3 highlight the message that even markets characterized by declining prices and oversupply (the coffee market is an example) offer opportunities for increased trade.

Even markets characterized by declining prices and oversupply, such as the coffee market, offer opportunities for increasing the value of exports.

'Success stories' among LDC entrepreneurs suggest that there are a number of common elements which other businesses can adopt in response to the challenge of making a mark in international business despite the small proportion of world trade in which LDCs have been competitive. For example, LDCs can move up the value chain by shifting resources to higher-value products, improving market positioning, shortening the distribution chain and downstream processing. LDCs can turn comparative advantage into competitive advantage by attending to productivity and quality issues. Addressing technical and structural barriers can turn a constraint into an opportunity.

The main types of opportunities available to LDCs can be grouped under five headings:

- Moving up the value chain;

- Niche markets and product innovation;

- The services revolution;

- Turning comparative into competitive advantage; and

- Overcoming technical and structural barriers.

The sixth element: South-South trade.

One other opportunity should be mentioned: South-South trade. Regional trade, as pointed out earlier, is growing faster than world trade and the potential it offers LDCs has already been highlighted. While transport can be a major obstacle to international trade, turning to neighbouring country markets can shorten the distribution chain and move a business up the profit ladder. Regional markets, because of similarities in consumption patterns, will often provide a company with a more easily satisfied customer than an advanced industrial market. In addition, as the Meet in Africa trade fair for the leather industry has shown (see box 15 at the end of this chapter), South-South trade has made it easier for many companies to climb the value chain by establishing business links across national borders within a region. The opportunity is often neglected, however, because so many institutions in developing countries focus on South-North trade rather than on exploiting less obvious markets.

Moving up the value chain

It is often argued that many LDCs have lost share in world export markets because their main exports have been primary commodities, the prices of which have, with few exceptions, fallen over the past 30 years. Thus the deterioration of terms of trade for LDCs has caused the decline in their shares in world trade. As a consequence, many countries have attempted to industrialize, often by stimulating downstream processing of their principal exports. The aim has been to increase value added and to position themselves in markets for manufactures that have not experienced as steep a decline in prices.

Focusing on commodity prices alone tends to detract attention from the many trade opportunities that are available to LDCs...

While the drop in commodity prices has no doubt contributed to poor export performance, focusing on this alone tends to detract attention from the many opportunities available to LDCs for improving the unit values of their exports. Downstream processing is only one method of increasing value, success in which may call for skills and resources that LDCs do not possess. And, sometimes, it may not even result in the highest rise in value.

Downstreaming policies – what not to do

...but downstream processing may call for high levels of capital investment, technical know-how and market knowledge that businesses in LDCs lack. It should not be the only strategy.

Policies intended to encourage downstream processing by banning or taxing the export of unprocessed primary commodities have, on occasion, resulted in a collapse of commodity exports without a commensurate increase in the output of manufactured goods. This is because downstream processing may call for high levels of capital investment, technical know-how and market knowledge that businesses in LDCs lack. In the case of certain commodities, the returns on processing may be so low as to make this unsuitable for capital-constrained LDCs.

Nevertheless, downstream processing may be a desirable or a suitable strategy. It can be not only a source of higher value added but also a means of keeping the business competitive.

These arguments notwithstanding, downstreaming should not be regarded as the only possible strategy for adding value. Instead, it should be seen as one of many ways to add value to traditional exports, such as:

- Shifting resources to higher-value products;

- Improving market positioning by targeting higher-value segments; and

- Shortening the distribution chain.

Box 3

United Republic of Tanzania: breaking into the tough market for gemstones

Company: *Glitter Gems Ltd, a company based in Arusha, in the northern part of the United Republic of Tanzania, has shown that a new company can establish itself in a difficult international market in 10 years. It currently exports 99% of its output. Tanzanites account for over 95% of these exports, rubies and sapphires most of the rest. Mining is carried out by about 100 workers. Cutting is the work of four, sorting another four. Purchasing and accounting employ another four. The products are sold mainly through agents in Germany, India, the Netherlands, the United Kingdom and the United States.*

Performance: *Initially, Glitter Gems was solely a dealer in rough stones, bought from small miners and sold to local buyers. Three years after its establishment in 1990, the company had developed a network of contacts with foreign buyers. By 1995 Glitter Gems had diversified its operations to include mining on its own account and cutting, using its own facilities.*

From then on production and exports grew fast. Specializing in all Tanzanian gemstones, the firm has a varied stock of rough and faceted gemstones. The selection ranges across sapphires, rubies, garnets, tanzanites (violet and blue gems) and lesser known gems such as spinel (a ruby-like gem) and alexandrite (which appears green in daylight and red under artificial light).

Its export business trebled from US$ 360,611 in 1997 to US$ 1.1 million in 1999. It is now the major mining, processing and exporting company in the country.

Key success factors:

❑ *Glitter Gems makes unceasing efforts to build relationships with its clients – essential in the gems industry for establishing a reputation for trustworthiness. The Managing Director makes sure he stays close to the market by visiting agents in Europe, the United States and Asia frequently, sometimes once a month.*

❑ *The firm has shown it knows how to adapt to proven marketing channels. It has also built up close relationships with workers and suppliers, and is recognized for treating workers decently.*

Constraints:

❑ *The gem business is one of the most difficult to break into. Personal relations count for a great deal in gaining customers. The distribution chain behaves like a club, pretty much barred to outsiders. Banks do not like to provide working capital to gem cutters, particularly newcomers. In fact, few banks have qualified valuers of precious stones, so they do not treat gems as collateral. The first three years of the company's existence demanded patience. The Managing Director believes most entrepreneurs would have quit or not considered further serious investment in such tough circumstances. On the other side of the coin, few Tanzanian entrepreneurs would have launched into such a venture, preferring less demanding and less risky activities such as trading.*

❑ *Glitter Gems has succeeded in breaking down the commercial barriers to a company from a least developed economy, establishing itself as a value-added finisher of products in a demanding industry. However, it estimates it could sell five times more gems than it is now able to export. The scarcity and uneven distribution of stones in the mines and within the mining area pose a problem. There is a shortage of trained cutters – the company has hired foreigners to fill the gap. The country also lacks qualified gemmologists for identifying stones and assessing their quality.*

❑ *Fuel prices are another burden, accounting for 50% of production costs.*

Shifting resources to higher-value products

As with economic development generally, export development requires a continuous shift of resources from lower-value to higher-value uses. Achieving this objective, in turn, calls for the development of efficient and flexible markets for production factors so that land, labour and capital can move as easily as possible to higher-value uses in response to price signals from the market. The conditions necessary for enabling such resource shifts are discussed in chapter 4.

Agricultural exports: higher-value exports

The agricultural sector provides perhaps the best illustration of how, in practice, flexible factor markets can contribute to higher-value exports. Value added per unit of land, labour and capital varies tremendously with the crop. Provided that climatic conditions permit it, that farmers have the requisite knowledge and that there are no insurmountable problems of market access, it should be possible continuously to increase the value of agricultural exports. For example, in the Tanzanian north, land used for cultivating low-value staples is gradually being turned over to growing vegetables for export to European Union (EU) markets. The more progressive farmers have also spotted new opportunities in floriculture, where returns on land and capital are higher. If the pattern followed in Kenya is replicated in the United Republic of Tanzania, the process of value addition will continue by widening the range of crops to include baby vegetables and off-season fruits for the EU market.

In agriculture, value-added per unit of land, labour and capital varies tremendously with the crop.

Two ITC case studies illustrate this process at the level of individual business. Mairye Estates of Uganda started by exporting vegetables. Finding that there were better returns from floriculture, the company has increasingly focused on that market. Terra Nova Farm of Zambia has evolved from supplying staples to the domestic market to producing and exporting vegetables, finally arriving at the choice of high-quality Arabica coffee as the most attractive crop.

Know the key success factors

Entrepreneurial businesses in other sectors also follow the same path. They are continuously searching for higher-value products in which to diversify. If such continuous searches for higher-value products are to become more widespread so that whole sectors, countries and regions take this approach, strategy-makers and entrepreneurs need to be aware of the key success factors: knowledge of market opportunities and cultivation/production methods, support in marketing and meeting standards and quality requirements, and the presence of entrepreneurial businesses.

Improving market positioning

At its simplest, improving the quality and design of a product or its presentation should strengthen its competitive position, allowing the exporter to increase market share. It is also possible that improvements in quality, design or presentation enable the exporter to target more attractive market segments, thus increasing the price that can be charged and the unit value of exports.

Some LDC entrepreneurs have been able to counter competitive pressures by astute reorganization and adjustment of their business.

The development of strong brands that can command premiums in the market or at least generate customer loyalty is another effective way to improve market positioning and increase value. There are numerous examples of exporters in LDCs who have developed new markets only to have competitors enter the market, cut prices and hence reduce the value added. Some LDC entrepreneurs have been able to counter such pressures by astute reorganization and adjustment of their business. Malawi's packaging champion PIM instituted a cost-cutting Total Productive Maintenance programme with worker support to recapture market share lost in its export and domestic markets (see box 4).

Box 4
Malawi: packaging champion beats the importers

Company: *Packaging Industries Malawi Limited (PIM) has become Malawi's leading manufacturer of paper-based packing materials for the domestic and export markets. It has 230 line workers. Its 1999 profits totalled over MK 52 million (about US$ 1 million). A growing percentage of its turnover is derived from exports.*

Performance: *Since it began operations in 1969, initially restricting itself to cement bags, PIM's product range has grown to include corrugated cartons, paper sacks, packing cartons for liquids, tea sacks, egg trays and toilet tissues. The bulk of these products is used for Malawi's main agricultural exports – tobacco and tea.*

The company's packaging materials are also used for domestic consumer goods such as beer and detergents. The company derived just under 90% of its turnover in 2000 from the domestic market. Mozambique, the United Republic of Tanzania, Zambia and Zimbabwe, its main export markets, accounted for the balance.

Key success factors: *PIM's current leading position is due to several factors. These include diversification of its product range, a duty-free agreement with neighbouring Zimbabwe, foreign investment and a nimble response to challenges in the market, especially in 1998.*

In that year, export earnings suffered when the company's products became too costly in key markets. Challenges included high inflation, big corporate taxes, prohibitive interest rates, devaluation of the local currency, the cost of importing raw materials and the emergence of imported packaging substitutes. But after cost-cutting measures were implemented under a Total Productive Maintenance programme which featured employee participation in the company, PIM regained its competitive advantage and recaptured lost market share in both its export and domestic markets.

Constraints: *Most of PIM's raw materials are imported from South Africa and Europe. Nevertheless, for Malawi, the company is considered a fine example of import substitution. Its strategy could well be emulated in other sectors of the economy to redress the current trend of closing or scaling down local factories in favour of importing finished goods.*

High returns from better positioning

It should be noted that the returns from improving market positioning through better quality, design, presentation and branding can be very high. For example, the CIF (cost, insurance and freight) price of a T-shirt with little design content, sold virtually as a commodity to a printer based in a developed country, is under US$ 1. The price of a 'designer' T-shirt printed in the country of origin can be several times this amount, representing a substantial return against the cost of design and printing. And, there need not be any proprietary knowledge involved. The difference in the price realized for a vegetable sold 'loose' as against the same vegetable sold washed and trimmed in consumer packs represents a highly attractive return to the investment in processing and packaging.

Shortening the distribution chain

Traditionally, LDCs have channelled their exports through importers which then market the product to wholesalers, end-users or retailers. The disadvantages of working through a large number of intermediaries include poor knowledge of market trends, inability to gain competitive advantage by adapting the product to specific customer needs and, of course, the margin lost at each stage of the distribution chain.

There is a trend in developed countries for shorter distribution chains. This offers opportunities for exporters in LDCs.

There is a trend in developed countries for shorter distribution chains. This is prompted by the use of supply-chain management to gain competitive advantage through specialization, total quality management and just-in-time supply. End-users and large retailers wish to be in close contact with their suppliers to be able to control more effectively the timeliness and quality of supply and avoid having to carry out processes in which they lack competitive advantage.

This offers opportunities for LDC exporters to shorten their distribution chains and, by doing so, to increase the value of their exports. The least that is possible is better understanding of customer requirements so that the product can be adapted to their needs and the exporter is better informed of market trends. At best, not only will the exporter benefit from better customer knowledge, but also the company will earn for itself the margin that previously went to the intermediary and take charge of its own marketing.

Bypassing intermediaries

By way of example, there is a growing trend in the cut-flower market to bypass the Netherlands flower auction (which still handles a large proportion of the flower trade) and to supply flowers direct to supermarkets. The main benefits are better understanding of customers and their requirements as well as improved marketing. Prices realized, net of the additional costs of serving the supermarkets, are practically the same. But exporters prefer to supply the supermarkets direct because of the stability and security of knowing what is happening to their product in the market.

The long-term benefits of shortening the distribution chain should not be underestimated. It can serve as a catalyst for change.

The long-term benefits of shortening the distribution chain should not be underestimated. It served as the catalytic change that has allowed Frager, based in Haiti, to become the world's largest supplier of vetiver (see box 5). Another example, taken from the tourism industry, is that of the large Jamaican all-inclusive chains that perform the role of tour operators in the United States and European source markets. They are thus better able to control the marketing of their product and earn tour operator margins.

Box 5

Haiti: adding value to vetiver through direct user contact

Company: *Frager is a family-owned business started in 1958. The current Chief Executive Officer, Pierre Léger, took charge in 1984. It produces vetiver, an essential oil used by perfumeries.*

Performance: *From its modest beginnings, Frager is now the world's largest supplier of vetiver. Exports have risen from 20 tons in 1991 to 80 tons, worth more than US$ 5 million.*

Key success factors: *The turning point in the business was the decision by Pierre Léger to look beyond its principal client, a United States supplier of essential oils, to end users of vetiver. He contacted European perfumeries, including a Swiss firm, and promoted the distinctive characteristics of Frager's product – 'the true Haitian vetiver, pure, natural and without additives'. The properties and quality of the product reinforced the claim and has resulted in a solid and loyal customer base. Frager's strong customer orientation is reflected in its tailoring its products to its clients' needs and sharing with them knowledge of the properties and characteristics of the product. Frager does not advertise but uses direct customer contact and the concept of customer partnership to cement its relations with customers.*

The other contributors to Frager' success are:

❑ *Frager's support to its out-growers. The business does not carry out farming activities, but has strong links with its suppliers.*

❑ *Respect for, and preservation of, the environment.*

❑ *Excellent employee relations.*

❑ *Investment in modern plant and equipment.*

❑ *Strong research and development capability.*

Constraints: *Frager's success has been achieved despite the most challenging circumstances. The years of neglect of investment in Haiti's physical and business support infrastructure, underdeveloped financial markets and a less than helpful business climate have been strong constraints to the growth of the business. Less than 2% of loans from Haitian banks are given to agricultural enterprises. Therefore, Frager has had to fund roads, power and water supply, telecommunications, plant and equipment, and the growth of the business largely from retained earnings. The country's trade facilitation services are underdeveloped.*

Downstream processing

The reservations expressed regarding downstream processing as the only way of adding value should not stop LDCs from examining this possibility. Where LDC exporters have been able to meet market requirements in terms of investment, market knowledge and know-how, the processing of commodities into manufactured products can be an effective way of adding value and developing strong and sustainable market positions. A convincing example comes from Turkey's leather goods industries. They have turned their country from an exporter of hides and skins to a net importer of leather whilst substantially increasing exports of leather garments and small leather goods.

The key success factor is to take each step in the value chain separately so that competitive advantage can be developed at each stage. There are many examples of successful diversification downstream by LDC exporters who continue to export both unprocessed and processed products, positioning each in different geographic markets. Nali Limited, a company that grows chillies and exports chillies to India and chilli sauce to neighbouring countries, exemplifies such strategies (see box 6). Its experience suggests that by addressing the markets for each product separately, it is possible to succeed in both.

Box 6
Malawi: exporting chilli sauce – turning comparative advantage into competitive advantage

Company: *Nali Limited is a family-owned business started in 1974, manufacturing mainly chilli sauces. Its founder, Nali-lo Alford Khoromana, died in 1997, and the company is now managed by his widow, Mrs Khoromana.*

Performance: *In 1974, Mr Khoromana bought 30 acres (12 hectares) of land and started producing and exporting whole chillis. From these humble beginnings, the company has grown into a US$ 2 million business, and employs 200 persons in chilli processing. More than 50% of turnover is exported, mainly in the form of sauces, to neighbouring countries and the United Kingdom.*

Key success factors: *Nali's main achievement has been the identification of a new niche market for a product produced in Malawi and based on the country's inherent comparative advantage. The first step was to identify the potential for growing chillis in the country, and to master its production. The second step was to identify a processing opportunity and potential export markets. The chillis are now sourced from local farmers within a short distance of the factory, and the main markets are neighbouring countries. So far, export marketing has been limited primarily to participation in local – and occasionally foreign – trade fairs. The continuing success of Nali can be attributed to the loyalty of the workforce and the retention of the accumulated experience of the company.*

Constraints: *The company has overcome many obstacles in its development, especially in recent years. It survived major devaluations of the national currency in 1998 and 2000, which substantially increased the cost of imported additives and packaging. While manufacturing in Malawi has generally declined, Nali has continued to grow. Not least, Nali has survived the death of its founder in 1997. His widow's success in continuing to expand and develop the business is testament to the solid foundations of the business and to her ability, and is an indication that gender need not be a barrier to entrepreneurial success.*

The company's main constraint is finance for expanding the business. Inquiries from trade fairs indicate that demand for its products outstrips supply.

Dangerous measures: the FDI alternative

Forcing exporters to process commodities before they have developed competitive advantage can be extremely damaging, as occurred in the Egyptian cotton industry. Spinning some of the world's best cotton (long-staple) competitively required know-how and investment in modern equipment. However the export of raw cotton was taxed (setting prices above world market levels) before the local industry was able to meet these requirements. Taxation simply resulted in a fall in raw-cotton output.

If domestic industry is not able to compete effectively in the downstream process, the practical solution may well be to attract foreign direct investment.

If domestic industry is not able to compete effectively in the downstream process, the practical solution may well be for companies with proven international competitiveness to attract foreign direct investment (FDI). Such investment can have a demonstration effect on domestic industry.

Niche marketing and product innovation

One weakness often cited as contributing to the LDCs' lack of success in world markets is the small size of their own markets and hence of domestic output. It is thought difficult to develop the economies of scale required for doing well in international markets.

In today's business environment, small size may actually be a source of competitive advantage.

In today's business environment, however, small size need not be a disadvantage and may actually be a source of competitive advantage. Increasingly, world markets are fragmenting into large numbers of small segments, with consumers demanding and willing to pay for choice. The small niche segments that have developed as a result of such fragmentation require products and services adapted to the criteria of their particular types of consumer. For suppliers, the implication is to be nimble and flexible, positioning different product offerings to meet the needs of the various segments.

For LDC exporters, the fragmentation of the market can be an advantage. They can develop strong market positions by specializing in niche segments which their larger rivals would find difficult to adapt to. Their product innovation can be more nimble. They can pick segments and address them with specific offerings, rather than attempt to make products that can be sold in the mainstream segment or in more than one segment, both of which are more demanding.

Identify products that larger-scale suppliers will find difficult to provide.

By definition, niche segments are specific to each product or geographic market and it is difficult to talk of opportunities in a general way. What is required is to identify products that larger-scale suppliers will find difficult to provide and to develop a product offer that meets the purchase criteria of the segment in which they are to be sold. Differentiation is the hallmark of niche marketing.

For example, the mass tourism destinations, based on large hotels and catering for the sun-and-sand consumer, find it difficult to offer the atmosphere and intimate contact with local people that are the criteria for success in the niche, cultural tourism segment. This provides an opportunity for a smaller hotel to make the most of its size and offer the intimacy and people-centred experience that consumers in this segment are looking for. Such hotels will also need to ensure that they offer the diversity of visitor experience and exposure to the arts, crafts, cuisine and other aspects of culture that are important success factors in this subsector.

Environmental and social concerns

A number of purchase criteria are becoming common across a large number of product markets. Two that are increasingly relevant to LDCs are environmental impact and ethical trade. The former is, along with concerns over health, the driving force behind the increase in the trade in organic foods. Provided problems of certification can be overcome, the supply of organic produce offers opportunities across a range of agricultural and food markets (see chapter 3). Nabekam Bio, a Guinean company (see box 7), shows what can be achieved.

'Naturally produced, naturally good'
– Slogan of DIPAG, exporter of tropical fruits and vegetables, Guinea

The opportunity to add value by adopting environmentally sensitive production methods extends to a wide array of products. Where it can be shown that a product is natural and produced by sustainable methods, the product is likely to fetch a premium or to be preferred to goods that are not. Through consumer pressure, the standards bodies of the developed countries have started introducing eco-labelling. To qualify, producers must be willing to submit their production methods to inspection and certification. This obviously disadvantages LDCs that do not operate certification schemes of their own. However, if it is possible to introduce internationally recognized systems of certification that are cost-effective, the rewards for exporters can be high. It opens up markets for products for which purchase criteria give priority to environmental impact rather than price.

Box 7
Guinea: niche marketing of organic fruits

Company: *Two friends, financial economist Ismael Nabe and agronomist Maurice Kamano – both working for the public authorities – took advantage of the liberalization of Guinea's economy in 1984 to set up Nabekam Bio in 1988. It is an exporter of organic fruits such as plantain, pineapples and mangoes, which are grown 160 km from the capital Conakry.*

Nabekam Bio targeted specific markets in advance, growing and packaging the fruit to meet European norms and signing exclusive contracts with a number of companies. In 1990-1993, Nabekam benefited from a government assistance scheme that helped finance marketing, packaging, local transport and participation in trade fairs. Further aid came from a French cooperation agency and the European Union in developing the techniques used.

Performance: *Between 1988 and 1997, Nabekam Bio exported 400 tons of fruit yearly to Belgium, France, Germany and the United Kingdom. To expand its scope, Nabekam Bio began working with local producers in Fria, providing them finance and technical support. Exports in 1999/00 amounted to 683 tons of organic fruit. Its annual turnover rose from US$ 281,000 in 1997/98 to US$ 365,000 in 1999/00. In addition, its exports of dried fruit rose from 12.2 tons to 21 tons over the period.*

Nabekam Bio's major export leap began after its founders took part in European trade fairs under a European Union scheme to support entrepreneurs taking part in such exhibitions. When news came back of their success, the firm secured Guinean francs 10 million in financing and set up a farm to grow organic fruit.

To meet the rigorous criteria of European certifying agencies, the company trained supervisors, who in turned passed on the techniques to local producers. A French certifying agency, ECOCERT, visited the enterprise regularly.

Key success factors: *Among the critical factors for the company's success was its creation and support of village cooperatives for the production of organic fruit. In the process, they stopped a decline in the local population. Further efforts to develop the cooperatives will include a guaranteed price for small planters. Nabekam has also opened up participation in the company to all its employees, enabling them to buy shares and feel a sense of ownership in company operations.*

The company's reliability enabled it to persuade clients to sign five-year contracts, with the stability these imply. In addition, the contracts provided for shared transport costs, credit facilities to enable the company to package its products according to European norms, study tours in Europe for Nabekam employees, and participation in trade fairs. Pre-financing facilities came in handy when the company needed to buy equipment to diversify into exports of dried fruit.

Constraints: *In 1997, economic difficulties in Guinea affected the enterprise. These led to a reduction in cargo-handling capacity and a rise in the cost of organic certification services. European expatriates about to give up their business sold Nabekam Bio their fruit-drying machines and passed on their knowledge of the European market, enabling the business to diversify.*

Consumer movements

In recent years, consumer movements in developed countries have extended their focus beyond the environment to the social impact of business practices, particularly in developing countries. Concerns over the use of forced labour and child workers and the impact of businesses on communities have led to the boycott of products made by major multinationals. There are strong views that a fair share of the price paid by the consumer should return to the developing country producer.

With the right response to ethical concerns, businesses can show their competitiveness even in an LDC.

Frequently, these concerns are viewed as yet another barrier imposed on exports from developing countries. In fact, with the right response, businesses can turn this into an opportunity. New segments of the market are emerging in which the ethical behaviour of suppliers is a major purchase criterion. The standard price/quality ratio still holds, but consumers prefer to purchase ethically produced and traded goods.

Voluntary standards are being introduced by consumer groups (such as the Clean Clothes Campaign which aims to improve working conditions in the garments industry worldwide. The adoption of such standards opens up new market segments. Compliance need not be any more onerous than conforming to local labour laws some of which may, in any case, prohibit the use of child labour.

Formation Carpets has a social code of conduct, under which it provides a day care centre, coaching with two teachers, a canteen, and health insurance for their employees and the children.

In Nepal, the company Formation Carpets (see box 8) has made the fair and ethical treatment of its workforce the basis of its competitive advantage. The manufacture of hand-made carpets is often attacked by consumer groups in developed countries as being exploitative of women and children. The case study shows that ethical behaviour can be a source of competitive advantage in that it differentiates the product in the market place and creates a more productive workforce.

Box 8

Nepal: exporting handmade rugs – combining ethical trade with niche marketing

Company: *Formation Carpets was established in 1991 by two women, Sulo Shrestha-Shah and Linda Gaenzle. It makes exclusive handmade rugs, which are exported to Germany and the United States.*

Performance: *Exports have grown from US$ 26,000 in 1990/91 to US$ 424,000 in 1999/00. The company now employs some 200 weavers (all women) and 60 other direct employees. In addition, it provides work indirectly to about 400 in wool spinning. It is widely viewed as a model factory which cares for its staff, providing better wages, reasonable working hours, care facilities for their children, a canteen and health insurance. Formation Carpets has also helped another entrepreneur to establish a separate business on a partnership basis.*

Key success factors:

❑ *The company was formed in response to inquiries from some German friends of Ms Shrestha-Shah, which enabled Formation Carpets to export direct to German retailers at good prices.*

❑ *Consequently the company has been able to pay fairly good wages, resulting in high-quality weaving.*

❑ *Despite paying piece rates, the company has adopted a policy of continuing to produce during periods of insufficient demand (often with new designs on a trial basis), so that permanent employment is provided. This has contributed to the maintenance of a high-quality output that can be sold at premium prices.*

❑ *The social code of conduct followed by the company, combined with campaigning by Ms Shrestha-Shah against the exploitation of child labour in rug-making in parts of South Asia, has provided much publicity for Formation Carpets and attracted further export orders.*

Constraints: *In 1993/94 there was a slump in trade and the number of weavers and their output fell. Fortunately, the owners managed to obtain a place on a marketing trip to the United States managed by the United States Agency for International Development (USAID). This resulted in a contract with an importer which is now the company's main customer (importing about 300 square metres a month). At first, Formation Carpets found it difficult to work with the American company, but patience and persistence were finally rewarded by the establishment of good and mutually beneficial relations.*

Differentiate products in fragmented markets

Product innovation is a tried and tested way of differentiating products to add value. The problem in the past has been that LDC exporters, far from end-use markets and lacking in know-how, have largely been followers rather than leaders in this field. The increasing fragmentation of markets and the worldwide linking of markets through globalization offer the opportunity for product innovation in ways that need not disadvantage LDCs.

The export of ethnic foods is an obvious opportunity for LDCs.

The greater variety of products being consumed in developed countries presents clear opportunities. The ITC product profile of medicinal plants (summarized in chapter 3) indicates that the use of traditional plants could form the basis for product innovation. Nonu chips from Samoa provides one example (see box 32, in chapter 3).

The export of ethnic foods is an obvious opportunity for LDCs. The export of a range of camel milk products by Tiviski (box 9) in Mauritania shows how a country not known for comparative advantage in dairy products can develop exports on the basis of its local produce.

Box 9

Mauritania: a camel dairy farm and its differentiated products

Company: *Tiviski is a private limited company started in 1989 by Nancy Abeiderrahmane, a British-born engineer. The company produces milk from its dairy farm and has commenced converting it into value-added products such as cheese. The main dairy farm is in Naukchott. This was the first dairy farm in Africa to pasteurize camel milk.*

Performance*: At first, the dairy processed camel milk, the only fresh milk available. Production of cow milk began in 1990 and goat milk was added in 1998. From its modest beginnings, Tiviski today produces 13,000 litres of milk and has a sales turnover of 557,665 ouguiyas. It will soon export camel cheese.*

Key success factors: *The turning point in the business was the decision of Nancy Abeiderrahmane to diversify from camel milk to milk from cows and goats, and eventually to produce camel cheese. In February 2001 construction began on a facility for UHT (Ultra High Temperature) cow milk. Eventually this milk will be exported to countries in the region. Camel milk will also be tested to find out whether it can be adapted to UHT processing for domestic sale and eventual export.*

In addition, Tiviski:

❑ *Received financing from France in 1990;*

❑ *Received assistance from the Food and Agriculture Organization of the United Nations (FAO) in setting up the cheese factory;*

❑ *Selected high-quality cows, camels and goats for the dairy farm;*

❑ *Carefully cross-bred local cattle;*

❑ *Operates state-of-the-art stainless steel continuous pasteurization equipment;*

❑ *Packages milk in gable-top cartons;*

❑ *Controls product quality in compliance with European standards;*

❑ *Can supply milk and cheese locally at prices lower than those of imported products;*

❑ *Imports packaging for cheese products from Europe and Saudi Arabia and is thus able to meet the design standards of its prospective markets;*

➡

➡

❑ *Signed a franchise agreement with a leading French company, CANDIA, to manufacture UHT milk under its brand;*

❑ *Launched a website, tiviski.com, to provide up-to-date information to its target markets;*

❑ *Received a Rolex award for enterprise in 1993; and*

❑ *Was awarded the Order of National Merit by the Mauritanian Government.*

Constraints:

❑ *Dairy farming is seasonal in the country, i.e. production is high in the dry and cooler periods and falls during the hot season.*

❑ *As European regulations do not cover camel milk, new regulations have to be drafted. Scientific research has been undertaken with a view to establishing suitable product tests.*

❑ *Saudi Arabia and the United Arab Emirates are prospective markets. However, their distance from Mauritania and the lack of direct flights with refrigeration facilities pose logistical problems.*

❑ *Southern Mauritanians do not drink camel milk (for cultural reasons). The same applies to Morocco.*

❑ *The local population in Mauritania and the region traditionally do not consume cheese.*

The services revolution

The international markets for business and professional services and tourism have become major markets, worth over US$ 700 billion in the case of the first two and approaching US$ 500 billion for tourism, far larger than the markets for most goods. There are other opportunities in offshore banking and other financial services, and in transport and other trade-related services. Duty-free shopping, often closely allied to tourism, is a market also valued in several billions of United States dollars.

Failure to address the services sector adequately now would leave LDCs poorly placed to participate in a sector that will dominate world trade.

The growth of trade in services reflects the domination of world GDP by the services sector and the overall trend towards globalization. The implication for LDCs is hugely significant. Policy-makers and businesses need to go beyond the limited view of exporting only merchandise to keep pace with, and benefit from, these trends. By doing so, it should become possible to identify areas of comparative and competitive advantage that have not been exploited in the past. Failure to address the services sector adequately now would leave LDCs poorly placed to participate in a sector that will dominate world trade, particularly in view of trade liberalization under GATS.

Moreover, the development of a competitive services sector should foster the growth of merchandise trade by improving the availability of finance and reducing transaction costs (for example, by cutting the cost of transport and other trade-related services).

Critical requirements for market entry

Skilled human resources, and adequate telecommunications facilities and Internet service providers are critical requirements for entering the services market.

The critical requirements for market entry are skilled human resources, and adequate telecommunications facilities and Internet service providers. In many countries, policy-makers are often unaware of the level of skills available in the country and hence may not give the sector the policy attention it deserves. So it is important that policy-makers inventory and understand the skills base available before they start to frame strategies for the development of this sector.

Services are tied closely to policies on education, vocational training and telecommunications. It is important for policies on business and professional services to link the skills supply with their commercialization.

Tourism provides opportunities for all LDCs. The product is the country itself, its natural, cultural and heritage assets, and its infrastructure. The sector's development, therefore, needs to be guided by comprehensive plans that tie in closely with national policies on environmental sustainability, culture and heritage, and physical planning.

Regulatory reforms needed

Growth of trade in financial services is often contingent on undertaking regulatory reform.

The growth of trade in financial services is often contingent on undertaking regulatory reform. While many LDCs have concerns over the consequences of liberalizing their financial sectors to widen participation in the services institutions, carefully planned and phased reform, including the building of regulatory capacity, can overcome many of these concerns. The upside is not just the potential export of financial services but also the major contribution that a competitive financial services sector can make to an efficient economy and to facilitating the growth of merchandise exports.

Deregulation and encouragement of wider participation in the provision of transport and other trade-related services to increase efficiency are crucial for the development of international trade generally. And many LDCs can earn substantial revenues from the export of these services.

GATS and FDI

Widening and strengthening the General Agreement on Trade in Services will be the subject of considerable attention in the ongoing process of deepening the WTO trade pacts. LDCs need to approach these discussions from the viewpoint that improved market access could provide major opportunities for the growth of their services exports. To a large extent, LDCs need to catch up with the revolutionary changes that are taking place in the services trade. The encouragement of FDI to bring in much needed investment and know-how has an important role to play in helping them catch up.

Turning comparative into competitive advantage

LDCs often have the same underlying comparative advantages as their more successful developing country counterparts.

A general theme that runs through the review of opportunities for LDCs to increase their share in world trade is that, often, they have the same underlying comparative advantages that have enabled more successful developing countries to benefit from the growth of world trade. Further, there should be an in-built momentum for LDCs to follow the path of their more successful counterparts in the form of a 'ladder of development': as the more advanced developing countries develop, they should move to the export of goods and services that make less use of factor-cost and resource-based advantages, leaving to LDCs the supply of goods and services that enabled them to increase trade.

However, the 'ladder of development' effect often takes considerable time to feed through to LDCs and their underlying comparative advantage may fail to be translated into strong export performance. The main reason for this is that LDCs are often slow to turn comparative advantage into competitive advantage. Opportunities for export growth are thus exploited either slowly or not fully.

Lessons from the newly industrializing economies

Studies of the export success of the newly industrializing countries show that they focused their export strategies on two critical factors:

- Building capacity and capability amongst their export-oriented businesses to compete internationally;

- Assisting these firms to exploit their international competitiveness in target export markets.

Lack of sufficient numbers of businesses with the capacity and capability to compete internationally is the main constraint that the LDCs need to address to turn comparative advantage into export success. Once this constraint is overcome, assistance in developing international markets will ensure that comparative advantage is turned into competitive advantage.

LDC companies use their comparative advantage

An example of how to use comparative advantage to become competitive is given by Meskel Flowers of Ethiopia, which has been able to turn the advantages of climate and cheap labour into major exports of cut flowers (see box 31 in chapter 3). The company was able to do so at a time when Ethiopia was only just turning from State planning to a market-led economy. The climate for private-sector investment was poor and there were huge obstacles to overcome in registering title to land, obtaining finance and developing the infrastructure for trade.

If countries wish to develop businesses with capacity and capability to compete internationally and help them market that competitiveness, authorities must improve the environment for private-sector development and trade.

The company's experience highlights the importance of establishing an enabling environment for private-sector development and trade. The two are inseparable in turning comparative advantage into competitive advantage. While gifted and committed entrepreneurs will always be able to overcome constraints, if countries wish to develop sufficient numbers of businesses with capacity and capability to compete internationally and help them market that competitiveness, authorities must address the environment for private-sector development and trade. The ways in which this can be achieved are presented in the next chapters.

Another example is provided by Magin Confecções of Mozambique (box 10). LDCs all have a comparative advantage in cheap labour to enable them to succeed in garment making, yet only a few have managed to become significant exporters. The performance of African LDCs has been particularly poor in this regard. The main problems have been the failure to make cheap labour sufficiently productive and to achieve acceptable levels of quality. Magin Confecções has succeeded in overcoming these problems.

These companies' experience shows that African LDCs need not give up hope of seizing this opportunity. What is required is to focus on improving the productivity of the labour force by vocational training, the use of incentive systems that reward productivity and focus, production methods that enable labour to be used productively, and quality assurance systems that build quality into each production process.

> **Box 10**
> **Mozambique: developing sources of competitive advantage in the garments sector**
>
> **Company:** *Magin Confecções Lda manufactures clothing for export. It started in 1974 as an importer of semi-manufactured piece goods with an assembly line. It is now one of the largest clothing manufacturers in Mozambique.*
>
> **Performance:** *The liberalization of imports of clothing in 1992 resulted in the collapse of some clothing manufacturers, but Magin Confecções turned this adversity into an opportunity. It acquired 80% of another company in 1994, and formed a strategic alliance with a company based in South Africa at the end of 1996 to broaden its customer base and to widen the range of products on offer. It now has 500 employees producing 3,500 garments a day, specializing in shirts and T-shirts. All output is exported, with about 95% accounted for by the company's South African distributor. The company has ambitious plans to continue to expand through strategic alliances and acquisitions. It believes that Africa has the potential to become a major source of garment exports to other parts of the world. The ratification of the SADC trade agreement on textiles and clothing is expected to bring significant benefits, and AGOA (the United States Africa Growth and Opportunities Act) holds the promise of duty-free access to American markets.*
>
> **Key success factors:** *Magin Confecções has focused on developing its workforce. The company recognizes the importance of addressing the aspirations and concerns of its employees, and of providing sufficient training and a supportive working environment. This policy has been rewarded with loyal and motivated staff at production and management levels. Magin gives the needs of its suppliers and customers similar attention. It believes in developing mutually beneficial relationships with all stakeholders, based on honesty and integrity.*
>
> **Constraints:** *In the past, Magin's progress was severely hampered by the civil war. Looking to the future, the management knows that productivity and efficiency levels remain below world levels, and that they must be raised if the company is to compete in markets outside Africa. Such improvements will require investment and access to technical know-how.*

Success factors changing

Recent trends in world trade show that, increasingly, success in export markets will be determined less by factor- and resource-based advantages and more by competitive advantage derived within individual firms. World trade in merchandise and services is increasingly dominated by what may be termed intra-industry trade. The supply of intermediate inputs or manufacture in a foreign country by subsidiaries of multinational corporations is now the dominant form of trade and its importance is increasing.

With this form of trade, the factors for success are:

The known success factors draw attention to the importance of interventions at the sectoral level.

- Know-how vested within the firm of both product and manufacturing technology;

- The competitiveness that results from this know-how through core competence;

- Structural linkages with suppliers and other firms in the industry that complement the firm's competence.

In turn, these success factors draw attention to the importance of interventions at the sectoral level in the form of comprehensive sectoral strategies which address:

- The policy environment;

- The structure of output and business linkages;

- The supply of factors of production and other inputs;

- Physical and business support infrastructure, including SQAM systems; and

- The development of competence and capability within firms.

The importance given to FDI in this book reflects its growing impact on world trade and the role it can play in transferring know-how and competence. While the capital it provides could be replaced from domestic sources, market knowledge and presence and FDI's potential role in transferring technology and competence, through a demonstration effect, are hard to obtain from domestic sources.

Overcoming technical barriers and structural constraints

Many successful LDCs remark on the challenges posed by increasing technical barriers to trade. More demanding sanitary and phytosanitary regulations, increasing insistence on certification to safety standards, and new regulations on compliance with environmental management and labour standards are becoming commonplace in most developed country markets. They may also spread soon to developing country markets.

There is evidence that LDCs are already finding it hard to comply with these technical barriers. The loss of a Ugandan market for fish as a result of an EU ban on the grounds of public health concerns is a prime example. While developing countries are no doubt going to resist in WTO and other trade forums any imposition of higher standards and certification requirements, to ensure that they do not constitute non-tariff barriers, technical barriers may well increase, driven by consumer concerns.

To cope with growing technical barriers, LDCs must develop programmes to:

- Disseminate information to exporters on product standards;

- Disseminate know-how on cost-effective ways of meeting standards and certification requirements;

- Undertake substantial investment in their SQAM systems;

- Address the issue of access to, and affordability of, SQAM systems and advisory services, particularly for SMEs.

Progressive exporters have already seen the need to meet the challenge of technical barriers to trade.

Despite the poorly developed SQAM systems of most LDCs, progressive exporters have already seen the need to meet the challenge of technical barriers to trade. A pertinent example is the Ugandan firm Greenfields (U) Ltd (see box 11) which has already invested in meeting HACCP (hazard analysis and critical control points) standards and is in the process of obtaining ISO 9000 certification to enable it to export to EU and other markets.

To establish an enabling environment, however, LDC Governments need to have active and effective programmes in place. The required know-how and investment are critically important for donor support.

Box 11

Uganda: exporting fish – market and product diversification to overcome TBTs

Company: *Greenfields (U) Ltd is a private company formed in 1989. It has four shareholders, two foreign (holding 83% of the shares) and two local (17%). It is one of the leading exporters of high-quality Nile perch fillets.*

Performance: *Following an analysis of the market, the company identified a major opportunity to export chilled fish fillets by air to Europe. Exports grew every year from 1989 until 1997, when the European Union imposed a ban on fresh fish imports for temporary health reasons. The company responded by going to new markets (United States and Japan) diversifying its products to include frozen fish, and investing heavily in quality assurance systems. Its annual turnover is currently about US$ 6 million. It employs over 200 in its fish-processing plant and supports many fishermen.*

Key success factors:

❑ *The location of the processing plant near Lake Victoria and 4 km from the Entebbe airport;*

❑ *Careful targeting of export markets;*

❑ *Meeting strict hygiene and quality standards, including ISO 9002, in the production process;*

❑ *Regular feedback from sales agents and clients, followed by responsive improvements in product quality, packing;*

❑ *Expansion by ploughing profits back into the business rather than depending on loans; and*

❑ *Formation of the Uganda Fish Exporters and Processors Association to tackle common problems in the Ugandan fish industry, such as fish poisoning in Lake Victoria and the chartering of airfreighters.*

Constraints:

❑ *Bans and restrictions on imports of Ugandan fish into Europe, and bankruptcies of some European importers;*

❑ *Shortage of capital for operations and expansion;*

❑ *Inadequate airfreight capacity;*

❑ *Absence of a quality packaging industry in Uganda; and*

❑ *High cost of complying with EC directives.*

Build linkages

A major problem for LDCs is that their exporters do not have the size to obtain economies of scale. What are considered large firms in LDCs may not have the capacity to supply the volume requirements of buyers in developed country markets. With the growth of large supermarket chains in the retail trade and the growing dominance of the multinationals as buyers of industrial products, the problem is likely to grow.

Small suppliers in LDCs are often competitive producers. They need a mechanism to ensure consistent quality of product and to market the output.

The solution lies in building business linkages to and from effective clusters. Small suppliers in LDCs are often competitive as producers. They need a mechanism for bringing together their outputs in ways that ensure consistent quality of product and to market the combined output to provide the scale required by the market. LDCs have examples of linkages that have been successful in several industries. COMEBU (box 12) has made a success of small-scale mining. It assists small miners to offer supplies consistently and cost-effectively and undertakes distribution and marketing. Mali has a group of artisanal producers selling through a gallery to Europe.

Box 12

Burundi: building confidence in the mining sector

Company: COMEBU was established in 1986 with an estimated capital of US$ 250,000 and 2,500 workers. This company exploits mines and exports minerals. In early 1993, it started exporting cassiterite (tin ore) and niobium-tantalum to Germany, Japan and the United States. One stakeholder is Belgian who holds 20% of the company's capital, and six others are Burundians.

Performance: From 1991 to 2000, the company exported 325 tons of cassiterite (worth US$ 739,000) and 313 tons of niobium-tantalum (US$ 6 million). The company paid US$ 1.7 million in tax and fees during the same period. Furthermore, the company has exported about 50 tons of tungsten (valued at US$ 70,000).

The company envisages doubling its exports (up to 80 tons) of concentrated niobium-tantalum. A programme of exploitation of mineral deposits is in progress to increase production and to exploit other minerals such as kaolin, phosphate, nickel and gold.

Key success factors:

❑ Persistence and determination of the promoters;

❑ Mutual confidence between the promoters and customers;

❑ Training provided to artisans by qualified technical staff;

❑ Granting of bonuses;

❑ Good working relationship with the workers (necessary for using the tools provided);

❑ Permanent contracts signed with well-established customers; and

❑ Application of environmental regulations. For example, there is a law lowering taxes on mining industries that meet these standards. They are also tax exempt on benefits and dividends for three years.

Constraints:

❑ Political instability in Burundi and civil war in the subregion;

❑ Inadequate local transport;

❑ Inability to use international transport because of the costs involved; and

❑ Unsupportive financing system in the country (high interest rates, complex administrative formalities).

Market power barrier

The other major structural barrier is market power. The dominance of buyers in particular markets can make it difficult for LDCs to penetrate new markets or diversify into downstream processing. The well-known example in this regard is the failed attempt by the Tanzanian cashew industry to process raw cashew in the face of the dominance of Indian purchasers of this product and which preferred to do the processing in their own plants.

The barrier, which is principally commercial in nature, can be overcome. The firm SEPT SA in Benin has achieved this (box 13). The solutions include alliances with buyers in end-use markets to circumvent the power of intermediaries (which is what SEPT did), the targeting of market segments that do not need large-scale supplies or are price sensitive, and adaptation of products to special customer requirements.

These responses to market power require initial investment by the LDC supplier and major efforts in market development.

> **Box 13**
>
> **Benin: breaking into the cashew nut market**
>
> **Company:** *SEPT SA is a public limited company started in 1992 by Sani Agatha Loukman. The company exports raw cashew kernels and processed cashew nuts.*
>
> **Performance:** *Up to 1994 SEPT exported raw cashew kernels to India. Today, it exports 2,000 tons of raw cashew kernels and 6 tons of cashew nuts per month.*
>
> **Key success factors:** *In response to the devaluation of the CFA franc, the national currency, the company developed a new business strategy to take advantage of market trends and improved competitiveness. It focused on processing cashew kernels, finding distribution outlets for them and raising the substantial additional finance required to compete successfully in the market for cashew nuts. SEPT's strategy was to:*
>
> ❑ *Invest in processing cashews using tried and tested technology that would enable it to compete against entrenched competitors. Several missions were undertaken to India to study cashew nut processing in the world's largest supplier.*
>
> ❑ *Forge an alliance with a French importer to market cashew nuts. The French company also assisted SEPT in setting up the processing plant and in training its staff.*
>
> ❑ *Develop a marketing strategy that enabled the company to continue to supply cashew kernels to Indian processors whilst competing against them in the French market.*
>
> ❑ *Train its labour force thoroughly in the new technology with the support of the ACP-EU Centre for the Development of Industry (CDI).*
>
> ❑ *Introduce rigorous quality control and verification procedures starting with control of the quality of raw materials (i.e. cashew kernels) through to the finished product.*
>
> ❑ *Obtain the backing of the Commercial Bank of Benin. Apart from investment in plant and equipment, the processing of cashews required a substantial increase in working capital. The procurement period for raw cashew kernels is short (4-6 weeks). All the kernels to be processed and exported for the rest of the year have to be obtained during this period. This is a capital-intensive business, so the support of the Bank was critical for success.*
>
> **Constraints:**
>
> ❑ *Difficulty in obtaining land for the processing plant;*
>
> ❑ *Electricity supply (which took over a year to procure);*
>
> ❑ *Resistance by Indian exporters, who are the main purchasers of cashew kernels and the main competitors in the trade in cashew nuts;*
>
> ❑ *High cost of technology and substantial working capital requirements;*
>
> ❑ *Difficulties in finding skilled labour; and*
>
> ❑ *High costs of training.*

South-South trade

With similar patterns in consumption and business practices, LDCs are finding that their best opportunities may be in trading with their neighbours and other developing countries rather than looking immediately to the industrial nations as their markets. A number of the successful entrepreneurs profiled in this book have found niche markets in developing countries. Nali Ltd of Malawi sells chilli sauce to Africa and India as well as Europe. Magin Confecções Lda of Mozambique did a deal with South Africa's major clothing distributors.

Nevertheless, the current low levels of trade among developing countries is often interpreted as a lack of market potential. Secondly, it is generally believed that developing countries produce similar goods, primarily raw materials and commodities, and that there are no trading complementarities. Thirdly, the notion prevails that low levels of GDP reflect limited market demand.

The range of tradable products between developing countries is considerably more diverse and complementary than believed.

The paucity of reliable trade information on countries of the South perpetuates such perceptions. In fact, statistical and field research by ITC has revealed that the range of tradable products in developing countries is considerably more diverse and complementary than believed. ITC has also found that countries in the South spend large amounts on importing goods from the North that are available under competitive conditions in other developing countries, often in the same region. In other words, markets in the South can offer important and real trading opportunities for other developing countries.

In some circumstances, South-South trade is a welcome fallback for a company struggling with environmental and health regulations that do not fit its product, as is the case of the Mauritanian camel milk producer mentioned in box 9. A Tanzanian automotive parts manufacturer has been able to sell to Zimbabwe, Zambia, the Sudan, Mozambique, Malawi and Burundi as well as to the United Kingdom. Here South-South trade is a welcome spin-off from its original activity. A Nepalese company, Around the World Services Ltd, has established itself as an overseas employment agency supplying Nepalese workers to the Middle East; it has the prospect of adding Malaysia to its clients. Its founder was an humanitarian worker who happened to meet a Qatar businessman looking for a guarantee of quality work and honest dealings. In this case, the employer came looking for workers in the South, while the Nepalese executive had experience in helping friends and relatives who were seeking work abroad. The challenge was to demonstrate his credibility and business capabilities (box 14).

Box 14

Mali, Nepal and the United Republic of Tanzania: three success stories in South-South trade

Company: *SOMAPIL, the Société Malienne de Piles, founded in February 1974, has outlasted its rivals in Côte d'Ivoire despite higher resource costs and fought off competition from cheaper Asian suppliers. Today it has established itself as the leading producer of batteries in the West African subregion. Producing batteries under licence, it more than doubled its overall sales to FCFA 12.3 billion between 1993 and 1998, using 93% of its capacity. The company employs 298 full-time and 70 part-time staff. Its biggest foreign client is Niger.*

SOMAPIL credits its export success – a fivefold increase in 1998 to reach FCFA 411 million – to the quality of its products compared to that of its regional competitors (making it easier to enter international commerce), competitive pricing and a sustained marketing effort. Its profits remain too low to finance investment in new equipment, and local banks are cautious in offering (expensive) credit. SOMAPIL was able to renovate and extend its facilities in 1994-1995 only under a governmental grant for rebuilding industry after the civil disturbances in Bamako in 1991. It has great hope of expanding its sales under regional customs union.

Company: *Around the World Services Ltd (AWS) was created in November 1997 by Dan B. Tamang, 44, a one-time Project Director for the United States Peace Corps in Nepal, a former Project Manager for Save the Children (United Kingdom), and most recently Executive Director of the Sustainable Development Centre in Kathmandu. His decade of experience with non-governmental organizations, which*

➡

---

included travelling widely, gave him an international outlook and personnel assessment skills despite a non-business background. Barely 20% of the 200,000 - 300,000 Nepalese entering the labour force each year can get jobs. Working abroad was highly regarded in Mr Tamang's home village and he often helped relatives and village acquaintances to get in touch with Kathmandu's overseas manpower agencies. This enabled him to see what the agencies were doing wrong, principally their lack of energetic management and focus.

One day he met a visitor from Qatar who operated a staffing agency and was looking for a professional to work with. The man suggested that Mr Tamang should start a business in that line. He thought it over for a day, then accepted. The man immediately gave him a contract to find 104 workers, did not demand any advance payment for his services, and suggested that Mr Tamang take over the name of his Qatar recruitment agency for Nepal.

In four years Mr Tamang has found jobs for 5,000 Nepalese and expected to place 3,000 workers in 2001, including labourers for Malaysia. 'We make it a point to hear regularly from our clients on the quality and job performance of the workers we send off,' the Managing Director of AWS comments. 'We hold this as the key to successfully sustaining our business relationship. We encourage the same from the workers we send off.' AWS also seeks to safeguard the interests of its workers and does not accept jobs that pay employees less than US$ 150 a month (the per capita annual income in Nepal is US$210).

Company: *Afro-Cooling Systems Ltd in the United Republic Tanzania was established in 1978 to manufacture radiators for the motor vehicle industry. It started with technology bought from an Indian firm that had been making radiators for 25 years and had adapted the technology to Indian needs. Initially the products, using Indian sources of material, were targeted at the local replacement market. Soon, however, the quality of the products captured the attention of foreign companies such as an assembler of trucks and an assembler of tractors. The vetting of the quality by two international companies enabled Afro-Cooling systems to penetrate export markets in the United Kingdom, Zimbabwe, Zambia, the Sudan, Mozambique, Malawi and Burundi.*

At first 12 expatriate experts helped the start-up. By 1983 they had trained local staff and left, but the Patel family who started the business kept up the strict quality control that had made the company's reputation. The product is labour-intensive and the equipment used is simple, but the Patels have made a speciality of small-batch production. Despite recent import liberalization, Afro-Cooling continues to dominate the local market and has now diversified into industrial coolers and heat exchanges. The company exports nearly half of its output.

Three-stage approach

A fundamental approach to promoting South-South trade should have three stages:

- Identification of import/export opportunities through statistical analysis of trade flows between a group of countries and the rest of the world. This provides data on products on a sector-by-sector basis that have South-South trade potential.

- Determining the needs of the target market as well as the supply constraints within the group through detailed field research.

- Dissemination of the information to the target groups and arranging buyers-sellers meetings.

This is followed up by complementary trade promotion activities, including support at the enterprise level such as help in product and market development, marketing missions, trade fairs and training events.

Box 15
Africa's greatest leather industry assembly: South-South trade

Meet in Africa (MIA 2000), a trade fair of the African leather industry, took place in Morocco at the end of September and the beginning of October 2000. The conference/exhibition was organized by ITC with the assistance of the SIC Group in Paris. Some 1,746 participants attended the Morocco forum, compared with 971 for the first MIA, held in Cape Town, South Africa, in 1998. MIA 2002 is scheduled for Tunis in September 2002.

The 1998 meeting produced a number of trade and joint venture agreements, one of which covered the construction of a wet-blue tannery in Benin for exports to Senegal. Contracts on semi-finished leather were concluded by entrepreneurs from Egypt, Ethiopia, Senegal, South Africa and Tunisia. Yassin Awale of ESALIA, the Eastern and Southern African Leather Industries Association, commented at Morocco that the show 'highlighted the integration of the African leather sector into the global leather market…by producing high-quality leathers'.

In Cape Town, the number of exhibiting companies totalled 193 (186 from Africa), while Morocco attracted 256 African firms and 105 others. Chris Spyron, Executive Director of Zambia's Kembe Group, saw the Morocco fair as a place to promote the benefits of long-term investment in his country through joint ventures. 'This is the way forward for Africa and is especially important to the image of Africa and African leather,' he declared.

Hailu Bezuneh, General Manager of Ethio Sung Bin Leather Garment Factory, Ethiopia's second-largest leather garment manufacturer, reported: 'We managed to achieve a number of small orders from the show and we made some good contacts in other markets such as South Africa and Mauritius.'

Other Ethiopian tanners found Meet in Africa a good place to learn about the latest techniques and technology in leather manufacturing. Mulugeta Atsebeha, General Manager of Addis Tannery, Ethiopia's oldest tannery, observed: 'Morocco was an excellent shop window for us to show our leathers to potential European customers. We also felt that by talking together we could learn lessons from each other particularly when dealing with the European market.'

A shoe manufacturer from South Africa visited modern shoe factories in Casablanca, an activity that formed part of the Meet in Africa 2000 programme, and started discussions to obtain technical assistance from the Moroccans. Mohamed El Pekkali, Director of the Somatam tannery, declared: 'We made contact with Nigerians, Tunisians, Algerians, Mauritians and Senegalese. Without Meet in Africa, this would not have been possible. We are working now on joint venture projects that would never have seen the light of day without this event.'

Eddie Wichmann, proprietor of Leather Impressions, a producer of high-quality leather handbags in Cape Town, destined mainly for the South African market, commented: 'I went along to the first meeting at Cape Town and I think it is fair to say that it changed the course of my business. At that time, we were a large-volume producer that had been hit badly by South Africa's signing the WTO Agreement, which essentially opened up the domestic market to a wave of cheap imports from Asia. By opening my eyes to what other African businesses were doing, the Meet in Africa helped me decide on a new course of action, which resulted in us becoming the much more focused niche player that we are today.'

– From magazine reports on Meet in Africa 2001.

Chapter 3

Export performance and prospects of LDCs: the sectoral opportunities

Despite the difficulties that LDCs face in expanding their international trade, most of these countries have at least one 'champion' product and many have entrepreneurial success stories. The 'champions' include veneer from Equatorial Guinea, women's trousers from the Lao People's Democratic Republic, nuts and tea from Malawi, and sardines from Mauritania.

Business-related and professional services bring in US\$ 1.2 billion annually to LDCs, and these exports could rise substantially if the digital divide narrows. Coffee is not just a mainstay commodity: it is also a product which innovative entrepreneurs have been able to move up the value chain with specialities such as gourmet and organic coffee. Already, 35 LDCs process and export oilseed crops and their derivatives. Annual exports of spices are likely to exceed US\$ 100 million, but their importance extends far beyond the size of their markets. Grown by smallholders, they provide employment in rural areas, particularly for women. Several other sectors offer major opportunities: processed wood products and computer software are examples.

In comparing the trade performance of 184 countries in 13, ITC found that LDCs are not systematically at the bottom of the rankings. Cambodia, for instance, is the thirty-seventh largest exporter of garments among 130 countries worldwide, and Haiti and Myanmar are among the 10 fastest-growing exporters of this product group. Madagascar is the biggest exporter of vanilla and cloves. Benin, Ethiopia, Senegal and the Sudan are important exporters of oilseed-based products.

Thirteen sectors are important to LDCs for their potential and their current trading performance.

To explore the LDCs' potential for improving their trade performance, ITC studied the broad range of their export products. Its aim was to identify which products held most promise for the future, which had a high share in current LDC exports and which had shown strong growth in the immediate past.

Eleven merchandise and two services sectors were identified as having export development potential. These were cotton fabrics, textiles and clothing; fish products; coffee; cotton and fibres; wood and wood products; oilseed products; vegetables; fruits and nuts; spices; cut flowers and foliage; medicinal plants; business-related and professional services; and tourism. This chapter considers these sectors from the viewpoint of their importance in the export trade of LDCs.

The list is not exhaustive. Petroleum and gemstones play a major part in the economies of several LDCs, but the complexities of the market structure make them difficult to review from the perspective of concrete opportunities that can be strategically addressed. Chapter 1 noted the reliance of oil-exporting LDCs on unrefined fuels, while the Indian experience in the strategic export promotion of precious and semi-precious stones may offer some encouragement to LDCs. The case study of Glitter Gems (box 3) indicates some of the constraints (as well as the opportunities) faced by businesses seeking to break into this market.

Leather is a growing sector for many LDCs and offers scope for South-South trade and joint ventures (box 15). The ITC-sponsored Meet in Africa trade fair provides a regional snapshot of the state of the sector in developing countries.

The sector for artisanal products, as some of the 'success stories' in this book indicate, also holds promise. Individual entrepreneurs, often linking groups of village craftworkers and operating with a social aim, have been able to make their mark on the international scene. Chapter 5 points to some of the problems of strategy-makers seeking to create an enabling environment for handicraft exporters. It also reports on the initiatives that have culminated in a recommendation to address the issues brought about by the absence of an agreed international nomenclature for the sector.

Table 2	LDCs: sectors with export development potential	
Sectors	**All LDCs: average annual exports, 1995-1999 (US$ million)**	**Major LDC exporters (in descending order of importance)**
GOODS		
Cotton fabrics, textiles and clothing	2,681	Bangladesh, Nepal, Malawi, Madagascar, Mozambique, Benin, Ethiopia
Fish products	1,800	Bangladesh, Myanmar, Madagascar, Mozambique, Solomon Islands, Equatorial Guinea, Mauritania, Senegal, Maldives
Coffee	1,300	Uganda, Ethiopia, United Republic of Tanzania, Democratic Republic of the Congo, Burundi, Madagascar
Cotton and fibres	1,010	Mali, Benin, Sudan, Chad, Burkina Faso, Togo, Zambia, Madagascar, United Republic of Tanzania
Wood and wood products	856	Myanmar, Solomon Islands, Cambodia, Equatorial Guinea, Democratic Republic of the Congo, Lao People's Democratic Republic, Myanmar, Madagascar
Oilseed products	405	Sudan, Senegal, Solomon Islands, Benin, Myanmar
Vegetables	288	Myanmar, Sudan, Ethiopia, Senegal, Bangladesh, Zambia, Burkina Faso, Gambia, Afghanistan, Madagascar
Fruits and nuts	249	United Republic of Tanzania, Mozambique, Madagascar, Guinea-Bissau, Afghanistan, Somalia, Bhutan, Malawi, Myanmar
Spices	92	Madagascar, Comoros, United Republic of Tanzania, Uganda, Myanmar, Malawi, Lao People's Democratic Republic, Niger, Zambia
Cut flowers and foliage	31	Zambia, United Republic of Tanzania, Uganda, Malawi, Ethiopia, Rwanda, Yemen, Haiti, Madagascar
Medicinal plants	31	Sudan, Democratic Republic of the Congo, Vanuatu, Myanmar, Madagascar, Lao People's Democratic Republic
SERVICES		
Tourism	2,360 (39 LDCs)	United Republic of Tanzania, Maldives, Nepal, Myanmar, Senegal, Uganda, Haiti, Lao People's Democratic Republic
Business-related services	1,254 (19 LDCs)	Myanmar, Nepal, Angola, Madagascar, Ethiopia, Yemen, Senegal, Solomon Islands, Togo, Vanuatu

Sources: ITC estimates based on COMTRADE and FAO statistics.

The sectors chosen for a close look in this chapter range from cotton fabrics, textiles and clothing, with annual exports from LDCs reaching US$ 2.7 billion, to cut flowers and medicinal plants, each contributing about US$ 31 million yearly to the LDC export ledger.

Cotton fabrics, textiles and clothing

This sector is fairly well developed in some LDCs, and exports from all LDCs averaged US$ 2.7 billion yearly between 1995 and 1999, contributing about 30% of the total for all the merchandise sectors considered in this chapter.

Madagascar, Mozambique, Benin, Zambia and Ethiopia supplied 85% of LDC exports of cotton fabrics. Bangladesh in particular has shown that it is possible to move successfully up the value chain by exporting finished products. In 1999, it was by far the largest single LDC exporter of finished woven fabrics of cotton. It also provided a hefty 83% of the value of all LDC exports of clothing. Benefiting from privileged access to the EU market and liberal quota allowances in the United States, the LDC trade in garments expanded rapidly over the period reviewed.

Full liberalization of the trade in 2005 (when implementation of the Agreement on Textiles and Clothing is completed) as well as the increasing management of supply chains over computer networks will have a critical impact on the development and competitiveness of the LDC trade.

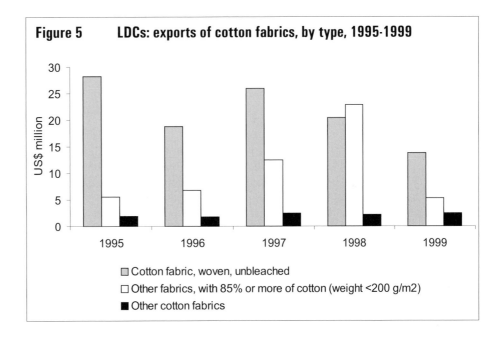

Figure 5   LDCs: exports of cotton fabrics, by type, 1995-1999

☐ Cotton fabric, woven, unbleached
☐ Other fabrics, with 85% or more of cotton (weight <200 g/m2)
■ Other cotton fabrics

Adapting to the demands of higher-quality markets

Bangladesh and Myanmar have succeeded in penetrating fairly sophisticated markets for textiles and clothing.

About 57% of LDC supplies of clothing consists of men's and women's clothing, not knitted or crocheted, in the low- and middle-quality levels. In clothing as in cotton fabrics, LDCs tend to focus on standard products, for which price is the main determinant of success and in-depth knowledge of fashion and design trends is not necessary. However, in recent years a shift has taken place in developed markets, away from cheap imports towards better-finished, higher-quality casual fashion and more individualized clothing. Countries like Bangladesh and Myanmar have already adapted to this shift, and have achieved remarkable success in penetrating fairly sophisticated markets for textiles and clothing.

Production moving to lower-cost countries

In the past decade, lower-cost clothing from Asia and from Mexico has increasingly made inroads into the main developed country markets (the United States, the European Union and Japan), eroding the role played by Turkey (a traditional supplier). To compete, leading manufacturers in these markets have begun to invest in the developing world, establishing joint ventures with their counterparts in Africa, Asia and Latin America to take advantage of the lower labour costs in these regions.

Labour shortages and the rising costs of labour have forced even the leading Asian exporters of textiles and clothing, such as India and the Republic of Korea, to move their production facilities to countries like Bangladesh, Cambodia, Lesotho, Madagascar and Nepal as well as to offshore processing zones in China.

The major world garment exporters are also becoming major importers.

The result is that the major world exporters are also becoming major importers, buying intermediate inputs to produce the products in which they specialize. Bangladesh, China, Mexico and Thailand, for example, import cotton yarns and fabrics to supply their expanding, export-oriented clothing manufacturers. This trend, together with the sharp import contraction in the United States, the European Union and Japan, has resulted in the increasing importance of developing countries as destinations for LDC exports.

World trade is restructuring, as increasing specialization takes place. As different products are moved backwards and forwards across the value chain, competition between exporters is becoming increasingly fierce.

Opportunities and constraints for LDCs

It has been estimated that trade liberalization under WTO will expand the value of the clothing trade by as much as 69%. A large part of this expansion is expected to accrue to developing and transition economies.

The European Union has recently taken steps to enhance market access for LDCs. An example is the provision on regional cumulation, which provides for a derogation from the rules of origin under the Generalized System of Preferences. It enables countries belonging to ASEAN, the Andean Community and the Central American Common Market to use raw materials from neighbouring countries to produce finished goods, including garments, that can then be exported duty free to Europe under GSP. Among the LDCs, this has benefited, for example, Bangladesh, Cambodia, the Lao People's Democratic Republic and Nepal.

However, preference erosion will continue to exert a downward pressure on import prices. The accession of China to WTO, which is expected to take place in 2002, should result in new competition for LDCs in Asia.

Export-oriented production of textiles and clothing has to be supported by vigorous strategies, including those that provide for a search for niche markets, strict quality control, and design and marketing innovations.

As the global market becomes more competitive with the phasing out of the Multifibre Arrangement (MFA), export-oriented textile production has to be supported by vigorous strategies that include a search for niche markets, strict quality control, and design and marketing innovations. LDC exporters could follow the example of Bangladesh, which is expanding its exports of items like quality suits, jackets and branded items. Future comparative advantages will depend not only on cheaper labour but also on technologically skilled labour. Increased investment in workforce training and skills development is now required as is the application of improved production technologies and marketing systems.

> **Box 16**
> **Bangladesh: exporting garments – securing competitive advantage**
>
> **Company**: *Fortuna Apparels Ltd was established in 1983 to manufacture and export garments. It has grown and diversified into a major industrial group in Bangladesh.*
>
> **Performance**: *Starting with 140 sewing machines and 250 workers in a rented house, the company now has 800 machines and 2,000 workers in its own 100,000 sq. ft building. It has diversified into a number of other products. From its first consignment of garments to the United States in 1984 – which was followed by a repeat order – annual exports have grown to their current US$ 10 million. The level would have been higher but for the exceptional floods of 1998/99, which affected output and deliveries. The company specializes in men's shirts, women's blouses and men's trousers.*
>
> **Key success factors**: *Success is attributed to four qualities:*
>
> ❑ *Entrepreneurial quality – the vision of the company's founder, combined with thorough analyses to identify target markets and products.*
>
> ❑ *Management quality – building up trusting relations with buyers, raw material suppliers and employees, based on honesty, integrity and sincerity.*
>
> ❑ *Product quality – meeting the buyers' requirements by working to their designs or cooperating closely at the design stage, purchasing quality materials, and ensuring that only top quality products are exported.*
>
> ❑ *Delivery quality – not being overbooked, so that commitments are met, the right product is delivered at the right time, and the company acquires the reputation of a trusted supplier.*
>
> **Constraints**: *Initially the greatest constraint was sourcing raw materials, but the problems were greatly alleviated by government measures to permit duty-free imports on a deferred payment basis. Other constraints have included port congestion, and delays associated with customs and/or quota regulations. The Bangladesh Garments Manufacturers and Exporters Association (BGMEA) has been particularly helpful in reducing such constraints.*

Tourism

World tourism grew by an estimated 7.4% in 2000 – its highest growth in nearly a decade and almost double the rise in 1999. Directly or indirectly, tourism is responsible for an estimated 245 million jobs and over US$ 5 trillion in economic activity worldwide, of which US$ 2.3 billion in 39 LDCs. Travel for leisure and recreation accounts for 62% of international tourism, business-cum-leisure trips 18%, and travel for other motives (visits to friends and relatives, for religious purposes, health treatment and other reasons) the remaining 20%.

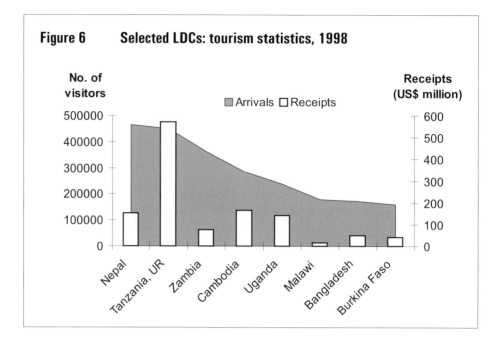

Figure 6   Selected LDCs: tourism statistics, 1998

Earnings per arrival lower for LDCs

Data from the World Tourism Organization for 1998, however, indicate that while developing countries, including LDCs, account for about 61% of international tourist arrivals, they draw only 53% of international receipts. Revenues per arrival averaged US$ 609 in developing countries, compared with US$ 827 for developed economies. The corresponding figure for LDCs was US$ 502.

Of the LDCs, only the United Republic of Tanzania is a significant tourist destination.

Of the LDCs, only the United Republic of Tanzania is a significant tourist destination, generating US$ 570 million in visitor expenditure. Cambodia, Nepal and Uganda are the only other countries to generate more than US$ 100 million. Zambia ranks alongside these countries in terms of visitor numbers but its receipts per arrival are much lower as it attracts large numbers of day trippers to Victoria Falls.

Tourism receipts as a percentage of export incomes in LDCs are highest in the United Republic of Tanzania with nearly 35%, followed by Vanuatu (33%) and the Gambia (24%). In countries like Bangladesh, Djibouti, Ethiopia, Guinea and Malawi, tourism receipts make up a very small proportion of export earnings. Compare this with tourism revenue in many Caribbean countries, which exceeds that of all other export sectors combined. Eight out of the 20 LDCs reviewed in a recent study of the World Tourism Organization have earnings from tourism above the average for the group.

Segmentation of leisure tourism

The market for leisure tourism is fragmenting into segments that include cultural tourism, eco-tourism and adventure sports. Nature travel, including eco-tourism, now accounts for over 10% of the market and culture is among Europe's leading tourist attractions. There are also important niches developing within the sun-and-sand segment, for families, the elderly and incentive travel. Sports tourism, including golf, yachting and diving, is gaining a significant slice of the leisure travel market in the United States, Europe and Japan.

Since two-thirds of business travellers extend their business trips for pleasure when they can, this is a huge potential market segment. Spending in this

---

Box 17
Bhutan: tailoring tourism products for diverse market segments

Company: *Etho Metho tours was established in the backdrop of the privatization of the tourism industry in Bhutan in 1990. Mrs Dago Bida, Managing Director, is a former marketing manager of the Department of Tourism in Bhutan. The company is a tour operator offering tailor-made itineraries covering cultural tours, trekking, eco-tourism, river rafting, mountain biking, bird watching and botanical tours.*

Performance: *The firm was formed with three partners, one support staff and just one computer. Now it employs over 50 regular staff. It was difficult for Etho Metho to gain a wide network of contacts in the international market rapidly, as no other private tour operator was established at that time in Bhutan. Today it is one of the top 10 private-sector revenue earners in the country and is the leader in the national tourism industry. Gross earnings for 2000 were estimated at US$ 450,000.*

Key success factors: *The enabling environment created by the Government contributed to the steady growth of this business. Such activities as training of tour guides, cookery and language courses, under bilateral and multilateral assistance programmes, also played a crucial role in the success of the firm. It also believes in establishing credibility through an excellent track record of timely payment of bills and personalized service which has earned it goodwill and credit worthiness in the business community and among overseas clients. The key success factors are:*

- ❏ *Effective marketing. Two sales promotion trips are undertaken each year to origin markets and the staff maintain close contacts with existing and new clients.*

- ❏ *Market responsiveness. The company anticipated the increasing fragmentation of the tourism market and has added new products in response. It started with cultural tours and trekking but now also offers eco-tourism, river rafting, mountain biking and bird watching to cater for niche markets.*

Constraints: *Despite the proprietor's previous experience in tourism, it was difficult to start from a modest beginning. The Government liberalized this sector in 1998. The number of tour operators increased, creating an oversupply. Though Bhutan is regarded as a favourite tourist destination by frequent visitors, it remains among the least visited places in the world. This is due to the lack of promotion and advertisement in other countries. Air links are a severe problem. The country's sole airport accommodates only small aircraft and is vulnerable to the weather. Internal roads are poor, so not all cultural and natural attractions are accessible to visitors. The country also lacks a tourism master plan.*

---

segment has increased in part because business travellers now tend to be accompanied by family members on their trips. Family visits and pilgrimages can be important for LDCs, many of which have large expatriate populations abroad. VFR (visiting family and friends) remains an underdeveloped segment of the market in many countries.

Health tourism, in spas and health resorts as well as for rest and recuperation purposes, is one of the fastest-growing segments of the market, though it is starting from a low base. There is strong interest in this segment in the world's largest origin markets, the United States and Germany. To date, the main destinations are developed countries but developing countries such as Cuba are demonstrating the potential for other countries, including LDCs.

Box 18
The Gambia: finding the right product – five-star luxury

Company: *The Coconut Residence is a five-star luxury hotel in Kololi, Gambia, with 18 suites, 24-hour room service, conference facilities, two swimming pools and two en suite pools. For the maximum of 36 guests there are 150 staff. Gambian-born Farid Bensouda, one of the enterprise's two proprietors, bought the land on which the Coconut stands some 15 years ago with the aim of investing in the tourism sector. But he waited for the right product and decided on the luxury hotel only in 1995. The investor originally intended to go to the Caribbean but was attracted to the Gambia partly because of the investment climate and partly because of Farid Bensouda's vision.*

Performance*: Operating in 1998, the Coconut Residence has since been almost fully booked in all seasons. With a la carte dining under a Spanish chef and individual attention from the highly trained staff, the Coconut (there are about 20 coconut varieties planted on the site, imported from different parts of the world) offers a departure from the conventional hotel setting in luxury surroundings.*

Mr Bensouda was convinced that the Gambia would be attractive to most Europeans. It is only six hours away from most European countries, with a perfect year-round climate and freedom from hurricanes. The business began marketing the hotel among small exclusive travel agencies in Germany and Switzerland soon after construction began and invited them to visit the site. In addition, the enterprise conducted direct marketing in Germany. By the time construction was finished, the Coconut Residence had received contracts from various agencies in Germany and the United Kingdom.

Key success factors:

❑ *The Coconut Residence pays particular attention to meeting the needs of individual guests and maintains contact with them after they have returned home.*

❑ *The Spanish chef has several years of experience and long managerial experience in Germany. He trains Gambian staff in the provision of first-class service. All the food is procured locally.*

❑ *The management takes a long-term view of the investment, paying particular attention to relations with both clients and staff. As well as priding itself on being frank and open with all staff, management pays performance-related bonuses. It is already training its future managers.*

Constraints:

❑ *Organizational difficulties during the construction period and start of operations.*

❑ *Staff were not used to offering the level of service required. With training and management openness, they quickly adapted to requirements.*

❑ *The company does not benefit like enterprises in conventional sectors from investment incentives such as waivers on customs duty or tax holidays.*

Impact of e-trade and industry consolidation

E-trade is having a profound effect on the tourism industry. Consumers have adopted online travel planning faster than any other online retail activity, and online leisure travel bookings are expected to exceed US$ 29 billion (or 12% of industry revenues) by 2003. Increasingly, tourist destinations are offering virtual samplings online of the ambience of their tourism products to entice consumers to make a travel commitment. Consumers now expect not only to make destination selections online but also to make arrangements for travel, accommodation and local transportation at the same website.

There is growing
consolidation within the
travel industry, with an
increasing part of the market
controlled by networks of
tour operators, hotel chains,
airlines, and rental car
companies.

There is growing consolidation within the travel industry, with an increasing part of the market controlled by networks of tour operators, hotel chains, airlines and car rental companies. Therefore even if individual tourism planning is on the rise, so is the use of intermediaries to guarantee value for money. The use of packaged tours, study trips, and cruises makes planning easier for the tourist but also decreases the in-country multiplier effects as all-inclusive fees are paid ahead of time in the country of origin. Also on the rise, as a form of packaged tour, is incentive travel awarded by corporations to their employees.

Opportunities and constraints for LDCs

Many LDCs have excellent tourism potential, with a rich diversity of natural, cultural and other heritage assets. However, in the majority of countries, including the United Republic of Tanzania, a high proportion of the assets remain undeveloped and inaccessible to visitors. LDCs have yet to make a significant impact in this industry, which is forecast to become one of the largest in the world. Their product offer is unknown and their industries are underdeveloped because of the following structural constraints:

- Lack of effective promotion, both of the destination and products offered by specific businesses.

- Weak tourism administration.

- Lack of basic facilities, proper infrastructure and social services.

One of the main challenges for LDCs is to let potential tourists know what they have to offer.

- Lack of investment in the tourism plant and the wider product (attractions, entertainment, shopping, etc.).

- Lack of qualified, trained and skilled human resources.

- High level of ecological fragility and vulnerability.

One of the main challenges for LDCs is to raise the awareness of potential tourists of their offerings. Most LDCs do not have an experienced tourist board to promote the destination, and the private sector lacks the expertise and resources to promote their products to the tourism trade and on the Internet. Online bookings are difficult or non-existent, owing to limitations in the telecommunications and Internet infrastructure. Information is not presented in a manner that helps the potential visitor to differentiate the country's market offerings from others.

In most LDCs, there has been little training of frontline tourism personnel.

In most LDCs, there has been little training of frontline personnel (e.g. taxi drivers, tour guides, interpreters, hotel and restaurant staff, attractions staff) in customer service standards. LDCs have also neglected two issues of primary importance to foreign visitors – health and safety. For this reason, most foreign tourists prefer to travel under prepaid arrangements where an intermediary is responsible for the quality of service that they receive. Such arrangements lower the multiplier effect in the host countries.

But perhaps most importantly, many LDCs have yet to embrace the concept of sustainable tourism. Conventional hotel-based tourism, restricted to the beach, is not sustainable, and it often builds resentment in the host community.

Fish products

About 30 LDCs export fish products of marine, freshwater and aquaculture origins, bringing them an annual turnover of US$ 1.8 billion between 1995 and 1999. Five countries (Bangladesh, Myanmar, Madagascar, Mozambique and Senegal) provided over 95% of the LDCs' exports of crustaceans and molluscs.

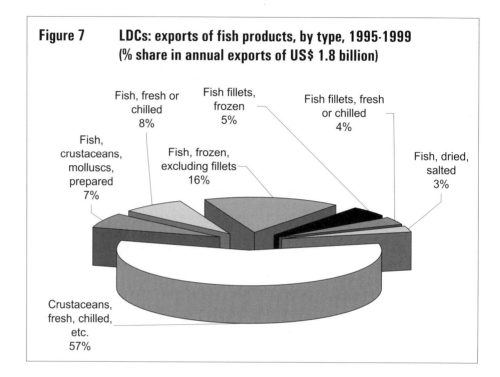

Figure 7   LDCs: exports of fish products, by type, 1995-1999 (% share in annual exports of US$ 1.8 billion)

LDCs are also significant sources of fresh, chilled and frozen fish (including tuna, sardines, herring, mackerel, flat fish and salmon). The major suppliers are the Solomon Islands, Equatorial Guinea, Kiribati, Maldives, Mauritania, Senegal, Bangladesh, Cambodia and Yemen.

Beyond the preparation of fish fillets and drying, fish processing in LDCs consists mainly of canning (of tuna in particular). However, LDC supplies of canned fish have not exceeded 0.6% of world imports in recent years. Senegal, Madagascar, Bangladesh, the United Republic of Tanzania, Uganda and the Solomon Islands are the largest LDC exporters of processed fish products.

The main factor affecting the form in which fish is consumed worldwide is convenience. Demand in developed countries is being driven increasingly by the preferences of an ageing, better-educated, health- and quality-conscious clientele. Exports will need to be tailored to the requirements of specific import market segments; innovative branding will be required; and better packaging to increase shelf-life will be essential.

Among direct consumers, the market is moving towards high-quality fresh fish products, and away from whole fish to time-saving fillets. Pre-packed and pre-cooked fish products are sold increasingly through restaurants and fast-food outlets. Demand for farmed fish, white fish, crustaceans and molluscs is rising faster in developed countries; import requirements in developing countries are tending to emphasize lower-value fish, such as the small pelagic species.

> ### Box 19
> ### *Madagascar: staying competitive against the multinationals*
>
> **Company:** *Unlike most fishing businesses in Madagascar, Manda does not belong to a multinational enterprise. It is wholly owned by Arthur and Bakoly Razakanavalona. A medium-sized company by Malagasy standards, with 1% of the domestic market for fish, it nevertheless remains competitive against the big companies. It handles 180 tons of exports and has an annual turnover of US$ 600,000.*
>
> **Performance:** *Founded in 1995, Manda specializes in exporting frozen fish. It has six sales outlets in the capital Antananarivo and four at the second largest industrial centre, Antsirabe. Its major markets are Mauritius, South Africa and Singapore. In all Manda has 32 permanent staff, 20 working on exports. Mahajanga, 650 km north-west of the capital, with its community of traditional fishers, is Manda's principal source of fish.*
>
> *Mme Razakanavalona has been in the fish business since 1990. She was a management executive in a big international fish import-export company at Antananarivo until she left in 1994 to set up her own business.*
>
> **Key success factor:** *Because of Manda's recognized reliability in delivery and supplies, its customers today are ready to pay for orders in advance, which is indispensable for the company's cash flow and a guarantee of healthy finances. Manda's customers normally put their own label on the fish after processing abroad.*
>
> *Other success factors:*
>
> ❏ *Manda operates a strategy of reinvestment in the business above a 15% profit on sales.*
>
> ❏ *Manda's concern for quality has obliged it to become more involved in monitoring the harvesting of fish and in assisting traditional communities to meet international standards.*
>
> ❏ *It has helped traditional fishermen to become more professional, providing boats and nets, and training them on freezing procedures, standards and quality control. It has put powerboats at their disposal to bring the catch quickly to shore.*
>
> ❏ *It has signed a contract with traditional entrepreneurs to ensure that the cold chain is not broken. In return, Manda guarantees to buy all the catch and to pay the fishermen cash on delivery. The company transports the fish by road to the capital in its own refrigerated trucks. Mr Razakanavalona, a driver-mechanic by trade, is responsible for maintenance and logistics.*
>
> **Constraints:** *Several foreign vessels, mainly European, harvest in Malagasy waters under an agreement with the European Union. However, this exploitation is now threatening to reduce the catch of artisanal fishermen considerably. Manda plans to start collecting fish from south and east Madagascar, which will require the extension of the processing plant. It also plans to bring its standards in line with European regulations to enable it to sell to the European market.*

Opportunities and constraints for LDCs

A large number of LDCs have the advantage of natural marine and freshwater resources, which yield high-value fish products, such as white fish, crustaceans, cephalopods and river fish. Moreover, the business community in several LDCs, grasping the importance of fish farming for ensuring the sustainability of fish supplies, has invested in aquaculture.

These countries have efficient and dynamic traditional fishing communities despite their many problems, and small-scale fish landings have risen in the last decade. By contrast, the export-oriented packaging and processing sector has often failed to perform competitively, notwithstanding financing and efforts to modernize. One result has been the emphasis on the export development of whole fish and fresh, chilled or frozen products.

The major challenge faced by LDCs is how to ensure that their products continue to meet the growing health and safety requirements of importing countries. Among the other constraints are:

• Lack of funds for the development of new harbours and the renovation or replacement of fleet;

• Inadequate infrastructure and facilities, and lack of skilled personnel;

• Over-fishing in several areas and a depletion of breeding stocks;

• Insufficient dissemination of reliable information on products, prices, markets and trade patterns;

• Irregular shipping and airfreight services, and scarcity of insurance cover;

• Inadequate inter-ministerial and sectoral consultation and coordination mechanisms for resolving institutional conflicts and differences in approaches and priorities; and

• Heavy dependence, for geographical and historical reasons, on European markets for higher-value fish products.

An increasing number of small and medium-sized specialized LDC operators have turned from capture of domestic market breeds (notably small pelagic fish) to coastal fishing for export, stimulated by official export incentives and encouraged by the recent devaluation of local currencies. This has resulted in domestic market supply shortages and triggered significant increases in prices, raising food security problems in several LDCs.

Several other problems have restricted the development of the intraregional trade in fishing products, despite rapidly increasing import demand. LDC African exporters have lost market shares in Africa and have been replaced by exporters from developed and developing countries. Their problems include landing and official language problems, frustrating administrative and customs difficulties, and financial trade restrictions. Moreover, product transport problems and non-operational clearing mechanisms have blocked the entry of LDC products into the African and Arab markets in particular.

The access of LDC exporters into markets abroad is influenced by national support measures as well as by tariffs, trade and fishing agreements. Several LDCs provide attractive investment, tax and customs conditions to export-oriented, labour-intensive fishing and fish-processing enterprises in industrial free zones, or to companies exporting a part of their output (for example, at least 80% of the output of enterprises benefit from this special status in Senegal). Fishing is subsidized through various measures, such as preferential pricing of fuel, duty-free or low-duty import of equipment and spare parts, and direct export subsidies.

Free or low-tax market access and the absence of quota restrictions under the Lomé Convention contributed to the competitiveness of fishery products from LDCs on the European market. Moreover, the three main import markets for fish products from LDCs have substantially reduced the tariffs applicable under the most-favoured-nation clause: average tariffs were lowered to 0.9% in the United States, to 4% in Japan and to 10.7% in the European Union.

Most LDCs with sea access have established fishing codes, in a bid to protect their stock of sea resources and to optimize their value, defining usage rights and standards of utilization. However, the codes are often difficult to apply, and shipowners and fishermen continue to try to obtain the biggest catches possible of species of high commercial value. This could lead in the medium- or long-term to over-exploitation and limit export resource availability.

Moreover, most coastal LDCs do not have sufficient means to exploit their marine resources and have given access to these resources to other countries. The latter have often resorted to over-fishing, slowing down the development of small-scale fishing in LDCs and reducing their export competitiveness. Local fishermen in Senegal, Mozambique and Cape Verde are already complaining that foreign trawlers are taking the best catch, to the detriment of local fishing and the supply for export.

Quality and health control measures imposed by the European Union in 1997 were perceived by fish exporters as non-tariff measures on their value-added products. These measures added to the already heavy burdens imposed by the increasingly stringent requirements on quality and grading, health certification, packaging, marking and labelling in all developed import markets and in advanced developing countries. The initial impact of these measures was severe on LDCs, creating substantial loss of employment and foreign exchange earnings and imposing major investment requirements.

Business, professional and related services

Without exception, all LDCs export business, professional and related services and, for some of them, the revenues thus generated are crucial. Bangladesh, Haiti, Madagascar and Nepal supply substantial back-office services to foreign clients. Nepal and some other LDCs have public and private organizations supplying labour under contract internationally. Consulting firms in LDCs work successfully for donor agencies, and there are some striking success stories: a Ugandan engineering firm, for example, won an international contract for regional hydropower management in open competition against major international engineering firms.

Exports of business, professional and related services can create skilled value-added jobs throughout the economy, diversify export revenues and reduce dependence on imports of services.

The development of exports of business and related services can create skilled value-added jobs throughout the economy, diversify export revenues and reduce dependence on imports of services. The main opportunities for LDCs are in the areas of business support services (including the rapidly emerging call-centre market) and computer and related services (software in particular). There is much that LDC Governments and international donor agencies can do to promote exports of these services.

The level of exports of business and related services from LDCs is probably higher than the official statistics record because of the difficulties of collecting accurate data. In addition, these services are rarely given prominence by LDC Governments, either in the allocation of public-sector finance and resources or in export promotion. For example, none of the LDCs provide examples of business and professional services expertise on their websites, and only Ethiopia offers a directory of local consultants on its investment website.

The global market for business and related services is estimated at US$ 3 trillion for 2001, or approximately 10% of global GDP. Exports of business services for 2001 are projected (based on IMF balance-of-payments data) to be US$ 734 billion, or 24% of total global production.

Table 3	LDCs: examples of tradable business-related services	
Exportable service	**Potential exporters**	**Potential importers**
Business support services	Djibouti, Ethiopia, Madagascar, Mozambique, Nepal	All other LDCs
Consultation services on creating back-office operations	Bangladesh, Madagascar	Djibouti, Mauritania, Mozambique Nepal, Uganda, United Republic of Tanzania
Agricultural services (e.g. soil testing)	Ethiopia, Malawi	Mozambique
Services incidental to hydropower production	Bhutan, Cambodia, Uganda, Zambia	Benin, Burkina Faso, Guinea, Nepal
Mining services (e.g. expertise on mining operations, gem valuation)	Ethiopia, Guinea, Mauritania, Uganda United Republic of Tanzania, Zambia	Burkina Faso, Cambodia, Malawi, Mali, Mozambique
Services incidental to oil and gas (e.g. field services)	Benin, Mauritania, United Republic of Tanzania	Madagascar, Mozambique
Services incidental to commodity processing (e.g. production management, industrial design, packaging)	Bangladesh	Guinea, Malawi, Mozambique
Consultation services on free trade zones and offshore operations	Djibouti, Vanuatu	Gambia, Mozambique
Consultation services on creating export processing zones	Bangladesh	Malawi
Consultation services on privatization	Ethiopia, Mozambique, Uganda	Burkina Faso, Madagascar
Convention planning and support services	Ethiopia, United Republic of Tanzania	Djibouti, Gambia, Zambia
Consultation services on eco-tourism development	Gambia, Malawi, Uganda	Benin, Ethiopia, Madagascar, Mali, Mauritania
Consultation services on developing port and trans-shipment services	Djibouti	Gambia
Consultation services on developing security services	Bangladesh, Guinea, Nepal, Zambia	Mauritania
Consultation services on strengthening health care systems	Uganda, United Republic of Tanzania	Burkina Faso, Malawi
Consultation services on environmental health hazards (e.g. bilharzia)	Uganda	Bangladesh, Burkina Faso, Ethiopia, Malawi
Consultation services on AIDS (acquired immunodeficiency syndrome) education and prevention	Uganda	Benin, Burkina Faso, Cambodia, Ethiopia, Haiti, Malawi, United Republic of Tanzania, Zambia
Consulting engineering services	Cambodia, Ethiopia	Mozambique
Consultation services on establishing professional associations	Bangladesh, Haiti, Malawi, Nepal, Zambia	All other LDCs
Consultation services on establishing an association of services exporters	Uganda	All other LDCs

Source: ITC.

Since 1990, exports of business services from developing economies have been 50% higher than those from developed countries, and have grown at an annual average of 10.5%, as against 6.9% for the developed world. Developing countries already account for approximately one-quarter of global exports of business services, and their share is expected to continue to rise.

> ### Box 20
> ### *Uganda: launching and sustaining a services coalition*
>
> *The Ugandan Government knows that services industries and exports form a largely invisible but key part of the economies of developing countries. Under GATS, trade in services will become increasingly liberalized. This will create new opportunities abroad for Ugandan service firms and increased foreign competition in Uganda's domestic market.*
>
> *In 1997, at an ITC workshop on GATS and because the Ugandan Government recognized the importance of services, a resolution was passed to form a services exporters' association to provide a strong voice for the needs and accomplishments of services exporters. Its objective was to raise the profile of Uganda's services industries. Since the existing services associations did not address export readiness nor the export information needs of member companies, the coalition would address this gap.*
>
> *Today, the Association has 30 members, with plans to expand its membership. All the other services coalitions in the world – totalling just seven – are in developed countries.*
>
> *ITC is currently working closely with the Uganda Services Exporters' Association to develop it further as a model for other developing countries.*

Constraints

In the sectors being reviewed, professional associations fulfil an important function by setting standards, enforcing codes of conduct, and providing ongoing education. In most LDCs, such associations do not exist. Exceptions include a management consultants' association in Bangladesh; accountancy associations (affiliated with the International Federation of Accountants, IFAC) in Haiti, Malawi and Zambia; and engineering associations in Bangladesh and Nepal. However, the focus tends to be on domestic regulatory matters rather than on supporting export initiatives by members through mutual recognition agreements with sister associations in export markets.

Services exporters in LDCs report that they are constrained by a lack of profile. Their own Governments are typically unaware of their capabilities.

Services exporters in LDCs also report that they are constrained by a lack of profile. Their own Governments are typically unaware of their capabilities, national websites make no mention of world-class service exports, and international donor agencies overlook the expertise that they have to offer.

When large projects and specialized work are consistently awarded to foreign firms, often because of tied aid, it is extremely difficult for local professionals (who have often been trained and licensed in those foreign countries before returning home) to maintain their specialized expertise.

Often national development planning focuses on transport infrastructure, forgetting the importance of telecommunications and Internet access for exports in the services sectors.

The costs of doing business are typically high for LDC business-related service firms. Cable television is now available in many LDCs, but cable modem access has not yet been made available. Often national development planning focuses on transport infrastructure, forgetting the importance of telecommunications and Internet access for the export trade in services.

Other associated costs include high import duties on computer and office equipment. Until local application service providers are developed in LDCs, business service firms will have to continue to bear the high costs of continuous upgrades in computer equipment and software.

Another major constraint relates to temporary business travel for conferences and other venues, where exporters can meet potential international clients and demonstrate their competence. Often host countries require business persons to present a letter of invitation or to provide financial statements from their bank or tax authority.

> **Box 21**
> *Togo: finding a niche for translation services*
>
> *Last summer, a translator in Togo, Mr Akoli Penoukou, realized that business was falling off and that he needed a way to bring in new revenue. A subscriber to the ITC Forum magazine, he read an article on how to innovate as a service provider to obtain new clients and differentiate oneself from competitors in services exporting.*
>
> *Following the article's advice, he looked for new opportunities. During a chance visit to a pharmacy, Mr Penoukou noticed that many of the products were imported from Europe and carried labels only in European languages.*
>
> *Though he had a small business, Mr Penoukou took the plunge and approached the large pharmaceutical producers abroad, offering to translate the labels online. He also contacted chambers of commerce and industry associations.*
>
> *Six months later, Mr Penoukou reports that he is now registered as a translation agency in Germany and is receiving work from that country. He is also in the final stages of being registered by firms in three other countries, including the United States. As a result of this international expansion, three new jobs were created for Togolese translators, all of whom were about to seek work abroad because of the economic situation at home.*

What can LDC Governments do?

Governments could provide incentives for start-ups of business service firms whether funded locally or through foreign direct investment.

The most important step that LDC Governments can take is to raise awareness of their countries' business and professional service capabilities among potential customers and foreign investors. These capabilities should be highlighted on all national websites (whether managed by the Government or hosted by others). Service firms should be registered in online directories and e-marketplaces. To help local businesses, government agencies should promote domestic capabilities among foreign-owned firms in export processing or free trade zones and offshore operations. Special incentives could be linked to the use of local service firms. Governments could also provide incentives for start-ups of service firms whether funded locally or through foreign direct investment.

Development funding needs to target relevant human resource development. This includes skills training of personnel for service firms.

Additional promotion is needed through networks of contacts. Some LDCs, such as Uganda, have post-secondary institutions where a number of regional business and political leaders have been trained. These alumni can form an excellent referral network.

Development funding needs to target human resource development. This includes skills training, and training in exporting services. An efficient and responsive communications industry is essential for most business services. International experience has indicated that this is best achieved by liberalizing the industry. Attention should also be given to providing high-speed broadband access to the Internet. Both wireless and cable modem Internet access can be cost-efficient alternatives to trying to extend wired capacity.

Most LDCs offer tax incentives or import duty concessions to new industries. Where appropriate, LDCs should consider similar incentives for service firms (e.g. such as reducing the cost of importing hardware).

Coffee

LDCs supply 10% of the
world's green coffee.

About half of LDCs produce and export robusta coffee, while Rwanda, Burundi, the United Republic of Tanzania, Yemen, Benin and Ethiopia provide over 80% of all the arabica exported worldwide. The LDCs' exports of green coffee during 1995-1999 averaged US$ 1.3 billion, equivalent to 10% of the global import trade. Their annual exports of processed coffee have been limited to US$ 1.9 million in coffee solubles and extracts, and US$ 1.5 million in roasted coffee.

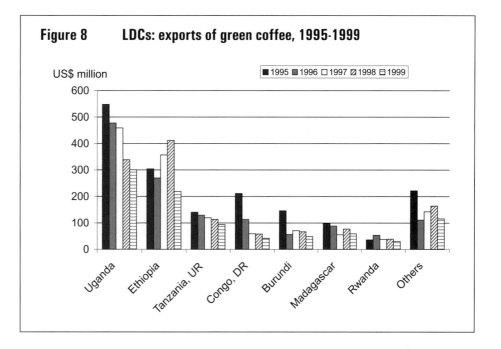

Figure 8   LDCs: exports of green coffee, 1995-1999

The largest exporters of green coffee are Uganda, Ethiopia, United Republic of Tanzania, Democratic Republic of the Congo, Burundi and Madagascar. The four leading suppliers of roasted coffee are Madagascar, Ethiopia, Uganda and United Republic of Tanzania. The bulk of the coffee solubles and extracts is provided by the United Republic of Tanzania, followed far behind by Togo, the Lao People's Democratic Republic, Uganda, Burundi and Myanmar.

Coffee provides over half of the export earnings of Uganda, Burundi, Rwanda and Ethiopia.

Although net world imports of coffee by volume increased by 4% a year in the five years to 1999, values fluctuated widely, declining over the period because of the slump in international market prices. The vagaries of international coffee prices provoked economic shocks in Uganda, Burundi, Rwanda and Ethiopia, where coffee provides over half of the national export earnings.

Stagnant consumption, but demand for speciality coffees is growing fast...

Consumption in developed countries has stagnated since the beginning of the 1990s. The slight increase in global consumption in volume terms, not exceeding 1% yearly since 1995, is occurring mainly in developing countries. The world's largest coffee consumers are developed and industrialized developing countries.

Box 22
Burundi: increasing exports of gourmet coffee

Coffee accounts for more than 50% of Burundi's exports. It is estimated that 800,000 persons grow at least some coffee, and for many farmers the arabica bean provides the family's only cash income. Grown on steep hillsides at altitudes of 1,500 - 2,000 metres, coffee helps prevent soil erosion. All work is done by hand and the cherries are delivered to washing stations on foot, often requiring a 7 km hike.

The three-year Gourmet Coffee Project, launched in 1997 by ITC, the International Coffee Organization (ICO) and the Common Fund for Commodities (CFC), looked at ways Burundi could earn more from its attractive, mild-tasting but rather small bean.

At the time the Burundi bean was accepted as a useful but not essential element in European coffees. The conclusion was that Burundi could earn more only by increasing yields and raising quality.

The official body coordinating the coffee business OCIBU (Office du café du Burundi) used the data from 10 years of records to select the most promising area in which to grow a speciality coffee that could be targeted to new markets in the United States and Japan. Since there were no growers' associations, OCIBU's staff prepared a number of 'grower messages' to be distributed at the washing stations on selective harvesting and handling.

The first harvest ran into technical problems, partly over quality control, and it was decided in 1999 to use a private mill that could handle small batches of coffee. Still, about one-third of beans had to be rejected.

But in February 1999, 33 tons of the 1998 harvest were sent to Japan, where Ngoma Mild was well received, and 68 tons of the 1999 crop were exported later that year, earning 30-35 cents a pound more than the coffee sent to Europe. Reactions were encouraging enough for Burundi to continue the experiment.

Five participants in the coffee project

In all, five very different coffee-producing countries, including three LDCs, participated in the US $1.4 million Gourmet Coffee Project: Brazil, Burundi, Ethiopia, Papua New Guinea and Uganda.

The project tested a range of activities from production methods to marketing tools. Market development work included cup-tasting panels, brochures and films, articles in the press and exhibitions. In addition to new sales outlets in the United States and Japan for Burundi, the results included better recognition of the gourmet coffee potential in Brazil; better coffee selection methods and premiums to farmers in Ethiopia; promotion support in Japan for Papua New Guinea producers and the identification of smallholders' quality coffees; and new processing methods in Uganda.

The most spectacular event of the project was an online worldwide Internet auction of coffees from the participating countries over 48 hours in December 1999. It was the first event of its kind. The technology worked, and coffees were sold at prices substantially above expectations. Brazil scheduled a second auction, which sold more coffee, in 2000 and planned a third for late 2001.

In the next four years or so, sales of speciality coffees in the United States are expected to reach 50% of all coffee sales. The cappucino varieties predominate among these coffees, achieving almost two-thirds of sales.

The United States is the largest single importer of coffee. According to the International Coffee Organization, demand there is stronger for roasted coffee and decaffeinated coffee. The speciality/gourmet market absorbed 22% of total sales by volume in 1997, and 27% by value (or 37% inclusive of instant speciality coffees). In the next four years or so, sales of speciality coffees in the United States are expected to reach US$ 3 billion - US$ 4 billion, or around 50% of all coffee sales in the country. The cappucino varieties predominate among these coffees, achieving almost two-thirds of sales.

The European Union is still the largest consuming region, but its share in world imports had fallen to 33% by 2000. About 95% of coffee consumption in Scandinavia consists of high-quality speciality/gourmet light roasts. Finland traditionally consumes 100% pure arabica of a gourmet quality. The recent growth in the Spanish coffee market has been largely due to speciality coffees, particularly espresso. *Torrefacto* and *mexcla* coffees, common in Spain, qualify as speciality coffees. Speciality instant coffees accounted for 56% of coffee sales in Germany in 1997. As in the United States, cappuccino varieties predominate in this category.

Japan is the fourth largest importer, after the United States, the European Union and Brazil. Its most popular products are soluble and canned coffees.

As in the past, growth in the global supply of coffee will outpace demand and depress international prices. Although it will be less volatile than supply, demand will fluctuate in response to price developments. Demand can be encouraged by coffee promotion, which will also soften the impact of higher prices on consumption. Domestic policies on coffee production, pricing, stocks and trade will continue to exert a strong influence on the world market.

Several consumer trends will persist in the medium term. These include a decline in the share of soluble coffee in world demand and the related fall in requirements for robusta coffee, the growth of the gourmet markets for high-quality and speciality coffees, and a general shift in preferences towards arabicas.

Over the long term, the markets with the strongest growth potential are the Russian Federation, China and the eastern European countries. For LDCs, these market trends have major implications.

Prospects and strategies for LDCs

The major achievement of the Uruguay Round negotiations in relation to coffee was the complete elimination of import tariffs on green, non-decaffeinated coffee by the European Union. However, tariff and non-tariff barriers, including internal taxes and tariff escalation, continue to restrict exports of processed coffee from LDCs to developed markets, with the exception of the United States and Sweden.

LDC coffee exporters could benefit if they:

LDC coffee exporters could increase their market shares by improving product quality, increasing their offer of gourmet, speciality and organic coffees, and of branded products or coffees of certified origins.

- Improve the quality of their coffee and establish themselves as reliable sources of supply.

- Promote gourmet coffee varieties. ITC has played a leading role in developing the markets for, and promoting, higher-value coffees. For example, it has recently assisted Uganda in developing and promoting some of its robusta coffee as gourmet varieties. There are similar opportunities for other LDCs to access premium coffee markets.

Ethiopia and Uganda have exported certified organic coffee.

- Promote exports of organic coffee. Provided a cost-efficient system of certification can be introduced, organic coffee can be produced and exported at little extra cost. The price premium for this coffee on international markets is currently around 15-20 cents/lb, although it can be as high as 40 cents/lb for some types of gourmet coffee. Several LDCs, such as Ethiopia and Uganda, have already succeeded in producing and exporting certified organic coffee.

- Promote branded coffees of certified origins. Demand for coffee of particular brands or from certified origins (e.g. coffee from the Kilimanjaro region of Kenya) is growing, and these can be positioned as premium coffee.

- Increase the export offer of processed coffee. Despite the strong concentration of coffee processors in developed countries, several LDCs, such as Madagascar, Ethiopia, Uganda and the United Republic of Tanzania, have installed domestic processing units and export processed (roasted) coffee. LDC exporters can form alliances with international processors, wholesalers and retailers in consuming countries in order to offer processed or branded products to the international market.

Box 23
Ethiopia: training to keep coffee quality high

Abraham Begashaw is Manager and Chief Liquorer at the Coffee and Tea Quality Inspection & Liquoring Centre in Ethiopia. He is one of the many young professionals who have benefited from ITC-financed and ITC-arranged training missions for promising young executives in the public and private sector to expand their skills and study the market abroad.

From 1983 to 1986 he was Regional Coordinator of coffee-producing cooperatives in Ethiopia, becoming a junior coffee grader and liquorer in 1987. In 1989, with the support of ITC, he was trained in coffee control analysis, sampling and roasting techniques, and warehouse management in Kenya. This was followed by training in the United States in the coffee trade and futures market.

'The training gave me an insight into importers' perception of quality, which I still use in my efforts to improve the quality and reputation of Ethiopian coffees,' he notes. The other Ethiopians who went abroad for training are today active in the country's private coffee business.

Mr Begashaw advanced to senior coffee-grader and liquorer with the Coffee and Tea Authority in 1990, where he was responsible for classifying and certifying the grade quality of all coffee prior to auction and export. He became head of the coffee and tea trade department in 1994. He earned a Bachelor of Science in agricultural economics at Alemaya College, Ethiopia, in 1994, following this with a Master of Science in food economics and marketing in 1999 from the University of Reading, United Kingdom.

He continued to explore coffee quality control techniques in Germany and Italy, and throughout the 1990s attended conferences, seminars and cupping sessions of the Specialty Coffee Association of America (SCAA). He also visited major coffee-producing countries such as Brazil, Côte d'Ivoire and Kenya to study their systems of processing, grading, quality control and marketing. He took part in an ISO quality assurance seminar organized by the Ethiopian Standards Institution.

Mr Begashaw has in turn trained others, leading to an increase in the number of coffee quality experts in the country. In 1994, he prepared an African coffee flavour profile manual under the sponsorship of the Inter-African Coffee Organization (IACO).

'The quality standard of export coffee from Ethiopia has improved, particularly sun-dried coffee, as a result of introducing better coffee grading and a quality control system,' Mr Begashaw states.

Cotton and cotton fibres

Thirty of the 49 LDCs produce and export cotton and cotton fibre, which are important foreign exchange earners for many of these countries.

Cotton consumption, stimulated by economic growth and lower prices (in comparison with man-made fibres), reached record levels in 1997 and again in 2000. However, world imports fell sharply from US$ 10.8 billion in 1998 to US$ 5.8 billion in 1999, mainly because of broader economic trends in East Asia and Turkey and the increasing relocation of textiles and clothing manufacture to developing countries. Over 92% of the trade consisted of cotton, not carded or combed, and 9% of cotton linters. Imports of cotton yarn averaged US$ 7.4 billion between 1995 and 1999.

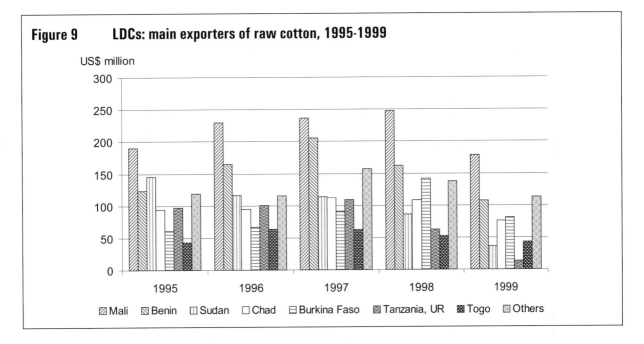

Figure 9   LDCs: main exporters of raw cotton, 1995-1999

US$ million

Legend: Mali, Benin, Sudan, Chad, Burkina Faso, Tanzania, UR, Togo, Others

The share of supplies from LDCs in world imports increased steadily, from nearly 9% in 1995 to 12% in 1999. However, the value of their exports dropped US$ 87 million in 1995, to US$ 65 million in 1999, as cotton prices fell drastically following the market developments mentioned above. The main exporters of cotton, contributing over 80% of the total for LDCs over the period, are Mali, Benin, the Sudan, Chad, Burkina Faso, Togo and the United Republic of Tanzania.

Annual exports of cotton fibre from LDCs averaged US$ 50.6 million a year, equivalent to less than 1% of world imports. Zambia, the Sudan, Madagascar and the United Republic of Tanzania provide nearly all of these supplies.

World market trends and development prospects for LDCs

The general increase in world production, yields and consumption of cotton, as well as in world import demand, will continue, sustained by the rise in world population and disposable incomes, and the revived international appreciation of the intrinsic properties of cotton relative to substitutes. Import demand for cotton and cotton fibre for the textile industries is expected to remain concentrated in Asia. Asian processors and exporters of textiles will cater for the rapidly growing regional demand, and expand   their shares in developed markets.

Provided the world economy stays buoyant and consumption rises, the long-term direction of cotton prices is upward. However, the significant additional production capacity for synthetic fibres foreseen to come on-stream in the medium term is likely to prevent any excessive increases in price levels. In the short term, however, much will depend on the evolution of China's stocks, imports and consumption.

Several marketing and technology issues will affect the cotton sector as a whole. These include industry restructuring, strengthening of global competition, biotechnology and consumer-related issues (e-commerce, labelling and ecological concerns).

Spinners, the primary raw cotton consumers, require competitively priced fibre of regular, standardized quality in order to supply plants which run at over 98% of capacity and reduce labour needs to a minimum. In the increasingly competitive world markets, these requirements are likely to become even more stringent. They will accelerate the need to set up a more coordinated worldwide marketing system for cotton and the application of global quality standards in the long term.

The tendency to control the supply of cotton at origin is likely to continue.

The tendency to try to control the supply of cotton at origin is also likely to continue, with spinners, processors and large traders promoting cotton in conjunction with governments in developing countries and LDCs with successful privatization programmes. Despite their often opposing short-term interests, cotton breeders, growers, spinners and traders will be constrained to follow the example of the United States and Brazil, and strengthen their partnership, in order to improve the profitability of all segments of the national cotton sectors.

Ginning and spinning are the first cotton upgrading processing stages. In most LDCs, these is where bottlenecks to development will have to be eliminated.

In LDCs, bottlenecks to development during ginning and spinning will have to be eliminated.

Cotton contamination has a major negative impact on the cost-effective use of LDC fibre in quality garments. International spinners increasingly refuse contaminated cotton lint and the LDCs' potential to add value to cotton is greatly impaired by their current incapacity to meet quality requirements abroad. Giving ginners access to adequate extension services and support in quality improvement can boost cotton processing in LDCs.

Certified organic cotton fibre has a lucrative niche market, with international market prices 1.5 to 2 times higher than those for ordinary fibre. However, growing cotton organically entails initial risks for farmers, as yields may be reduced and costs are 15% to 20% higher than those of conventional cultivation methods.

The main distortions in the world cotton trade have resulted from direct or indirect subsidization of production in cotton-producing countries. The small number of countries following free market policies (Australia, Argentina, Paraguay, Mexico, Peru, Nigeria, Israel and some other small cotton producers) together account for less than 5% of the world cotton output.

Trade in processed cotton has also been subject to distortions brought about by tariff escalation and the Multifibre Arrangement. However, the trade-weighted nominal tariffs on cotton yarn from developing countries entering the EU market dropped from 6% in 1992 to 4% in the post-Uruguay Round period. Under the African Growth and Opportunity Act, the United States has granted quota-free and/or duty-free treatment to selected goods from all African LDCs. Textiles, apparel and cotton seed are among these goods, although raw cotton is not. By lowering United States import tariffs on alternative crops and providing greater access to the American textiles and clothing market, AGOA may result

> **Box 24**
> **Chad: direct marketing pays**
>
> **Company:** CotonTchad, officially known as the Société cotonnière du Tchad and formerly 75% State-owned, is being privatized. About 90% of its operations is carried out by nine mills capable of handling 230,000 tons of raw cotton a year. In addition, it has a large modern complex that can produce 16,000 tons of oil and 4,000 tons of soap yearly. It sells cotton fibre to the European Union, Asia and Latin America as well as to the Middle East and North Africa.
>
> **Performance:** From 1993/94 to 1999/00, its exports of fibre rose from 33,205 tons to 71,189 tons.
>
> **Key success factors:**
>
> ❑ Direct marketing to spinning mills without passing through wholesalers.
>
> ❑ CotonTchad has commercial representatives who promote its product and identify potential clients.
>
> ❑ The company also has a portfolio of regular clients in Europe, the Middle East, Asia, Latin America and North Africa.
>
> ❑ Dynamic and aggressive customer development and sales strategies.
>
> **Constraints:**
>
> ❑ Infrastructural: poor roads and other facilities which increase the cost of producing and moving goods.
>
> ❑ Financial: poor availability of finance.
>
> ❑ Rigid banking regulations: these require full repatriation of the company's export revenues.
>
> ❑ International constraints: the agricultural subsidies granted by developed countries to their farmers are an obstacle to the expansion of its sales.

in an increase in the acreage planted to cotton by African LDC farmers in the future. A number of these countries have already submitted applications for eligibility for special treatment under the Act.

Compliance with strict quality standards will remain a critical requirement for increased market penetration.

In conclusion, most LDCs have many of the factors for the successful cultivation, processing and export of cotton and fibre. World markets have the capacity to absorb exports from these countries. However, compliance with the increasingly strict quality standards in importing markets will remain a critical requirement for market penetration.

Wood and wood products

Annual world imports of wood and wood products averaged US$ 100.3 billion between 1995 and 1999, with global demand increasing by a healthy 2.5% yearly over the period. Trade in higher value-added products, such as furniture and builders' joinery and carpentry, grew much faster, while demand for semi-processed or unprocessed products (logs, sawn wood and fuel wood) stagnated.

LDCs supplied less than 1% of world imports over the period at a value of US$ 858 million a year. The bulk of these supplies consisted of hard

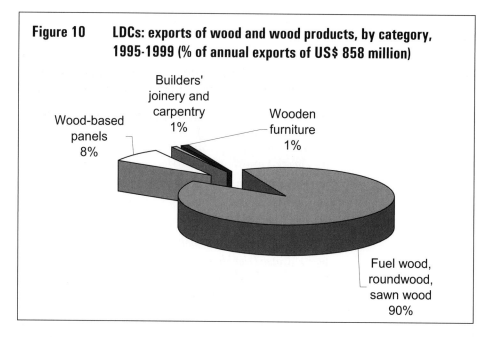

Figure 10   LDCs: exports of wood and wood products, by category, 1995-1999 (% of annual exports of US$ 858 million)

Builders' joinery and carpentry 1%

Wooden furniture 1%

Wood-based panels 8%

Fuel wood, roundwood, sawn wood 90%

roundwood (60% of the total), hard sawn wood (20%) and fuel wood (10%). Exports of value-added products (wood-based panels, builders' joinery and furniture) did not exceed 2% of the total.

Import demand for the main LDC exports is stagnating.

The value of LDC exports declined by 11% a year, from US$ 1,107 million in 1995 to US$ 695 million in 1999. The main causes were the very high share (90%) of unprocessed and semi-processed products, for which import demand was stagnating, and the fall in the international prices of these products between 1995 and 1998. While the volume and value of LDC exports of furniture and wood-based panels rose during the period, this was not enough to compensate for the losses in the main sector.

Myanmar is a traditional source of teak, and the leading LDC exporter of wood and wood products, mainly logs and sawn timber. However, the country's supplies of teak logs from natural forests is falling, following the large-scale exploitation of this species. Plantation teak (of inferior quality) is now being grown. The Solomon Islands is the second biggest LDC exporter of logs. Cambodia holds second place as a source of sawn hardwood; the Solomon Islands, Equatorial Guinea and the Lao People's Democractic Republic are smaller suppliers of this product.

Cambodia, Equatorial Guinea and the Democratic Republic of the Congo are the top three LDC exporters of veneer and sheets for plywood, while Madagascar, Haiti and Myanmar are the leading suppliers of wooden furniture and manufactures for domestic use.

Opportunities and constraints for LDCs

There is a closer physical and economic linkage between primary wood processing (saw milling and veneer/plywood production) and forest management, than between primary and further processing. Semi-finished products, such as rough sawn lumber, veneer or standard plywood, can be efficiently transported over long distances and further processed practically anywhere. Therefore, the comparative advantage derived purely from resource endowment tends to fall with further processing. Economies of scale behave similarly, i.e. the higher the degree of processing, the lower the dependence on plant size as a factor of cost competitiveness.

For LDCs to gain competitiveness in value-added wood products, they will therefore have to balance the following factors:

- The excellent quality of their many tropical timbers, well adapted for further processing, and the widening base of sustainable plantation forests;

- The low costs of raw wood and labour, which can compensate for the high costs of other local and imported inputs, and ensure price competitiveness;

- Quality in the product and the design;

- Alternative strategies for gaining better control over distribution channels by shortening them and reducing the number of intermediaries (thus cutting the incidence of mark-ups on prices).

Africa's demand for sawn wood is expected to rise from 11 million m^3 in 1997 to 12 million m^3 in 2010, outstripping supply by 1 million m^3. The supply gap, mainly in North Africa, will be filled by imports from Europe. Major export flows are expected to take place between Western Africa and Europe and Asia for tropical wood, and between southern Africa and Europe for plantation-grown timber (mainly pine, and some eucalyptus). Good demand for sawn soft wood also exists in North Africa and in the Middle East.

During the same period, the African demand for plywood is expected to more than double, from 650,000 m^3 to 1.4 million m^3. Foreign investment in additional processing units and government support of value addition are increasing West Africa's potential for export. North Africa, the main importer of construction plywood, will offer increased market opportunities for this product.

LDCs have opportunities for increased trade in builders' joinery and carpentry as well as wood flooring.

As far as builders' joinery and carpentry are concerned, LDCs should maximize the use of fast-growing wood species and sustainable high-quality timber as raw materials. Pine and eucalyptus from southern Africa, for example, have already been successfully used for mouldings, interior finishings, shelving, wall and ceiling panelling. Exports of doors and mouldings from the region are rapidly increasing.

Several LDCs have high-value timber which can be adapted for hardwood flooring, although many of the species available are not currently in fashion in the highly conservative flooring markets. Several Madagascar exporters have established joint ventures with French flooring companies and are currently exporting most of their output to their partners' captive markets. This timber also provides raw material for wood carvings and wood handicrafts. The diversification of export destinations remains a key challenge in improving the profitability of exports.

Eucalyptus and acacia may develop into viable flooring materials.

Eucalyptus and acacia plantations may prove much more viable as sources of flooring materials in the coming years, because of the technological progress made being made in processing these fast-growing species. Effective marketing communications, focusing on sustainability and certification of forest management, will provide valuable sales support for fast-growing woods. Eucalyptus flooring producers in Spain and Portugal are providing examples of this new direction.

LDCs need to diversify their markets for furniture.

At present, Myanmar, Samoa and the Lao People's Democratic Republic are the only LDC exporters of wooden furniture. Myanmar exports mainly chairs to the European Union, while the Lao exports consist almost entirely of bedroom furniture for the Russian Federation. This country is also the only buyer of Samoan wooden chairs. LDCs need to diversify their markets for furniture.

Some African LDCs, such as Mozambique, have bamboo resources at their disposal. This under-utilized material is becoming more fashionable as a furniture raw material and could offer interesting export development potential.

Wooden manufactures for domestic use: value-added products for niche markets

Wooden manufactures offer a viable export development opportunity for many LDCs.

Wooden manufactures for domestic use are a good example of value-added products for niche markets which LDCs could exploit. They comprise low-volume, but high-value, consumer-ready products, such as wooden frames, table- and kitchen-ware, wood ornaments, as well as inlaid wood and marquetry. These products offer a viable export development alternative for many LDCs, where the establishment of export-oriented, large-scale wood processing units may be uneconomic. The volume traded on international markets is low, but a large share of the value added remains in the exporting LDCs, leveraging employment and revenue-creation better than the trade in bulk wood products. The level of processing is often advanced, requiring woodworking skills and long traditions of craftsmanship.

Box 25

Mozambique: product costing for artisans

Product costing and pricing are key skills for business survival. Numerous aids have been produced for formal small businesses and larger enterprises, but they have not helped artisanal producers in developing countries to learn elementary techniques.

In 2000, the International Trade Centre produced a training module on basic costing and pricing for artisans who are entrepreneurs, using the experience of Aid to Artisans, Inc. (ATA), a non-profit organization that provides training and collaboration in product development, production and marketing to foster artistic traditions, cultural vitality and community well-being. One African country is already exploring the possibility of producing a local language version of this collection of advice and exercises, case studies and contacts.

One case study concerns Chamania, a group in Nampula, Mozambique, which makes sugar bowls from turned blackwood. The group is a loose union of four men who share and pass on orders, and who are trained to produce each other's products if necessary to ensure they can always fulfil an order.

When Chamani was first asked how much its materials cost, the men replied: 'Nothing. We gather the wood for our products ourselves.' However, each of the four producers was travelling quite a distance to gather enough wood for one month of production. Each man would be gone for a week at a time, leaving the others to cover the incoming orders. The costs in fact included transportation, accommodation and food, and the cost of hiring help to load wood onto a truck, as well as the loss of one week's production.

Chamaria learned that it could reduce costs and increase production by sending out two members of the group to gather a month's supply for all four producers or by hiring less-skilled workers at a lower hourly rate to gather wood.

Chamania had never considered items like sandpaper, chisels, glue and wax in the group's material costs. After doing a proper costing, Chamania worked out that it had been covering only half of its expenses in the price of a sugar bowl.

Increased functionality and better finishing are important to producing exportable wooden products.

For certain products, success in exporting may require the upgrading of equipment and exposure to modern methods of woodworking. In addition, though traditional skills in carving may result in attractive products, their functionality could be increased by better training in cabinet-making and other woodworking skills. Finishing technology is of a crucial importance in producing exportable consumer products of wood.

Oilseed products

Thirty-five LDCs cultivate and export oilseed crops and derived products, and a large part of their populations depend heavily on oil-crop cultivation, processing and trade for their livelihood. Despite the constraints to a more rapid development of the sector, exports of oilseed products from LDCs are expanding, making up between 1% to 5% of merchandise exports in over 30 LDCs. They provide 42%, 26% and 15% respectively of foreign exchange in Vanuatu, the Gambia and the Sudan.

The main oilseeds cultivated in LDCs are groundnut, cottonseed, sesame, oil palm, coconut and shea nut. Some countries also cultivate sunflower, soybean, rape and mustard seed.

LDCs supplied 1.2% of the volume of world imports of oilseed and 0.4% to 0.5% of all imports of oils and cakes over the 1995-1999 period. Under the combined effects of reduced export availability (because of adverse climatic conditions) and depressed international demand and prices, LDC exports of oilseeds fell by 14%, from 706 million tons in 1997 to 608 million tons in 1999. Exports by value rose from US$ 394 million in 1995 to US$ 488 million in 1997, but dropped to US$ 328 million in 1999.

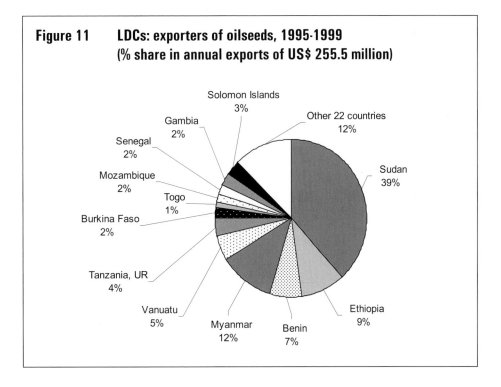

**Figure 11   LDCs: exporters of oilseeds, 1995-1999
(% share in annual exports of US$ 255.5 million)**

Performance in specific oilseeds was much stronger. LDCs supplied about 85% of global imports of shea nuts, 25% of copra, 33% of sesame seed and 16% of palm kernels during the period.

In value terms, the largest LDC exporter of oilseeds was the Sudan (39% of total exports between 1995 and 1997), followed by Myanmar (12%), Ethiopia (9%), Benin (7%) and Vanuatu (5%).

Domestic processing of oilseeds for export is generally not so competitive in LDCs. Therefore, the bulk of their exports over the period consisted of oilseeds (62%). Oil cakes, oils and other oilseed-based products made up 29%, 9% and 1% respectively of total exports. The main LDC exporters of vegetable oils were

Senegal (32% of overall trade by value), the Sudan (25%), Solomon Islands (16%), Benin (7%) and Mali (6%). Twenty-one other LDCs supplied the remaining 14%.

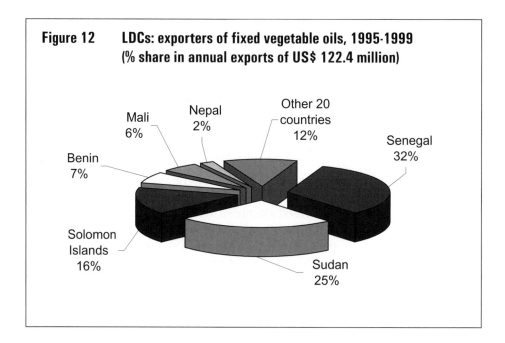

Figure 12   LDCs: exporters of fixed vegetable oils, 1995-1999 (% share in annual exports of US$ 122.4 million)

The LDC export trade in oil cakes rose rapidly, from US$ 31 million in 1995 to over US$ 42 million in 1998, but dropped by nearly 40% to US$ 28 million in 1999. The reason was the crisis in the livestock sector in Europe and the resulting sharp fall in import demand for oil meals. The major exporters were the Sudan (32% of total exports over the period), Senegal (16%), United Republic of Tanzania (9%) and Togo (9%). Twenty-four other LDCs provided the remaining 43%.

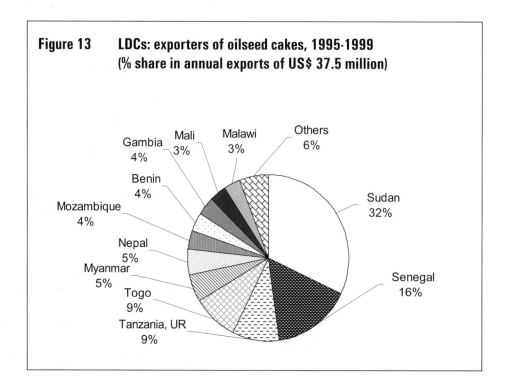

Figure 13   LDCs: exporters of oilseed cakes, 1995-1999 (% share in annual exports of US$ 37.5 million)

Government policies have a major impact on the development of the sector

Several Governments support oilseed production, consumption and trade.

Policies have a major impact on the development of the sector. Governments of both developing and developed countries have tended to intervene in production, consumption and trade in oil crops and derived products through price support and payment schemes, ceilings on cultivated areas, export and market promotion, and other support measures. However, the role of the public sector has now been reappraised in several countries. Governments have reduced market intervention either in the context of general economic reforms or in order to reduce public spending. Several restrictions to the free movement of oil crops have been lifted, many State-dominated processing and trade companies have been privatized and marketing is increasingly being taken over by the private sector.

Such policies are expected to remain in place and continued reforms should bring domestic prices more into line with world market prices, strengthening the transmission of price signals between producers/exporters and consumers/importers. Among LDCs, Senegal has adopted policy measures leading to reduced consumer protection and consumer prices, thereby cutting public expenditure and accelerating economic liberalization.

Main market trends

The sector has traditionally expanded at a faster pace than most other agricultural commodity sectors, and the growth of production, consumption and trade has been stronger in developing than in developed countries. This trend is expected to continue.

A rise in productivity will be essential in LDCs with already high utilization of agricultural land.

Although production growth will continue to result from increases in both the area planted and the productivity of oil crops, the latter will steadily assume greater significance, because the scope for expanded plantings is shrinking, especially in many developing countries and LDCs with a high rate of utilization of agricultural land. There is therefore an acute need to boost productivity in all LDCs where yields per hectare are well below average.

The growth of the LDC output of oilseed products will be increasingly dependent on the development and diffusion of improved cultivation methods, processing technologies, and research and development results.

Environmental protection issues have been attracting increasing attention since the beginning of the 1990s. New approaches should address the possible undesirable effects of some production and extraction techniques on the environment, in particular those of cotton cultivation and oil palm crushing. Moreover, the increasing substitution of petroleum-based raw materials with environment-friendly oilseed-based 'green' products for the manufacture of detergents and fuel substitutes is another important environment-related aspect supporting the rise in demand for oilseeds.

Competition among exporting countries will intensify, and developing countries are expected to take an increasing market share.

The trend for American and Japanese multinationals and for large international food and commodity groups, such as Unilever, Cargill and Arthur Daniel Midlands, to invest or develop partnerships with overseas producers/exporters can support the development of exports of oilseed products from LDCs.

Fruits and nuts

Several LDCs rely heavily on exports of fruits and nuts for foreign earnings.

The development of the fruit and nut sector is important to LDCs in the context of improving nutrition, poverty alleviation and as a source of foreign exchange. In 1997, cashew nuts provided nearly 86% of the total export income of Guinea-Bissau and 13% of that of Mozambique. Over 50% of Afghanistan's foreign exchange earnings in the same year came from dried fruits and nuts; and bananas provided nearly 7% of Somalia's export earnings. The improved economic environment in several LDCs and supportive government policies favoured the rapid expansion of their exports of both fresh and higher-value processed products.

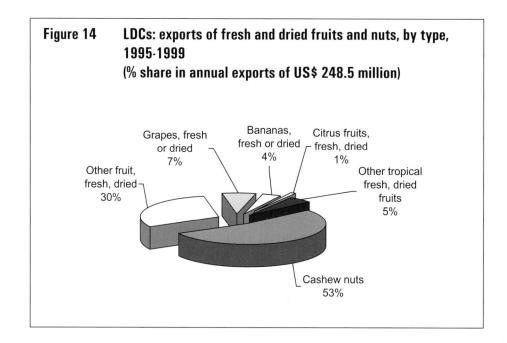

Figure 14   LDCs: exports of fresh and dried fruits and nuts, by type, 1995-1999
(% share in annual exports of US$ 248.5 million)

Average annual LDC exports of fruits and nuts amounted to US$ 248.5 million, equivalent to less than 1% of global imports in 1995-1999. Cashew nuts were the largest export, accounting for 53% of LDC exports of fresh and dried edible nuts. The major African exporters of edible nuts were the United Republic of Tanzania (44% of exports over the period), Mozambique (22%), Guinea-Bissau (16%) and Benin (6%). Afghanistan, Myanmar, Senegal and Malawi were among the smaller exporters.

Exports of fresh and dried tropical fruits consisted of melon, papaya, pineapple, avocado, litchi, guava, mangosteen (30% of the total), fresh and dried grapes (7%), other fresh and dried temperate fruits (5%), bananas (4%) and citrus fruits (1%). The main LDC suppliers were Madagascar and Haiti (with 62% and 13% respectively of exports of other tropical fresh fruits); Bhutan and Mozambique (70% and 19% of exports of fresh and dried citrus); Somalia (88% of exports of bananas), and Afghanistan (almost all exports of fresh apples, grapes and sultanas).

Annual LDC exports of processed fruits and nuts averaged US$ 3.4 million between 1995 and 1999. Over half (58%) were preserved and prepared products, 26% were frozen fruits, and 16% were provisionally preserved products. Haiti was the largest supplier of processed nuts, followed far behind by Malawi, Senegal, Togo and Bhutan.

LDC exports of fruit juices (17% orange juice and 83% other tropical fruit juices) increased steadily, from US$ 303,000 in 1995 to US$ 3.5 million in 1999. Bhutan and Nepal were the main exporters of both citrus and other tropical juices, followed by the Central African Republic, Myanmar and Djibouti for other tropical fruit juices.

Main market trends

The main export problem for LDCs is price competition from other developing countries.

The main problem for LDCs is that many developing countries have already penetrated import markets successfully, establishing a dominant position particularly in fresh and processed tropical fruits. Cashew nuts from LDCs have a good export development potential, as the Indian domestic crop is foreseen to remain short of demand from the local processing sector and the North American and the South African markets should remain open to quality cashew nuts of declared origins. The export development of the sector is of special interest to Guinea Bissau, Mozambique and the United Republic of Tanzania, not least because of the impact of this development on poverty alleviation (family smallholders produce almost all the commercialized crop).

Although contrasting market developments cloud the international market outlook for bananas, the market for fresh, certified organic bananas is growing rapidly and the products fetch substantial price premiums. Cape Verde has already penetrated European markets and supportive government policies in other LDCs could lead to increased exports of organic bananas.

As regards other fruit, the best opportunities for LDCs lie in the supply of fresh fruits, prepared fresh fruits and partially dried fruits. The largest export potential is in the fresh fruit sector, where demand is sustained by consumer interest in healthy eating in all seasons. There is a year-round demand for pineapple, mango, baby banana, lychee and ramboutan, to cite some examples, and for off-season (November to March) temperate products such as melon, strawberry, grape, citrus and stone fruits.

Any expansion in LDC exports of fruits and nuts to developed markets is fully dependent on the quality delivered to consumers. These give the highest importance to the uniformity and specificity of fruit characteristics (colour, size, taste, typical flavour and origin), to the quality of packing, and to attractive and informative labelling of products.

In addition LDC suppliers must meet the requirements of importers, processors and retailers. These include regularity of supply, consistency in quality, compliance with phytosanitary regulations and competitive pricing.

LDC export development opportunities

The favourable climatic and soil conditions in several LDCs for growing varieties of fruits and nuts which could command better prices if their origin is certified, as well as the increasingly beneficial environment created by the liberalization and privatization of their economies, are their main comparative advantages. Moreover, the cultivation and collection of fruits and nuts is labour intensive, and labour is generally abundant in these countries. The sector can ensure regular supplies of quality products for export by securing the output of smallholders under advantageous contractual conditions.

The markets for organic nuts, fruits, juices and pulps offer possibilities for LDCs.

The potential for industrial value added and for the export of organic products is eliciting great interest among local entrepreneurs. Burkina Faso, Mali and Guinea are already processing fruit into fruit drinks (juices, syrups), jams and dried fruit. Likewise, exporters from Cape Verde and the Gambia have penetrated the EU market for fresh organic fruits.

> **Box 26**
>
> **ITC's pioneering study on organic food products**
>
> *On the subject of organic products, a 1999 ITC study,[7] the first report to cover the world market for organic food products, concluded: 'It seems clear – at least in the short to medium term – that an insufficient supply of organic products will be the main problem rather than lack of demand…', at least for most items. The survey found 15 LDCs among the developing countries that produce certified organic food and beverages in commercial quantities. In 2000 about 20 LDCs were producing for this market.*
>
> *Since that pioneering 270-page study, ITC has organized a series of seminars on the export development of organic products in 16 developing countries – 14 of them LDCs – in Africa and Asia, with financial support from the Government of Denmark. The seminars were put together in cooperation with local organic trade and farming associations wherever possible.*
>
> *With FAO and the Technical Centre for Agricultural and Rural Cooperation (CTA), ITC is carrying out a joint survey of the market for organic fruits and vegetables in Europe, the United States and Japan, to be issued in late 2001.*

ITC has organized seminars on the export development of organic products in 14 LDCs.

Adequate export development strategies should make it possible for LDCs to follow in the footsteps of their successful developing country competitors.

LDC exports of air-dried or lyophilized (freeze-dried) fruits sold in bulk, or in pre-packed cellophane bags, could also be expanded, provided they can comply with the stringent standards of high and uniform quality applicable to fresh produce. The main end-users of these products are processors of dried fruits and nuts, manufacturers of breakfast cereals and yoghurt, and producers of baby food and candy bars in Europe, the United States and Japan. These end-users are pushing growth in import demand, as they develop new products based on dried fruit that can be rehydrated, with a lower sugar content, in new physical forms, or with a longer shelf life. Most of their needs are imported direct from supplying countries.

Certain LDC exporters could also specialize in supplying tropical fruit pulps and concentrates to niche markets, which are likely to have sustained growth not only in EU, the United States and Japan, but also in developing Asian and Latin American countries. These markets import deep-frozen tropical fruits (pineapple, mango, papaya, etc.) for use as ingredients in baby food, bakery and milk products, and fruit salads.

Export development strategies should envisage means to increase exporters' knowledge of consumer requirements and preferences, market access conditions, and the most appropriate marketing channels and techniques.

> **Box 27**
>
> **Burundi: exporting agricultural products from a country in crisis**
>
> ***Company:*** *Cotriex started operations in January 1998, in the midst of an embargo against Burundi by neighbouring countries. The company objective for exporting agricultural and craft products was to help diversify sources of foreign exchange earnings and increase incomes in rural areas. It works with local peasant organizations in producing and processing coffee and passion fruit, and in exporting dried fruits, jams and fruit juices, as well as medicinal plants and ethnic products. Cotriex concentrates on logistics and quality control. The idea for the company came to Adrien Sibomana, a young entrepreneur in 1997, who wanted to help Burundi export more, starting with traditional products and then moving on to other goods.*
>
> ➡

---

7   *Organic Food and Beverages: World Supply and Major European Markets.*

> ➡
>
> ***Performance:*** *The export volume grew from 90 tons in 1998 to 596 tons in 2000. Turnover between 1998 and 1999 went up fourfold. Until air flights improve, and while the Bujumbura airport lacks cool-storage facilities, Cotriex is putting more emphasis on processing products in non-perishable form. It has also launched a project for own-label coffee.*
>
> ***Key success factors:*** *Cotriex ascribes its success to its openness with its partners, even giving buyers a rebate if it can purchase products at lower cost than originally foreseen. Its marketing strategy is based on partnership confidence, building up relationships and respecting its commitments as regards both quality and price. If goods are damaged in transit, Cotriex is proud that it delivers a note of credit to clients.*
>
> ***Constraints:*** *Because of the embargo, Mr Sibomana had to convince buyers that the company could still respect its delivery commitments by making new land and air-cargo arrangements. He received positive responses from Switzerland and the Netherlands and the first contracts for coffee were signed when the company was established.*
>
> *Cotriex believes it could double or even triple its exports by air if flights were available. Administrative procedures are also often slow and onerous. In addition, banking charges are high, while payments can take some time to come through.*
>
> *Another big problem is meeting European standards of packaging and design. Local materials are expensive and of a lower quality. To give customers attractively packaged products, Cotriex has gone into association with other exporters to order packages from abroad.*

Vegetables

LDCs grow both tropical and subtropical vegetables for export, generally on smallholdings. The most cultivated crops are sweet potatoes and yams, followed by leguminous vegetables, cabbage, eggplants, onions and tomatoes. The soil is fertile and water is available the year round in most cultivating areas. Yields of several crops, including beans, chickpeas and eggplants, are close to world averages, indicating comparative land productivity in many LDCs. However, labour productivity is highly dependent on the farming systems in use, while crop productivity under non-irrigated conditions varies with the weather.

Vegetables are of considerable interest to LDCs as export products. Several LDCs can harvest several crops a year and are able to supply off-season products at premium prices. Moreover, vegetables of guaranteed origins and certified organic products have promising markets in the developed world, particularly in Western Europe. Import demand in Africa and Asia is growing rapidly. Intraregional trade in these areas is being facilitated by regional integration agreements (WAEMU, ECOWAS,[8] ASEAN, among others) and the rising buying power of consumers there.

The LDC export trade

Despite their comparative advantages, LDCs supply only 1.4% of world imports of fresh, dried and simply preserved vegetables.

Despite their comparative advantages, LDC exports of fresh, dried and simply preserved vegetables, roots and tubers declined by 15% a year from US$ 302.5 million in 1995 to US$ 161.5 million in 1999, covering only 1.4% of world imports over the period. The share of dry leguminous vegetables taken on their own was much higher, amounting to 8% of the global total.

---

8   WAEMU: West African Economic and Monetary Union; ECOWAS: Economic Community of West African States.

The decline was due to adverse climatic conditions in 1998 and 1999, the fall in international prices, and shrinking export availability as a result of rapid population growth, urbanization and increased local consumption of vegetables.

Nearly 70% of LDC exports by value consisted of dried, shelled leguminous vegetables. About 20% comprised fresh and chilled vegetables (mainly cabbage, onions, cucumbers, green beans, peas and tomatoes) and 9% were roots and tubers. It is evident that there is a serious mismatch between what LDCs export and what world markets demand: during 1995-1999, 68% of these markets' requirements were for fresh, chilled vegetables.

There is a serious mismatch between the LDC offer and world demand.

Myanmar was the largest LDC exporter of fresh and dried vegetables (accounting for 56% of all LDC exports in 1995-1999), followed by the Sudan (7%), Ethiopia (6%), and Senegal, the United Republic of Tanzania and Bangladesh (4% each). The remaining exports were provided by a large number of smaller exporters, such as Nepal, Madagascar, Zambia, Burkina Faso, Afghanistan, Malawi, Mali, Togo, Uganda and the Gambia.

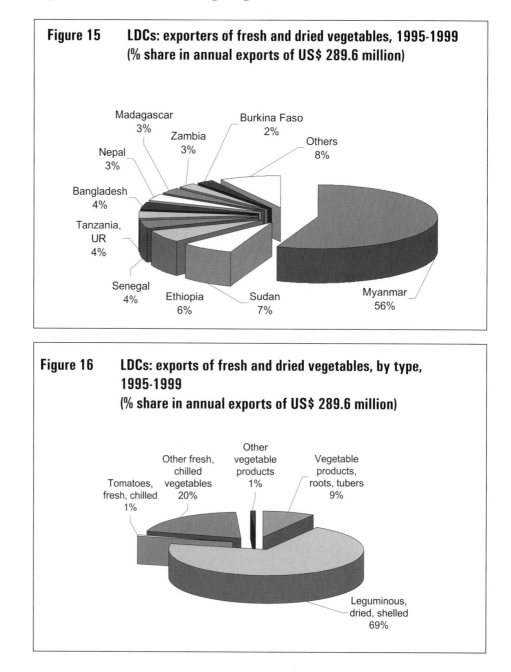

Figure 15   LDCs: exporters of fresh and dried vegetables, 1995-1999 (% share in annual exports of US$ 289.6 million)

Madagascar 3%
Burkina Faso 2%
Zambia 3%
Others 8%
Nepal 3%
Bangladesh 4%
Tanzania, UR 4%
Senegal 4%
Ethiopia 6%
Sudan 7%
Myanmar 56%

Figure 16   LDCs: exports of fresh and dried vegetables, by type, 1995-1999 (% share in annual exports of US$ 289.6 million)

Other fresh, chilled vegetables 20%
Other vegetable products 1%
Vegetable products, roots, tubers 9%
Tomatoes, fresh, chilled 1%
Leguminous, dried, shelled 69%

Annual LDC exports of processed vegetables averaged US$ 4.7 million between 1995 and 1999. Of these, 80% comprised canned products and other preparations, 12% flours and meals, and 8% dried products. Over 82% of the processed vegetables were exported from Madagascar to the European Union, about 12% were sent from Myanmar to Singapore and 2% from the Lao People's Democratic Republic, Bangladesh and Cambodia to the Russian Federation.

Market trends and opportunities

Consumers in the developed and the more advanced developing countries are willing to pay a premium for fresh, healthy vegetable products that can be prepared easily and are attractively packaged. Traditional vegetables are under pressure from exotic varieties receiving promotional support and premium prices. Niche markets for pre-packed green vegetables and organically grown products are growing rapidly in the developed world.

The globalization of the market for fresh vegetables is slowed down by the perishability of these products. The immediate prospects are in regional trade.

LDC exporters face strong competition on import markets from an increasing number of developing country suppliers. Global import demand is supported by the expanding market for imported off-season produce, and falling sea transport costs.

Import markets are becoming increasingly strict about their requirements for regular supplies of fresh and processed vegetables of consistent quality. These impose a considerable challenge for LDCs in terms of post-harvest handling and transport logistics. Following the entry into force of food safety acts in the European Union and the United States and the issuance of strict organic food standards, importers and retailers (supermarkets in particular) have developed systems for tracing products from growers to retailers' shelves.

Consumer pressure for conformity with food safety regulations, quality and labelling standards and tracing systems will increase. Moreover, consumers in developed economies, who have the decisive say on sources of supply and the range of products to be imported, impose labour and environmental standards that are rapidly gaining ground.

The need for economies of scale is bringing about changes in trade chains. Growers and exporters are investing downstream, while importers/distributors are tending to invest upstream. Wholesalers are increasingly importing direct and are establishing close links with growers/exporters and with providers of transport, pre-packing, packaging and other services. Over 60% of LDC supplies are distributed through supermarkets. This has required them to have access to real-time information networks, as well as multimodal warehousing and shipping platforms.

Strategies for value adding

Various strategies for value adding are described below.

Proper use of comparative advantages. The favourable climatic and soil conditions and abundant labour in several LDCs are major comparative advantages. However, these are not enough to sustain export competitiveness in world markets. LDCs should ensure regular supplies of consistent quality by offering smallholders incentives under mutually advantageous contracts and by adopting improved marketing systems and techniques. Producers and exporters should be trained in post-harvest handling, sorting and grading, cool-chain management, packing and shipping to enable them to meet customer requirements.

The need to provide products of consistent quality requires the integration of many stages of vegetable production.

Improve market knowledge. Export development strategies should envisage means to increase the exporters' knowledge of consumer requirements and preferences, market access conditions, and modern marketing systems and techniques. Export promotion agencies and sectoral associations are expected to play a crucial role in this respect and their capacity needs to be strengthened.

Increase research and development, and establish quality control programmes. Coordinated government and private-sector support for research programmes and the implementation and monitoring of standardization and certification programmes are necessary for ensuring that exports comply with quality and phytosanitary regulations in importing markets.

Improve infrastructure. Adequate facilities are required for harvesting, post-harvest handling and storage, intermediate processing (chilling, freezing, drying, cutting, trimming) and packaging; temperature-controlled land and air transport are also essential. While growing vegetables need not be scale-intensive, the setting up of efficient cool chains and logistics systems often requires the development of larger-scale units and installations.

Value addition in the trade in fresh vegetables is possible.

Develop higher value-added products. The trade in fresh vegetables and in speciality products (certified organic), which attract lower tariff rates, offers opportunities for value adding and creating employment. Value can be added to fresh products in two ways. The first is to shift to the more sophisticated market niches: for instance, away from loose fresh green beans in bulk towards ready-packed, cleaned and pre-weighed beans for distribution in supermarkets. The second option is to extend the range of activities undertaken by LDC companies, allocating to local subsidiaries, for example, the responsibility for regional coordination, procurement or training, or for product innovation, packaging, logistics, branding and marketing. The larger LDC exporters are already carrying out additional processing operations such as washing, trimming, bar coding and labelling, and are responsible for ensuring traceability and the quality of their products.

Diversification for value addition may take the form of downstream investments in processing (canning, pickling, dehydrating, freezing) or transformation into new products, such as vegetable juices. However, this type of diversification faces three major obstacles:

- Import tariffs on processed products in developed markets were bound at high levels during the Uruguay Round, restricting export opportunities for processed products;

- LDCs wishing to expand into competitive processing of vegetables should be able to attract foreign investment from the dominant processors. However, certain processing chains require economies of scale and are therefore capital- and technology-intensive;

- Demand for processed products in the industrialized world is stagnating, as consumers are switching to fresh products, in particular to high-value off-season temperate vegetables.

Vertical integration is already taking place in the export supply chain. LDC exporters of vegetables are increasingly taking control of arable land, in order to guarantee the regularity of supplies to foreign markets and to control production. Moreover, the need to provide products of consistent quality is pushing the integration of harvesting, provisional processing (chilling, freezing, drying), storage, and land and air transport in temperature-controlled conditions. As has been said earlier, while the cultivation of vegetables is usually not scale-intensive, the use of cool chains and local quality and logistics systems

---

Box 28

Uganda: exporting vegetables and cut flowers – adding value and overcoming technical barriers to trade

Company: *Originally established in 1952, Mairye Estates Ltd was re-established in 1972 as one of Uganda's major exporters of cut flowers and vegetables, after the return of its original owners.*

Performance: *In 1989, with the help of its Export Analysis Development Unit, the company identified a number of high-value crops suitable for export to Europe. Since then, Mairye Estates has experienced steady growth, and its annual turnover now exceeds US$ 2 million, produced by 3,000 workers on 500 acres of land. The company exports roses and French beans.*

Key success factors:

❑ *Targeting supermarket chains to secure higher prices than can be obtained from re-exporters in the Netherlands.*

❑ *Adopting ISO 9002 in order to become an EU-approved supermarket supplier. By September 2001 company operations were expected to be certified to ISO environmental standards.*

❑ *Introducing an integrated production and marketing system and acquiring shares in an airport handling company.*

❑ *Establishing a nursery for planting materials in order to take control of quality from the beginning of the production chain.*

❑ *Sustaining the regularity and quality of export supplies, handling customer complaints speedily, and seeking feedback for possible improvements.*

❑ *Showing a keen interest in the welfare of the workforce, by providing, for example, permanent housing on the estate.*

❑ *The Government's sound macroeconomic and trade liberalization policies.*

Constraints:

❑ *Shortages of air cargo space, and high airfreight costs.*

❑ *Some of the roads to the farm remain poor (but efforts are being made to improve them).*

❑ *Electricity supply fluctuations.*

❑ *Shortages of well-trained middle managers.*

---

is favouring the development of large exporters and cooperative farms. Some of the big exporters in LDCs have set up close links with European importers and supermarket chains.

Spices

Most spices traded internationally are grown in tropical and subtropical developing countries. Several LDCs have competitive advantages in these smaller-volume, relatively high-value commodities, for which importing markets have less scope for seeking alternative origins. Countries like the Comoros, Madagascar and the United Republic of Tanzania earn a substantial part of their foreign exchange from spice exports. LDCs can expand their export trade, provided that they are able to offer regular supplies complying with the increasingly stringent quality, packaging and phytosanitary requirements of importing countries.

The LDC export trade

LDCs supplied about 5.5% of global imports between 1995 and 1999, with average annual exports amounting to US$ 91.5 million. However, while world imports by value rose by 8.5% yearly over the period, LDC exports fell by 8.5% in quantity and 4% in value. One reason was the severe drop in world vanilla prices, following an oversupply situation in Indonesia, and the other was the poor weather conditions in several African producing countries in 1998 and 1999.

Only 10 LDCs are significant suppliers of spices to the world market.

The main LDC exports are vanilla, whole cloves, chillies, cardamoms, nutmeg and mace. Since 1995, LDCs have provided over half of world imports of vanilla, and over a fifth of the cloves. Although more than a third of the LDCs are involved in the commercial production and export of spices, only 10 are significant suppliers. Madagascar has a dominant position, supplying 72% of all LDC exports between 1995 and 1999, followed by the Comoros (6%), the United Republic of Tanzania (5%), Myanmar, Nepal and Malawi.

The international prices of most spices are volatile for various reasons, some of them unavoidable. The sharp drop in vanilla prices in 1997 has led several end-users to shift to synthetic substitutes and to diversify their supply sources. These have had a negative effect on export revenues and farmers' incomes in Madagascar and the Comoros.

**Figure 17   LDCs: exports of spices, by type, 1995-1999
(% share in annual exports of US$ 91.5 million)**

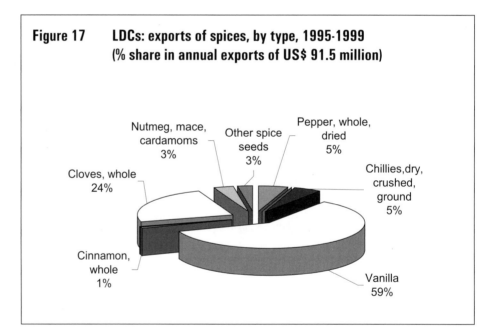

Figure 18   LDCs: unit price of vanilla, 1995-1999

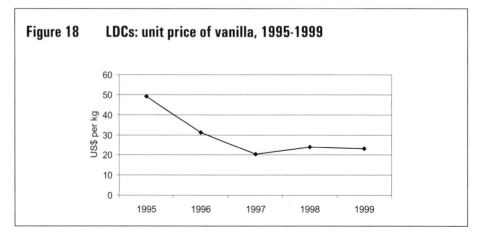

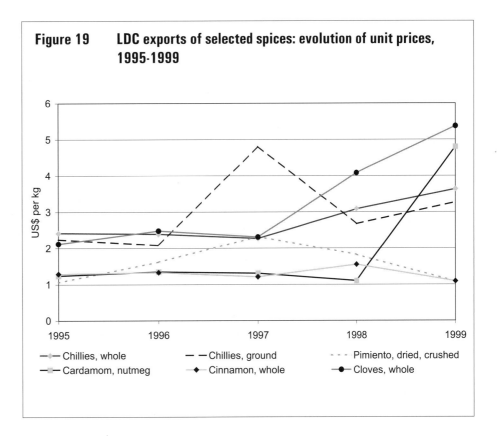

Figure 19   LDC exports of selected spices: evolution of unit prices, 1995-1999

Legend:
—◆— Chillies, whole
— — Chillies, ground
- - - Pimiento, dried, crushed
—■— Cardamom, nutmeg
—◆— Cinnamon, whole
—●— Cloves, whole

The unit prices of LDC exports of chillies, cloves, cardamom, mace and nutmeg have risen since 1996, those of cinnamon and pimiento have fallen slightly since 1997. The closer the specifications of exports are to quality requirements abroad, the higher the price they command.

Market trends and export development prospects

Consumption of individual spices is influenced mainly by the structure of the food industry and social habits. The growing number of ethnic communities abroad, the increasing number of travellers who seek to replicate foreign dishes at home and the influence of the media on buying habits have all induced changes in eating habits. This will fuel the rise of import demand for an expanded range of spices.

Households are the main consumers of spices in developing countries. In developed countries, the bulk of demand comes from the industrial food processing sector.

The rapid rise of the industrial food processing and the food service sectors in both developing and developed countries is leading to a modification of trade channels. The end-users and large spice processors in these sectors trade much less through dealers and brokers, preferring direct contacts with growers/exporters. Moreover, spice processing in developed markets is increasingly concentrated in a small number of multinationals, which often enter into joint ventures with spice producers and exporters in developing countries. These developments have direct implications for the formulation of spice export strategies in LDCs.

Despite the serious constraints to the development of spice exports from LDCs, liberalization offers their private sector larger scope for action. Governments should seek to create synergies between the players in the sector, coordinating and supporting research and development, extension activities and export-related services, including standardization, quality control and certification.

From the economic point of view, bulk-packed, ground spices remain the most profitable export alternative for LDCs. Although spices can be ground, retailed packed and labelled at origin to standards fully acceptable to developed markets, bulk and intermediate packing is often the most cost-effective means to reach new markets. Any effort to develop exports of consumer-packed spices will be hampered by the wide range of products required and the fact that their market segment makes up only 20% - 30% of the overall market in most countries. The margins are lower than for domestic branded products, and the cost of providing satisfactory promotional packing, technical and warehousing services abroad eliminates the possible gains from grinding at origin.

Two alternatives could, however, allow origin grinders and packers to supply both the industrial and consumer segments in importing countries. One would be the purchase of packaging units in import markets, delivery of bulk ground spices from origin together with whole spices, and repackaging these products in the importing country. This would result in better utilization of cleaning and grinding equipment and greater flexibility in blending at origin, while ensuring prompt delivery to end-users of technical services and products held in stocks in

---

Box 29

Zambia: exporting paprika – turning comparative advantage into competitive advantage with the support of foreign investment

Company: *Cheetah is the producer organization and subsidiary of a Netherlands-based company operating in Zambia and Malawi. The main product is paprika, supplied dried, for the food ingredient industry (food colouring and spice), mainly in Europe.*

Performance: *In six years Cheetah's output has risen to 2,000 tons of paprika yearly (2% of the world market), grown by 30,000 contract farmers. By 2002, a further investment of US$ 3 million is expected to double production and increase the number of growers to 50,000.*

Key success factors:

❑ *Solid market, agronomic and feasibility studies before start up.*

❑ *Training and strong support for contract farmers to ensure supplies of quality raw materials.*

❑ *Thorough understanding of the quality standards required by importers of food ingredients.*

❑ *Concentration on markets with a large import potential.*

❑ *Use of advanced technology and emphasis on quality control at all production stages.*

❑ *Motivated and highly capable team of managers and staff.*

Constraints:

❑ *Inadequte and expensive logistics and communications.*

❑ *Lack of processing equipment and spare parts, consumables and the related services.*

❑ *High cost of skilled managerial and technical staff.*

❑ *Low level of education of contract growers.*

the import market. The second alternative would be a joint venture or partnership between LDC grinders and packers at origin and established grinders in importing markets.

Under current market conditions, LDC exporters should probably concentrate on supplying whole spices to industrial end-users, grinders, processors and packers. Ground spices could be supplied to specialized market niches in intermediate wholesale packs for the catering sector and ethnic trade and in retail packs for the regional Asian and African markets.

LDC exporters need to understand the WTO provisions on domestic and export subsidies and countervailing duties to be able to draw up realistic export strategies and take the right decisions on investments and the location of their production facilities. Moreover, they need to monitor in detail the sanitary and phytosanitary (SPS) regulations and technical standards in their target markets. Compliance with SPS regulations and importers' quality and packaging specifications remain the biggest market access problems for LDC exporters of spices.

Box 30
Export packaging: playing it safe – the ITC story

For reasons of hygiene, environmental regulation and design, packaging has become a significant part of the trade equation. Exporters must meet an enormous variety of packaging requirements, and most small businesses do not have the skills or finances to adopt the best packaging options. Nor do they always have access to appropriate materials or technologies.

ITC's Export Packaging Service was set up to help exporters in developing countries, including LDCs, to meet the packaging requirements of their target markets. This ITC Service has trained more than 5,000 exporters and government officers in packaging technology and promotion. It has established packaging, testing and certification laboratories for the use of small enterprises. It has helped create packaging institutions and associations for local industry. It has supported the development of the packaging information base in various countries, including the United Republic of Tanzania.

The Service provides several materials free of charge:

❑ *Training kits and manuals, guides, newsletters, bulletins and resource documents – currently distributed to more than 500 packaging-related institutions in developing countries.*

❑ *Information on technical and commercial aspects of packaging manufacture and use through bibliographic databases such as PackData, PackFairs and Pack Experts. These are used by over 20 information units in developing countries.*

❑ *The ITC Export Packaging question-and-answer service. More than 800 queries are handled each year.*

Cut flowers and foliage

Several least developed countries have competitive advantages that they can exploit to develop their exports of cut flowers and foliage. But they need the right export development strategies.

World imports of cut flowers exceeded US$ 4.7 billion a year on average during the 1995-1999 period. The six largest importing countries (Germany, the

United States, the United Kingdom, France, the Netherlands and Switzerland) continue to account for nearly 80% of global imports. Imports into several developing countries are growing rapidly, despite high import duties and non-tariff trade barriers.

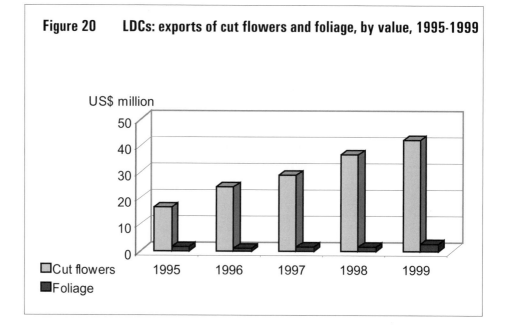

Figure 20   LDCs: exports of cut flowers and foliage, by value, 1995-1999

Exports from LDCs rose at an average of 32% yearly, from US$ 18 million in 1995 to over US$ 44.9 million in 1999, supported by the competitive advantages of these countries, the export development efforts of their business communities, and appropriate government strategies and support measures. About 95% of these exports consisted of cut flowers and buds, and 5% of foliage and other plant parts. The number of significant LDC exporters is small; they include Zambia, the United Republic of Tanzania, Uganda, Malawi, Ethiopia, Rwanda and Yemen for cut flowers, and Haiti, Ethiopia, Madagascar and Malawi for foliage and other plant parts. Exports are shipped mainly to Europe (Germany, the United Kingdom, the Netherlands, Belgium, Ireland, Italy, Norway, Poland and Switzerland). Small shipments go from Zambia to South Africa, from Yemen and the Sudan to Saudi Arabia and from Madagascar to India. With the exception of Yemen, the LDC exporters are members of the ACP group of countries enjoying preferential tariffs in the European Union.

Market trends and export development prospects

World import demand for cut flowers and foliage is expected to rise by 0.5% to 0.6% a year over the next five years, fuelled by increasing consumer impulse buying for the home and for special occasions.

Consumer demand is rapidly shifting from temperate varieties of flowers (roses, gladioli and carnations) to hot-climate types (orchids, anthurium, etc.) and cut foliage. Consumers are becoming highly quality-conscious, preferring flowers and foliage products with a long vase life. In addition, they are increasingly oriented towards environmentally friendly products that are produced under best manufacturing and labour practices, and are commercialized through fairer trade circuits.

The big buyers/importers (supermarkets, chain stores and cooperatives) are gaining shares in the market and tend to develop direct contacts with exporters.

The flower auctions (in the Netherlands in particular) are tending to lower their commission rates but to enlarge lots and raise handling charges. While this will facilitate the access of large suppliers from developing countries to the international market, it will also increase the selling costs and render more difficult market penetration by smaller exporters.

In general, the quality of LDC exports of cut flowers and foliage has to be raised. Exporters need to gain a reputation for products of consistently high quality, particularly as several import markets for temperate flowers are now showing signs of saturation. They will have to master such logistical aspects as packaging and the maintenance of cold chains and have access to suitable transport facilities.

The challenge for national research programmes is to develop new lines of cultivated fast-growing flowers and foliage, as well as native varieties for export. Moreover, the strategy for the selection of export varieties should be based on the development of high-yielding crops with a long vase life, which are adapted to domestic growing conditions and can be cultivated at low cost.

One of the main factors that will determine the LDCs' position in the cut flower markets is how they adapt their commercial strategies to the changing conditions in these markets. Both export marketing methods existing at present could be developed further, i.e. the Netherlands clock auction markets and direct sales by exporters to importers.[9] In both instances, LDC producers should avoid the use of intermediate agents, who take a large share of the profits.

LDCs with low-altitude cultivating areas and tropical climates could focus on tropical varieties (such as anthurium, successfully exported by Mauritius), or on native varieties with a long vase life. Moreover, the market segments for both 'ecological cut flowers' and the native flowers and foliage that last a long time in water are faster growing, boosted by widespread commercialization through supermarkets. The introduction of the 'Flower-Label' programme has offered exporters a new marketing tool to satisfy demand in specific market segments.

The signs of over-supply in European markets for certain temperate flower varieties indicate that only strongly organized LDC exporters, in direct contact with the markets, can penetrate these markets or increase their current shares. Their export development strategies should provide for the adaptation of their supplies to buyers' requirements in terms of range, quality and phytosanitary characteristics. They will also have to have adequate plans (and facilities) for production, the flow of supplies, packaging and the logistics of transporting their products to their markets.

---

9   While the Netherlands auction markets allow growers from LDCs to concentrate their efforts on production, the prices fetched are neither stable nor very high and producers/exporters lack information on, and control over, their export markets. Direct sales offer the advantages of higher prices and shorter distribution chains, which reduce the risk of damage to the quality of products on arrival.

> **Box 31**
>
> ***Ethiopia: overcoming constraints on the export of cut flowers***
>
> **Company:** *Meskel Flowers was incorporated in 1992 as a private company, and started to export cut flowers to European markets in 1993.*
>
> **Performance:** *The company started by exporting low-value outdoor summer flowers, but decided to switch to high-value indoor cut roses after facing crippling competition from a Kenyan exporter. It currently exports 5.5 million stems of cut roses a year at a value of US$ 1 million, and has 500 employees. Turnover was expected to quadruple to US$ 4 million in the 2000-2001 season, and the company has plans to reach US$ 20 million in five years.*
>
> **Key success factors:**
>
> ❑ *The founder spent 10 years in the United States and developed a clear idea of the business he wanted to start before returning to Ethiopia. He was inspired by Kenya's success as a cut flower exporter. His visits to various markets helped him obtain an appreciation of market requirements.*
>
> ❑ *Market responsiveness, illustrated by the switch from summer flowers to roses in the face of competition.*
>
> ❑ *Feasibility studies carried out by the African Project Development Facility (APDF) in Nairobi helped secure finance, and technical assistance from the EU's Centre for the Development of Industry was instrumental in achieving the switch to cut roses.*
>
> ❑ *Meskel is essentially a family company with a strong commitment to its success.*
>
> **Constraints:** *The company was established at the time when Ethiopia was striving to move to a free market economy, a period of massive change. New laws and regulations were being introduced, but the business environment remained difficult for private companies. Current constraints include import restrictions on certain chemicals and fertilizers, which expose production to disease and losses.*

Medicinal plants

Over three-quarters of the population in developing countries meet their primary health care needs through traditional medicine based on the use of medicinal plants. The traditional medicine systems[10] officially recognized and fully licensed by Governments of several Asian countries are fully comparable to the modern medicine systems of developed countries in Europe and North America in their degree of organization and research. The World Health Organization adopted in 1977 a resolution urging interested governments to give 'adequate importance to the utilization of their traditional systems of medicine, with appropriate regulations as suited to their national health systems'. Both developing and developed countries have since considerably increased the use of traditional and indigenous health care resources in national health programmes and have backed the development of appropriate legislation.

In Europe and North America, increased demand for medicinal plants is being fuelled primarily by consumer interest in 'natural' products and remedies and by aggressive promotion and marketing of traditional medicines and herbal remedies. 'Phytomedicines' have already linked traditional medicine and

---

10 Including the Ayurvedic, Unani and Siddhi medicines in India, Kampo in Japan, Yamu in Indonesia, as well as Chinese, Tibetan, African and Arab traditional medicines.

modern (allopatic) medicine, supported by sophisticated pharmaceutical laboratories, which analyse herbal ingredients and their effects. Some developed countries have introduced into their national curricula medical and pharmaceutical research into a number of alternative health systems, while traditional medicine is being developed in parallel with allopathic medicine in some developing countries (China, India, Mexico, Myanmar, Nigeria and Thailand).

Market trends

It is not possible to quantify the value of global trade in all medicinal plants, because a substantial part of this trade is not recorded and the recorded trade statistics either do not identify the plants individually, or do not separate their medicinal usage from others[11]. Moreover, taxonomic confusions are still found in some national customs declarations and legislation, allowing trade in a given plant species under several trade names.

World trade in medicinal plants and part of plants is estimated by various sources to have averaged US$ 1.28 billion during the 1995-1999 period. Recorded imports rose slightly from US$ 1.3 billion in 1995 to nearly US$ 1.4 billion in 1996, but decreased thereafter to US$ 1.1 billion annually.

Three-quarters of all imports by value were other medicinal plants (although the statistics also covered pyrethrum and other culinary and perfumery plants), a fifth consisted of ginseng root and just under 3% were liquorice root. The six leading importers in volume terms were Hong Kong (China), Japan, Germany, the United States, the Republic of Korea and France.

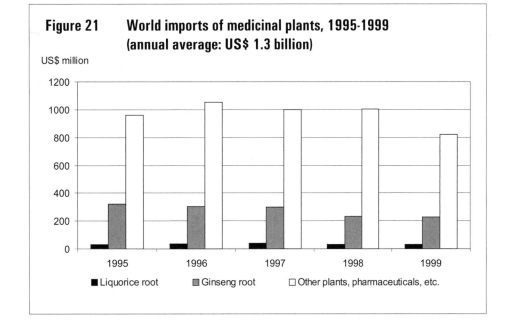

Figure 21   World imports of medicinal plants, 1995-1999 (annual average: US$ 1.3 billion)

US$ million

■ Liquorice root   ■ Ginseng root   □ Other plants, pharmaceuticals, etc.

---

11   Such as perfumes, essential oils, culinary herbs and spices, insecticides and fungicides. For example, liquorice is used as an expectorant and anti-inflammatory, but has other uses, from flavouring cigarettes, chocolate, beer and toothpaste, to stabilizing the foam in fire extinguishers. Papaya extract (papain) is a common enzyme used in the treatment of dyspepsia, intestinal and gastric disorders and blood clots, but is also widely utilized as tenderizer in the food industry.

LDCs supplied about 12% of the liquorice and 3% of the other medicinal plants imported over the period, amounting to a total annual trade of US$ 31 million on the average. Afghanistan is the only LDC exporting liquorice. Its exports, averaging US$ 4 million a year, are shipped mainly to the United States (two-thirds of the total between 1995 and 1999), as well as to Japan, France and India. The only LDC exporter of small amounts of ginseng root during the 1990s was Myanmar; India was the only importer of this product.

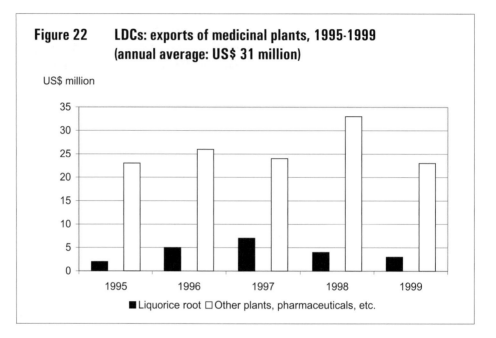

Figure 22   LDCs: exports of medicinal plants, 1995-1999 (annual average: US$ 31 million)

A large number of LDCs supply other medicinal plants. The Sudan is the largest exporter, supplying about 37% of all LDC exports, valued at US$ 27 million a year during 1995-1999 period. The other exporters are the Democratic Republic of the Congo (16%), Vanuatu, Myanmar, Madagascar and the Lao People's Democratic Republic.

There are good prospects for the growth of exports from LDCs. However, the markets for herbal medicine in developed countries – especially in Europe and the United States – are highly regulated and difficult to penetrate, as most LDC products do not undergo the stringent tests required by pharmaceutical manufacturers in developed countries.

Demand for medicinal plants is expected to continue to expand rapidly, fuelled by population growth and increasing awareness and support among environmentally conscious consumers who are also concerned with the possible side effects of allopathic medicines. Their basic uses in medicine will continue to be the same: direct, as a source of therapeutic agents, as well as a raw material for extraction or elaboration of semi-synthetic chemical compounds.

In developing countries, the use of medicinal plants will continue to compensate for shortages in, and the high costs of, allopatic medicines. As far as developed countries are concerned, the allopathic health care sector is currently facing economic and structural problems. These include the high cost of developing and bringing into the market synthetic pharmaceutical products, the period of exclusivity granted under patent protection legislation, the varying degrees of government involvement in social security systems, and the favourable treatment granted to certain generic pharmaceutical products.

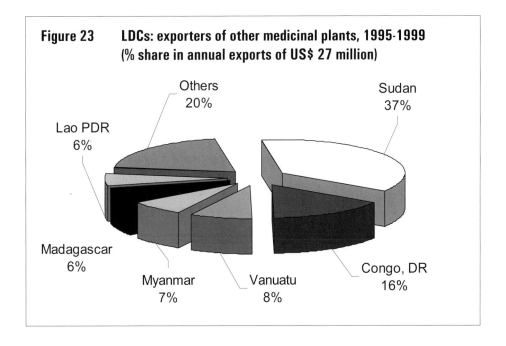

**Figure 23   LDCs: exporters of other medicinal plants, 1995-1999
(% share in annual exports of US$ 27 million)**

An increased use of medicinal plants is offering a solution to some of these problems. The trend towards more 'natural' self-medication in developed countries will therefore continue, supported by their governments' will to reduce the costs of subsidized health care and by consumers, who are increasingly taking responsibility for their own health. National legislation is tending to improve the status of the medicinal plant industries and enforce standards for their more generalized use.

The aggressive marketing and promotion of 'natural' pharmaceutical products and nutraceuticals by several large manufacturers are also expected to support further growth of the market for medicinal plants in developed countries. Moreover, pharmaceutical companies seem to be increasingly interested in the isolation of new compounds and active substances from plants, in particular to complement the use of allopathic drugs in the treatment of long-term, chronic diseases[12]. They are also expected to continue the highly profitable business of licensing the use of other companies' natural drugs, setting up subsidiaries based on herbal products, or entering the herbal medicine industry.

The therapeutic use of medicinal plants in developed markets will continue to differ from use in developing countries practising traditional medicine, whether or not subject to regulations. In developing countries where traditional medicine is subject to regulations (India, China, Malaysia, among others), medicinal plants are already codified in pharmacopoeias and imports are often strictly regulated. In countries where traditional medicine is not subject to regulations, the choice and utilization of medicinal plants is the exclusive field of indigenous medicine men, who are repositories of traditional secrets and techniques. Import demand in these markets is expected to grow faster in the medium term than in developed countries. In the latter, the use of medicinal plants for therapeutic treatments is likely to continue to be largely limited to over-the-counter prescriptions and self-medication.

An additional factor that will sustain the growth of demand for medicinal plants is their rising worldwide consumption in perfumery, cosmetics and food industries.

---

12   Including viral diseases, arthritis, cancer, diabetes, asthma, rheumatism and heart disease.

The depletion of medicinal plant resources in developing and least developed countries will increase concern about their conservation. The initiatives aimed at evaluating, screening and cultivating (farming) medicinal plants, as opposed to wild harvesting, in particular for protected or endangered varieties are expected to amplify in the future.

Market opportunities and constraints for LDCs

A large number of the medicinal plants entering world trade are endemic to specific geographical zones in LDCs, where they grow in a wild state. In contrast with major field crops, these plants can be profitably harvested on small scale and exploited on a sustainable basis. Their traditional wild harvesting provides cash resources. This is done mostly by women, who play a vital role in collecting the plants and dispensing traditional therapeutic knowledge.

The commercial cultivation of medicinal plants in LDCs is small, scattered and largely informal, although it allows the production of uniform plant material for export and relieves some of the pressure on wild harvesting of endangered varieties. However, an increasing number of LDCs encourage commercial farming and community participation in rural development projects based on medicinal plants. Farming medicinal plants in marginal, remote or degraded areas may also increase land values, promote better soil conservation and environmentally friendly land-management practices, providing better alternatives to low-value food crops.

Few LDCs have the resources and the institutional capability to develop their local processing base and to export products of consistent quality.

Practically all LDCs export medicinal plant raw materials and import finished drugs at high prices. Domestic value-addition through processing toward extracts and intermediary or final compounds is often not feasible, because of insufficient economies of scale and the lack of technology and capital.

Direct linkages exist between the medicinal plant sector and three other areas of activity: national research and development, conservation practices and health care.

Several LDC Governments have taken several measures to protect their medicinal plants, including improving methods of wild collection, deliberate cultivation and education of the population. In Ethiopia, for instance, the Diversity Institute plays a leading role in supporting the farming of medicinal plants and the conservation of plant genetic resources. In Bangladesh, the Research Institute on Herbal Medicines has established protocols for the evaluation of traditional medicines, as well as for the processing, production, licensing and marketing of medicinal plants. In Nepal, wildlife harvest and trade controls are undertaken under the National Parks and Wildlife Conservation Act in national parks and protected areas, and under the Forest Act and Forest Rules elsewhere in the country. The Mali Phytotherapy Society, created in 1998, seeks to promote and support the rational utilization of medicinal plants, and to contribute to the protection and conservation of the environment through rational wild harvesting. In Bhutan, protection and conservation of wild medicinal plants are provided under the Forest and Nature Conservation Act. Exports of endangered species of medicinal plants from the country are banned, while the collection and transit of permitted species are carried out under strict regulations, supervision and control. Moreover, national health care programmes in many LDCs recognize and promote the use of medicinal plants through traditional medicine.

Threats to the development of medicinal plant exports from LDCs are related to both the structure of the major import markets and to their own management of the resource base and the sector. Despite the very large import potential for medicinal plants in developed countries, export development in LDCs is constrained by several factors:

- National and multinational pharmaceutical companies exert a heavy influence on the registration and licensing of drugs and on the extent of research and development activities on medicinal plants. In addition, recent acquisitions of herbal companies by pharmaceutical companies with no allegiance to the related philosophy of medical treatments have undermined the credibility of the medicinal plants sector.

- Imports of medicinal plants not previously used in the European Union have been banned. Revision of the existing list of permitted active substances is not envisaged in the near future, and new registrations are limited to mono-substances.

- The capital requirements and research and development experience for entering developed allopathic markets, such as Germany or France, are beyond the resources of small LDC exporters. Their entry into countries where herbal medicines are not sold over the counter is also difficult, because distribution channels outside food outlets are hard to access and selling in unlicensed markets is risky.

- Doctors in developed markets (in the European Union in particular) often oppose the use of medicinal plants. Likewise, many consumers do not have sufficient knowledge of the therapeutic benefits of medicinal plants.

Box 32
Samoa: adding value through the development of new products

Company: *Nonu Samoa Enterprises Ltd was formed by Mr and Mrs Siaosi-Tinielu in 1995 to develop and test for export products from the nonu tree, which is indigenous to the region and has long been known locally to have medicinal properties.*

Performance: *The company originated from brainstorming by the Siaosi-Tinielu family to identify a traditional Samoan plant that might have export potential. The development stage lasted three years (1995-1998), including the testing of samples by potential clients in the United States (with the help of the Siaosi-Tinielu children). The company now exports about 10,000 pounds of nonu chips (sun-dried nonu) monthly to the United States and 400 - 500 kg of nonu juice a month to its distributor in New Zealand. Farmers from all over the country supply the nonu for the chips; the nonu for the juice is grown organically on the Siaosi-Tinielu's three-acre (1.2 ha) plantation. The company has 10 permanent employees, but provides further employment for casual workers at peak times as well as for local farmers.*

Key success factors:

❑ *Belief in the product, and determination and hard work to develop and promote it.*

❑ *Thorough experimentation and testing during the development stage to ensure that a successful formula had been identified.*

❑ *Emphasis on quality, which has been rewarded with an excellent reputation.*

❑ *Determination to build the company at a pace at which high quality and service can be maintained.*

❑ *Treating suppliers, employees and all stakeholders as one 'family' to harness their energies fully.*

Constraints:

❑ *The rapid emergence of increasing competition after exports of nonu began. The company has been able to build up its market position by insisting on quality and service.*

❑ *The supply of nonu is becoming an increasing constraint on the growth of the business. The company hopes that the Government will take measures to promote nonu production and improve quality control.*

The LDC trade in medicinal plants is largely unorganized. Matters are not helped much by fluctuations in national and international prices which result from variable supply and demand and which bring into conflict the interests of growers/collectors and end-use industries. Traders say that the international prices of medicinal plants tend to vary in cycles of six to seven years, determined by the time it takes for the market to go from over-supply to scarcity. These price fluctuations in a highly competitive market discourage small-farm cultivation and encourage over-harvesting of wild plants during periods of high prices.

The quality of medicinal plants for local consumption and for export is another matter of concern for LDCs. The quantity of active compounds in medicinal plants vary with weather conditions (temperature, humidity, luminosity, etc.), the time of harvest and the way the crop is harvested, handled and packed. Inadequate post-harvest handling and the length of storage prior to processing or shipping always results in a loss of efficacy. Moreover, insufficient sectoral regulation and organization brings about the indiscriminate harvest of wild plants, damages eco-systems and reduces bio-diversity.

Commercial farming of medicinal plants is rendered difficult by the absence of adequate development policies and strategies for the sector, as well as by the lack of standardized, sustainable agronomic practices. Quality planting materials are difficult to find at accessible prices, and farmers lack technical and financial support.

Intellectual property rights are another issue of importance to LDCs. Medicinal plant varieties have been used in traditional medicines for centuries and cannot be protected by patents. However, they can be registered as individual or regional trademarks, with declared origins.

Export development strategies should seek to increase exporters' knowledge of the product and the quality requirements of end-users.

Export development strategies should seek to increase the knowledge of LDC exporters on the following aspects: product and quality requirements of end-users, market access conditions, and appropriate marketing techniques. Business associations and export promotion agencies are expected to play a crucial role in this respect, and should be increasingly involved in training producers and exporters in sustainable harvesting techniques, grading and packing.

Table 4	Some medicinal plants and their uses

Selected LDCs: medicinal plants used in the traditional treatment of diseases

LESOTHO	MALAWI	UNITED REPUBLIC OF TANZANIA	ZAMBIA
Tuberculosis (leading cause of death) *Alepidea amatymbica* *Helichrysum capitatum* with *Scabiosa columbaria* *Casearia aspera* (reported to be as psychotropic as *Cannabis sativa*) **Respiratory infections, upper tract** *Artemisia afra* (for common colds and coughs) **Skin infections** *Dicoma anomala* **Wounds and sores** *Geranium caffrum* **Diarrhoea and vomiting in children** *Geranium caffrum* General body aches and pains; arthritis and rheumatism *Malva parviflora* **Hypertension and diabetes** *Sutherlandia frutescens* *Trifolium burchelianum* *Melolobiun alpinium* *Tephrosia semiglabra*	**Malaria** *Aristolochia petersiana* **Anaemia** *Eulophia species* **Tapeworm infestation (a major cause of anaemia in Africa)** *Albizia versicolor* **Respiratory tract infections** *Cassia petersiana Bolle* (pneumonia) **Diarrhoea** *Acalypha sinensis* **Childhood diseases, such as measles** *Ceratotheca sesamoides* **Sexually transmitted diseases** General: *Tamarindus indica* Syphilis: *Cassia petersiana*	**Malaria** *Cinchona succirubra* *Cinchona ledgeriana* *Cinchona hybrid* *Artemisia afra* *Azadirachta indica* **Diabetes mellitus** *Centella asiatica* *Runex urambarensis* **Epilepsy** *Hyptis suaveolens* *Vismianthus punctatus* *Ficus bursei* **Gonorrhoea** *Ozoroa mucronata* *Markhania obtusfolia* **Asthma** *Grewia sulcata*	**Malaria** *Dialiopsis africana* *Pterocarpus angolensis* **Upper respiratory tract infections (bronchitis)** *Mangifera indica* **Diarrhoea** *Mangifera indica* with *Cassia abbreviata* **Malnutrition** *Pterocarpus angolensis* (used to treat mouth ulcers in malnutrition) **Gonorrhoea** *Erythrina abyssinica*

Medicinal plant-based products sold over the counter in developed countries

Medicinal product	Plant source	Use
Quinidine	*Cinchona sp.*	Suppressor of out-of-sequence heartbeats
Quinine	*Cinchona sp.*	Antimalarial
Pilocarpine	*Pilocarpus* sp.	Treatment for glaucoma (from Brazil)
Picrotoxin	*Anamirta* sp.	Stimulant for the nervous system
L-Dopa	*Mucuna* sp.	Treatment for Parkinson's diseas
Bromelain	*Ananas* sp. [pineapple])	Anti-inflammatory
Scopolamine	*Datura* sp.	Sedative

Medicinal plant-based products sold in developing countries

Digitalin and digoxin	Digitalis sp. [foxglove])	Heart drugs
Atropine	*Atropa* sp. [belladonna])	Pupil-dilator
Curare	*Chondrodendron* sp.	Muscle relaxant (notably used in surgery)
Ephedrine	*Ephedra* sp. [from China])	Decongestant
Ipecac	*Cephaelis* spp. [from Central America])	Emetic; a cure for dysentery
Sennosides	*Senna* sp.)	Laxative

Chapter 4

Building an enabling environment

Policy-makers, export strategists and the private sector seeking to build an enabling environment for export development have several key questions to answer:

'Addressing trade policy alone will not create the necessary enabling environment for export development. Sound policies accompanied by a product-specific sectoral action plan to give impetus to export development will create a conducive atmosphere for the exporters to perform not only efficiently but profitably.'
Dawa T Sherpa, Bhutan, in the ITC e-Discussion

- Which markets and market segments should be given priority, defined in terms of location, products and type of customer?

- How should one build a strong and sustainable position in priority markets by out-competing rivals?

- How should one strengthen one's supply capacity?

In considering the technology that needs to be introduced for better production, strategy-makers also need to be sure that the local industry can acquire, absorb and use this capacity. A number of successful entrepreneurs in LDCs have devoted considerable resources to providing training and support to workers and independent suppliers to ensure that production is up to international standards. Several are moving deliberately ahead of their rivals in introducing quality controls that are being implemented only now even in the United States and the European Union.

National policy and enterprise-level strategy, therefore, most go together.

Factors contributing to failure in international trade

LDCs, with the right strategy, can out-compete rivals even when a market is declining.

Broad trends in the market, whether favourable or unfavourable, serve only to form part of the trading environment in which LDC exporters operate. While success is no doubt easier in markets in which the trading environment is favourable in terms of growth of export volumes and price formation, appropriate strategies should enable LDC exporters to improve market position and performance and hence accelerate export growth irrespective of these broad trends.

Several major factors, apart from lack of international market access, have contributed to the failure of many LDCs to take greater advantage of the rapid growth in world trade. These are domestic policies, poor infrastructure, lack of coherent export strategies or trade support services, and constraints within firms. These aspects are interrelated.

Policies for private-sector development

The policies that build an enabling environment include ensuring that there is sufficient incentive to invest and earn profit, competition to ensure efficiency, and open access to land and other production resources. They also cover such aspects as the competence and capability of the private sector. Collectively, they may be referred to as policies for private-sector development (PSD).

PSD policies help determine the economy's capacity level and competitiveness; trade policy sets the level of incentive to export. The two go hand in hand in ensuring export success, and are vital components for establishing an enabling environment for exporting.

There is growing recognition that the constraints to exporting in developing countries go well beyond policy barriers. A series of infrastructural, service-related and bureaucratic weaknesses have been identified as general supply constraints and specific constraints to exporting (World Bank, 1994[13]).

Weaknesses in infrastructure

In many developing countries, weaknesses in the basic national infrastructure (transport, utilities, telecommunications) are major constraints on investment and operations. They clearly affect the cost and continuity of production and product quality. If water supply problems, power breakdowns or voltage fluctuations, for instance, occur more frequently than in other countries, then export-oriented investment is likely to be diverted from the affected countries. Similar arguments apply where poor internal transport systems affect the cost and supply of intermediate goods and raw materials, and the cost and speed of delivering final goods to distribution centres and ports.

Export strategies: how important?

Views on the importance of export strategies vary. Some say that once the appropriate policies are in place and constraints placed by trade-related business services are reduced, businesses can develop their own export strategies. The sum of the individual decisions constitutes the national export strategy, making explicit national export strategy superfluous.

'The problem is not that of good policies but of putting the policies into action.'
– Emmarita Z. Mijares, Deputy Executive Director, Export Development Council, Philippines, in the ITC e-Discussion

On the other hand, export strategist Michael Porter and others have recognized the need for an explicit national strategy that identifies priority sectors and coordinates the actions required to improve the policy environment and trade-related business services. Export strategies for priority sectors would then address constraints within the firm. Such approaches appear indeed to be necessary in LDCs.

A national strategy can provide the private sector with a clear indication of the priority the country attaches to exporting and make government commit itself to a course of action that includes policy reform and programmes to ease constraints imposed by inadequate trade-related business services. It also serves as a framework for further elaboration by sectoral strategies which can address the sector-specific actions required to alleviate constraints within the firm.

Constraints within the firm

In the past, many interventions at the level of the firm have distorted markets by selecting a few firms for support and providing subsidized services to them.

However, there is also debate on whether programmes should be designed to address constraints within the firm. It is generally accepted that factors within local enterprises have an important bearing on export success, constituting one of the four elements[14] that make up Porter's 'diamond' of attributes of national advantage. Nevertheless, it is thought that interventions at the level of the firm may distort markets and doubts are being expressed about their sustainability

---

13   World Bank, *East Africa: Survey of Foreign Investors* (Washington, 1994).
14   The other attributes are demand conditions, related and supporting industries, and firm strategy, structure and rivalry. See M.Porter, *The Competitive Advantage of Nations* (Macmillan, 1990, 1998).

and cost-effectiveness. Further, it is argued that, provided policies lead to efficient and effective markets and trade-related business service constraints are addressed, firms will learn to tackle their own shortcomings.

In the past, many interventions at the level of the firm have distorted markets by selecting a few firms for support and providing subsidized services to them in a way that has adversely affected the supply of these services from the private sector. They have also proved unsustainable, ceasing when donor assistance comes to an end. But policy-makers are learning how these interventions can be designed so that they do not distort markets and can be provided cost-effectively and sustainably.

The overwhelming reason for intervening at the level of the firm is to serve as catalyst and enabler in accelerating the development of competence and competitiveness. Left to themselves, LDC firms may well develop competence and competitiveness. But the time required to do so would be very long, given their current level of development. If the prime objective of establishing an enabling environment is to accelerate the growth of exports, then measures aimed at addressing the constraints to competitiveness within the firm have a role to play.

Trade support services

Programmes to address constraints at the level of the firm through trade support services can form part of the enabling environment. Measures include the improvement of industry structure by supporting SMEs, promoting FDI and developing clusters. Benchmarking is also useful in diagnostics of export competitiveness. Assistance needs to be given to develop and implement firm-level export strategies. This can be provided under matching grant schemes, the costs of which are shared by public funds and the entrepreneur.

Viewing this issue as one simply of the availability of business support services, there should be no question that these are a necessary part of an enabling environment. In this respect, decision-makers should not neglect the institutional dimension of support services. Trade support institutions these days are understood to go well beyond dedicated trade promotion organizations and are more effective if they network the whole range of business services available even within LDCs to support export development. They can include information, training and quality standards bodies; financial agencies; packaging institutions and promotional services. Recent years have seen a move away from activities focused offshore to a more balanced and responsive programme of onshore facilities also available through such networks.

Trade support services are covered in chapter 5. This chapter focuses on the policy instruments that strategists and decision-makers can use to improve the environment for export development.

Progress in trade policy

New multilateral, plurilateral and regional trade agreements have induced major changes in national trade policies. In addition, there have been major unilateral initiatives to liberalize national trade policy, often prompted by structural adjustment initiatives under the International Monetary Fund and the World Bank.

Progress has by no means been uniform. There is some evidence of back-sliding: countries have replaced tariffs with contingent measures. It should be noted that import policies impact strongly on the incentive to export, as they affect the cost of manufacturing inputs and the relative terms of trade of exports and import substitutes.

Export policies

Implicit and direct taxes on exports

Direct taxation of exports has in general been substantially lowered or eliminated in most developing countries in recent decades, as part of their trade liberalization and export promotion initiatives. Such taxation had generally been aimed at traditional exports, and was either explicit (for example a sugar tax in Mauritius or a coffee tax in Uganda) or implicit (effected by export marketing boards which had the power to set prices to local producers below world levels). Both forms of taxation have tended to be eliminated either through abolition of the tax or deregulation and privatization of the marketing of export products.

Minimum export prices

'Export taxes on agricultural products... penalize peasant farmers because exporters have to pay the tax at the moment of taking goods onboard, so they deduct this sum from the price paid to producers. This reduces the farmers' revenues, therefore reducing the incentive to produce, whose consequence is a diminution of agriculture production – and therefore of exports.'
Christiane Leong, Head, Export Support Service, Madagascar Ministry of Commerce, in the ITC e-Discussion

In many countries, however, local taxes and other levies continue to affect the cost of exports. Some LDCs set minimum export prices; these may have much the same effect as export taxes. In addition to their making exports uncompetitive, these measures may form the basis for gate-keeping (corrupt) practices on the part of officials, which add to the risks of exporting and serve as a major disincentive to the trade.

Export marketing boards

Not all countries have abolished export marketing boards. Where they remain as inefficient parastatals, they reduce the share of the FOB (free on board) price paid to producers, thus effectively serving as a tax on exports. The gain to be had from abolishing such boards is illustrated by the coffee business in Uganda. The abolition of the monopoly on coffee marketing has increased the proportion of the FOB price paid to producers from 35% to 65%, according to a study by the International Coffee Organization. The change resulted in a substantial rise in exports.

Export licensing

Other countries continue to implement export licensing regimes which add to transaction costs (in time if not money) and may also be subject to corrupt practices. The original purpose of such regimes, to monitor exports and to prevent the export of national treasures, can be achieved through better customs administration.

'Incentives'

Most developing countries have implemented incentives aimed at promoting exports and export-oriented investment. Broadly they have been of three major types: input-related, output-related and externality-related incentives (including information). Such incentives can be useful in offsetting unusually high input or transport costs that have been brought about by market distortions. However, what is questionable is reliance on these measures to stimulate trade rather than addressing the fundamental causes of low competitiveness in an economy.

Often incentives or export subsidies affect the composition of exports rather than their scale. Indeed, given difficulties in targeting export incentives and their inherently discretionary nature, the net value of exports to an economy may be lower in the presence of subsidies than in their absence.

Many of these incentives, and certainly the subsidies, are not permitted by the WTO Agreement. In addition to the international constraints on their use, there is little evidence that interventionist export measures have been very successful in promoting exports. Using scarce resources to create an environment conducive to efficient production and competitive exporting is more important than trying to subsidize exports that would otherwise not pass the market test.

There is little evidence that interventionist export measures have been very successful in promoting international sales.

Artificial exchange rates and retention schemes

Ironically, many of the countries that have introduced incentive systems follow exchange rate policies that discourage exports. The maintenance of artificially high exchange rates (though much less prevalent or severe than in the past) continues, making exports less competitive. Many LDCs operate retention schemes which oblige exporters to remit foreign exchange earnings, allowing them to retain a small part (often less than half and sometimes as little as 10%) of their export earnings. This restricts their ability to import or hedge their currency earnings effectively.

Import policies

In the case of non-traditional exports, the main tax has not been on outputs but on inputs. In manufacturing activities with substantial requirements for imported intermediate or capital goods, price-raising import barriers reduce the value-added on exporting activities (the final prices of which are fixed by international competition).

To counter this adverse effect, many countries have sought to put exporting on an approximately free-trade basis. Imported intermediate and capital goods have (in principle at least) been free of import constraints and duties, either through duty exemption mechanisms (export processing zones, bonded warehouses) or through duty drawbacks.

The failings of drawback mechanisms

Duty drawback mechanisms have often been ineffective, because of delays caused by administrative deficiencies or revenue shortages.

Drawbacks in particular have often been ineffective, because of delays caused by administrative deficiencies or revenue shortages. It should be recognized that, even when exemption or drawback schemes have been effective, relief from taxation of imported goods is achieved only for inputs that are imported directly. Inputs of goods and services from local producers may be priced higher than they would be under free trade conditions (as opposed to special zones or schemes attempting to compensate for the absence of this trade).

In addition to eliminating or reducing direct taxation of inputs for export production, the liberalization of imports reduces indirect taxation of exports. An import tax effectively subsidizes producers of import-competing goods. It raises the prices (in gross and net terms) of importables relative to the prices of other domestic goods (including exportable ones), thus causing the terms of trade between exports and import substitutes to favour the latter.

Disprotection of exports

Import barriers effectively disprotect or tax exports. In the absence of export subsidies (whose use is limited by revenue constraints and international trade rules), the prices that export producers receive are fixed by world prices. If import barriers drive up the prices of non-export goods while export prices remain fixed, then the import barrier indirectly taxes the exporters by reducing the domestic purchasing power of a unit of foreign exchange earnings.

Import tariffs remain

The reduction of this source of anti-export bias in many developing countries' trade regimes has been a central aim of the trade liberalization adopted in recent decades (often as part of the World Bank's structural adjustment programmes).

The lowering or elimination of quantitative restrictions is particularly evident in some African countries, as reflected in the dramatic falls in the black market premium on foreign exchange.

It is certainly true that import barriers have been substantially reduced in many developing countries. The lowering or elimination of quantitative restrictions (import and foreign exchange licensing or quotas) is particularly evident in some African countries, and is reflected in the dramatic falls in the black market premium on foreign exchange. However, it is also evident that import tariffs are still not negligible, especially when compared with tariffs in developed countries. Average nominal tariffs often exceed 30%. They tend to escalate with the level of processing and vary across and within sectors, with higher tariffs applied where there is import-competing production. The net or effective rates of protection for import-substituting or competing production are likely to be considerably higher in general than the average nominal tariffs recorded.

Table 5	**Africa: import policy reforms**			
Countries/Dates of policy reform	**Average nominal tariff: %[a]**		**Coverage of quantitative restrictions (%)[b]**	
	Pre-reform	**Current**	**Pre-reform**	**Current**
Ghana (1983, 1991)	30	17	100	Low
Kenya (1987, 1991)	40	34	71	0
Malawi (1986, 1991)	26	n.a.	100	Low
Madagascar (1988, 1990)	46	36	100	0
Nigeria (1984, 1990)	35	33	100	Low
South Africa (1984, 1993)	n.a.	29	55	23
Uganda (1986)	30	n.a.	n.a.	Low
Tanzania, UR (1986, 1992)	30	33	100	100
Zaire (1984, 1990)	24	25	100	100

Source: *Adapted from J. Dean, 'The trade policy revolution in developing countries', The World Economy: Global Trade Policy, S. Arndt and C. Milner, eds. (London, Blackwell, 1995).*
a/ Unweighted.
b/ Percentage of tariff lines subject to quantitative restrictions and licensing requirements.

The clear implication is that sustaining and deepening trade liberalization programmes in developing countries are an important means of further lowering domestic policy barriers to exporting.

Improving policies and market efficiency

The Uruguay Round and regional trade agreements have made substantial progress in dismantling trade barriers. In the new trading environment, trade policies that provide the incentive to export need to go hand in hand with policies for private-sector development (PSD) which influence both the capacity to export and international competitiveness.

Although there has been substantial progress in reducing taxes on exports (direct and implicit) and import barriers, there remains considerable scope for improving trade policies. Much greater attention needs to be paid to PSD policies to make markets count, improve the overall incentive for investment and provide access to factors of production.

Economic efficiency

The key to economic efficiency lies in allowing markets to function effectively and efficiently. The role of the State should not be to intervene directly in markets to affect prices and allocate resources but, instead, to correct for failures brought about by the actions of government (government failure) and market imperfections (market failure).

Minimal barriers to entry and exit

For the private sector to be flexible in aligning resources to market requirements, there must be minimal barriers to entry and exit. Thus barriers to entry, in terms of laws on business establishment (company acts, and registration and licensing regulations), should be as liberal as possible. Further, there should be a hard budget constraint that prevents unviable firms from continuing to tie up resources in unproductive uses. Bankruptcy laws should provide minimal barriers to exit whilst protecting creditors.

Market failures

Market failures such as monopoly, unfair or restrictive trade practices, the sale of products that are unsafe, false claims for product performance and poor information are prevalent, particularly in LDCs. Effective competition policy and consumer protection laws are thus essential for markets to function efficiently. Moreover, the State has a major role to play in ensuring that information on markets reaches businesses, other producers and consumers.

Governments continue to intervene in markets, reserving parts of the economy for the State, setting prices, and allocating land or other resources to particular crops and uses.

Governments, nevertheless, continue to intervene in markets, reserving parts of the economy for the State, setting prices, and allocating land or other resources to particular crops and uses. At the same time, LDC Governments have been addressing incidences of market failure with inadequate competition and consumer protection systems and poor flows of information. These shortcomings need to be rectified.

Restrictive company regulations

In many LDCs, company acts and regulations on business formation are unnecessarily restrictive. Concerns over the social effects of business failure have led Governments to impose high barriers to exit and to intervene to keep afloat unviable businesses. Such measures are detrimental to economic efficiency. There are ways to mitigate adverse social consequences that do not undermine economic efficiency.

There is thus a considerable agenda that needs to be addressed if LDCs are to move towards economic efficiency and allow markets to lead the private sector to economically desirable outcomes. The reform of economic policies requires a healthy debate for the private and public sectors to arrive at a consensus.

Level of incentive

As opposed to a narrow focus on tax and non-tax incentives and subsidies, the factors that determine an economy's incentive level are economic stability and sound governance. The goal of governance should be to reduce risk and transaction costs, cut levels of aggregate taxation and increase access to productive resources. Unless the overall incentive level is sufficiently high, a country's productive capacity and competition level will not be sufficient to enable it to compete internationally. Under these conditions, the use of narrow tax and other incentives to stimulate exports may well detract from economic efficiency.

Macroeconomic instability leads to risk and undermines the supply of savings for investment. Businesses are likely to respond by engaging only in activities with short payback periods and those with sufficient returns to compensate for risk. Thus, trading in export commodities is likely to be preferred to investment in processing, manufacturing, tourism and knowledge-based industries with long lead-times. The fact that this is the characteristic behaviour of businesses in many LDCs speaks volumes for the degree of perceived risk in these countries brought about by economic instability and governance.

Many LDCs have embarked on programmes to improve macroeconomic stability and the results are encouraging. Nevertheless, inflation and exchange rate volatility remain much higher in these countries than in their more successful developing country competitors.

Macroeconomic instability leads to risk and undermines the supply of savings for investment.

Governance and corruption

The World Bank's *World Development Report 2000* offers strong evidence of the link between good governance and levels of economic growth. The political system, the soundness of economic laws and the enforcement of the rule of law are potentially important sources of risk. Corruption imposes both risk and higher transaction costs.

Despite major efforts, inflation and exchange rate volatility remain much higher in LDCs than in their more successful developing country competitors.

Some governments have embarked on programmes to improve governance and reduce regulatory burdens through deregulation. But much remains to be done. For example, the World Economic Forum, in its *Africa Competitiveness Report*, reveals that in a sample of six East African countries – Ethiopia, Kenya, Madagascar, Mozambique, Uganda and the United Republic of Tanzania – managers spent an average 15% of their time negotiating with officials on obtaining licences and permits, complying with regulations and discussing tax assessments. This is time that should have been spent developing the business.

The regulatory burden

Allied to governance is the issue of regulatory burden. This is the expense, in time and money, imposed on businesses by the need to comply with government regulations. There is always a need for regulations to ensure health and safety, protecting consumers and workers and the environment. But the way that these regulations are framed and implemented can have a major bearing on the incentive to invest and competitiveness.

Apart from their effect on
private-sector development,
governance and regulatory
burden have a direct bearing
on the orientation of the
economy.

High transaction costs

Apart from their effect on private-sector development generally, governance and regulatory burden have a direct bearing on the orientation of the economy. As Collier argues[15], transaction intensity increases in the move from traditional exporting to the processing of primary products and the export of manufactures. Transaction costs in many developing countries are high, partly because activities are comparatively low scale and often because government policies induce distortions. These high costs deter investment in production for riskier and more distant export markets, and tend to encourage investment in less transaction-intensive activities and in the less risky and less distant domestic market.

Title to assets

Lack of title to assets and
the poor enforceability of
titles and contracts in many
countries serve as major
disincentives to the
development of the private
sector.

In many countries, the lack of title to assets and the poor enforceability of titles and contracts are major disincentives to the development of the private sector. If they can be mitigated, it should result in higher and more sustainable levels of investment and less rent-seeking behaviour on the part of firms.

Foreign direct investment

Finally, as discussed in UNCTAD's *World Investment Report 2000*, it is the economy's overall incentive level, rather than narrow tax concessions, that influences the inflow of FDI. FDI does not usually lead investment, but rather, flows to countries experiencing strong economic growth as a result of domestic investment. Therefore, countries need to address the general level of incentive for private-sector activity rather than give away future tax revenues in a vain attempt to attract investment.

Resources for competitiveness

Access to factors of production is critically important to both the level of development of the private sector and its competitiveness in international markets. The evidence shows that poor access to factors of production has played a major role in limiting the productive base of LDCs. The LDCs need to take major initiatives to make the markets for these factors efficient and effective. Achieving this objective is vital if these countries are to be able to use their underlying comparative advantage for developing international competitiveness.

Access to finance, loans and equity is vital for investment to take place. The supply of funds for investment is determined by the level of savings, which is governed by such factors as macroeconomic conditions and interest rates. The extent to which these savings are made available for investment by the private sector depends on how much government borrowing takes away financial resources that could be loaned to businesses.

The financial sector's crucial role

The financial sector plays the crucial role of channelling savings to investment possibilities and allocating them to competing ends. Evidence of the link between the development of the sector and economic growth is mounting. Studies also show that the degree to which creditors and investors are protected determines the depth and breadth of financial markets.

15   P. Collier, 'Africa's comparative advantage,' *Industrial Development and Policy in Africa*, H. Jalilian, M. Tribe and J. Weiss, eds. (Cheltenham, Edward Elgar, 2000).

The efficiency of financial markets can be judged by the level of loans and equity finance that they are able to raise in relation to GDP. It is also judged by the impact of their investments on competitiveness within the economy. The two tend to be interlinked.

Investor and creditor protection is highest in countries where financial markets have breadth and depth.

Studies show that the depth of financial markets (i.e. the proportion of GDP accounted for by loans and stock market transactions) and their breadth (indicated by the number of investors) are highest in the United States and the United Kingdom, where investor and creditor protection is greatest. These countries also tend to have lower concentration of ownership of output, and hence the highest level of competition within the economy.

Entrepreneurs in LDCs need access to trade finance

One of the greatest problems in LDCs is access to finance. In an ITC survey (1997) of exporters and business associations in East African LDCs, access to trade finance was rated the largest obstacle to international trade, far ahead of government policies (the second biggest constraint).

Box 33

LDCs: trade financing for exporters

Surveys regularly find that obtaining financing worries exporters in LDCs more than any other problem. Nothing can be more frustrating than working hard to obtain a first order from a new customer far away, and then having to turn the order down because it cannot be financed.

Four basic types of finance are important to LDC exporters:

❑ *Finance for investment, i.e. for purchasing production equipment (capital goods);*

❑ *Finance for working capital (i.e. for funding the normal production cycle);*

❑ *Finance for specific transactions (including export or import financing);*

❑ *Incentive finance: grants and other schemes to enable businesses to become internationally competitive.*

Perhaps what matters most is what ITC calls 'transaction-based finance'. Rather than basing their financing decisions on a study of balance sheets, banks should understand what a business transaction involves and what it takes to enable exporters to respond to an order.

This leads to three basic principles for financing entrepreneurs who have a chance to enter the international market:

❑ *No exporter holding a genuine order should be allowed to lose it for lack of capital.*

❑ *Banks should help clients in every possible way, including advising them on how to reduce their risks.*

❑ *Policy-makers should concentrate on providing access to finance, even if cost issues need to be left until later.*

The financial sector in LDCs is often weak, and has become highly risk-averse, preferring to invest in government securities and large stable businesses. High levels of collateral are required for loans, effectively denying SMEs access to finance. This, in turn, blocks SME growth, undermining competition in the economy and reducing exports.

Though businesses often
complain of the high cost of
finance, studies show that
access rather than cost is
the major bottleneck.

Though businesses often complain of the high cost of finance, studies show that access rather than cost is the major bottleneck. There are many examples of credit lines with high interest rates which are fully subscribed and have low default rates. While it is true that when interest rates are kept high in pursuit of monetary policy, cost does become a factor in international competitiveness, but it merely restricts demand to the most profitable ventures. Limiting the access itself prevents even the most profitable businesses from acquiring resources.

Improving the financial sector

Measures are being taken to broaden and deepen the financial sectors in LDCs. The liberalization of local and foreign participation in the financial sector, of access to savings and of the instruments open to participation is one of the main initiatives to date. The other is the establishment of stock exchanges. Much more needs to be done. Liberalization is confined to a few countries and is restrained even in the most progressive of these countries.

Moreover, investor and creditor protection, financial transparency and corporate governance have yet to receive serious attention. The failure to address these issues was manifest in the Asian financial crisis.

Whatever measures are taken to broaden and deepen capital markets, it will take time for them to have an impact on the SMEs' access to finance.

Land problems

The allocation of land as a production factor in LDCs is both underdeveloped and inflexible. The lack of secure title, poorly developed systems of tenure which deny security to users, problems of obtaining development approvals and cumbersome procedures for registering title are major constraints to investment.

Government policies on
national self-sufficiency in
certain goods do not
encourage the efficient
allocation of land and are
outdated in today's global
trading environment.

For agriculture, the important issues are title, tenure and registration. In addition, governments may restrict moves to higher-value uses by insisting that a proportion of land be set aside for the production of staples in order to achieve or maintain national self-sufficiency in these goods.

The absence of title and secure tenure is most acute in societies where land was traditionally owned collectively or where collective ownership was imposed by the State. There is an urgent need in such countries for laws allowing more secure forms of ownership and tenure.

Government policies on national self-sufficiency in certain goods do not encourage the efficient allocation of land and are outdated in today's global trading environment. National food security can be achieved by having the funds for importing and by maintaining small, strategic reserves, the economic costs of which are likely to be much lower than forced attempts at national self-sufficiency.

Development approvals

Development approvals are a bottleneck for investment. The investor is forced to seek pre-investment approvals from a large number of agencies, in a process sometimes consisting of up to 30 steps. The cost and time involved could put off all but the most committed investor. It is certainly one of the main causes of the low rates of FDI in many LDCs. Where reforms have been attempted, the so-called one-stop-shops have often become one-more-stop-shops.

Development approvals are necessary to ensure rational land use and to minimize conflicts between users of adjacent land. However, much can be achieved by streamlining the process, reducing the numbers of agencies that must be involved and shifting the emphasis from paper-based pre-investment approval to post-investment monitoring and enforcement.

Cost of labour

The availability and cost of labour are cited as the obvious comparative advantage of LDCs. Yet it is precisely the cost of labour and, most importantly, its productivity which indicate that few LDCs have been able to translate a possible advantage into a competitive advantage for businesses.

Many LDCs are in a paradoxical position in that, although their GDP per capita low, their labour costs are higher than in countries with better GDP per capita figures.

Many LDCs are in a paradoxical position in that, although their GDP per capita is low, their labour costs are higher than in countries with better GDP per capita figures. African LDCs have labour costs similar to those of countries with per capita incomes several times higher than theirs. The cost of labour in the formal sector is kept high by collective wage bargaining as well as by government regulations on workers' benefits and working hours and conditions. Labour mobility is low because of poor information on job opportunities.

These policies and conditions result in a lack of incentive to use labour. Unemployment is high when formal wages are high. Comparatively high rates of capital intensity are prevalent in capital-scarce economies. The investment needed to create a job in an LDC in Africa is similar to that required in the more advanced developing countries. Thus, a potential comparative advantage fails to be converted into competitive advantage.

Productivity levels

In many manufacturing and service activities, productivity levels are as important as the absolute cost of labour in determining labour cost per unit of output. For competitiveness, what matters is the cost of labour per unit of output and not the cost of labour per hour worked.

The causes of low productivity lie in a host of factors starting with the system of education. Illiteracy rates are high, making it difficult to train the workforce to make it productive. Health problems lower productivity. Absenteeism is rife owing to the difficulties of encouraging a work ethic in the labour force. Labour skills are poor as a result of inadequate systems of vocational training. Even if these problems can be overcome, the poor organization of production within firms reduces productivity.

Infrastructure

The availability and cost of utilities and transport infrastructure are important determinants of competitiveness. Transport and communications play a vital role in bringing goods and services to and from international markets. This section evaluates their role in export development and identifies measures that can be taken to address constraints.

'Natural' barriers – transport

The transport and other transaction costs of doing business internationally help determine a country's ability to integrate fully into the world economy. This is especially true of the more complex manufactured goods, for which the geographical fragmentation of production processes is increasing and the trade in components and other intermediate inputs is expanding. This means that the value-added in a particular export activity will be sensitive to the costs of transporting both imports of the intermediates and exports of final products (Radelet and Sachs, 1998). Remoteness and poor transport and communications infrastructure isolate countries, and inhibit their ability to participate in global production networks.

Thus even when trade barriers are falling in export markets or countries are reducing the policy-induced costs of importing through liberalization measures, important 'natural' barriers to trade may remain.

'Bhutan has little
infrastructure for exporters.
The absence of a dry port
makes deliveries more
expensive. Rice has to be
packed into secure wooden
boxes, reducing the volume
that can be loaded into a
container.'
– Dasho Tshewang Penjore,
Bhutanese exporter of red rice

The issue of 'natural' barriers to exporting is particularly relevant in land-locked countries like Uganda, Zambia and Bhutan, which have also experienced long periods of under-investment in their infrastructure and transport systems. But it is clear that the issues have wider relevance in Africa and other regions where countries suffer from inadequate internal road and rail networks, poor air links, substandard ports and high costs of shipping.

Policy effects

One can certainly understand why some developing countries have higher transport costs than others. The scale of trade, a comparative disadvantage in capital or technologically intensive transport (e.g. containers), may bring this about.

But the differences are not likely to be wholly independent of public policies. This is so in an indirect and direct sense. The scale of a country's trade is not independent of its trade and other policies. Thus the costs of importing and exporting could decline for a particular LDC over time as the volume of trade rises following liberalization, for example. With expanded trade, the bargaining power of countries may improve, reducing the power of monopoly suppliers to fix freight rates.

Policies have an even greater direct influence on trade competitiveness and the cost of transport services. Many developing economies have in the past adopted cargo reservation policies in order to stimulate the development of their own national fleets and preserve foreign exchange. Such policies give preference to national lines and reduce competition for shipping services. Bennathan et al. (1989) estimate that the removal of such anti-competitive measures can reduce transport costs by up to 50%[16]. A non-negligible amount, therefore, of the total costs of international trading, described as arising from 'natural' barriers, may be better viewed as 'unnatural' or at least avoidable. In this respect, the analysis of 'natural' (and 'unnatural') trade barriers has considerable potential policy relevance for reforming economies.

The improvement of port
infrastructure and operations
is receiving policy attention
only now. LDCs, among
them the United Republic of
Tanzania, are opening up
their ports to private
ownership.

Empirical work in modelling trade flows shows that transport and infrastructure have an important quantitative impact on trade. A study by Limão and Venables (1999) suggests that halving transport costs would increase the volume of the average developing country's exports by a factor of five[17]. The same study shows that improving a country's infrastructure as well as the infrastructure in transit countries overcomes about two-thirds of the trade disadvantage associated with being landlocked.

Reducing transport costs is of major importance

This suggests the major importance of developing policies to reduce international transport costs, by sea and air. The improvement of port infrastructure and operations is only now receiving policy attention. LDCs such as the United Republic of Tanzania are opening up their ports to private ownership. Other developing countries have provided incentives for the major

16   E. Bennathan et al., 'Deregulation of shipping: What is to be learned from Chile', working paper (Washington, World Bank, 1989.
17   N. Limão and A.J. Venables, 'Infrastructure, geographical disadvantage and transport cost' (1999).

shipping lines to open up new routes. Provided these incentives are for finite periods, and directed only at facilitating new routes, they can to serve as an important part of maritime policy.

Air links and freight costs are becoming important for LDCs as many now supply fresh or perishable goods to export markets and most are tourist destinations. The economical supply of air services is critical for tourism. Air links and capacity determine the air freight capacity of the country, and freight is most economically carried on passenger flights. Like maritime policy, air policy has, in the past, been restrictive, limiting competition to national carriers.

Reform of these policies is necessary: while they may not serve their intended purpose, they certainly limit the development of important export industries. The viability of small national carriers in an industry experiencing major consolidation under the imperative of economies of scale is now increasingly in doubt. With the exception of Ethiopia and perhaps a few other countries, it is doubtful whether any national carriers in LDCs come close to breaking even. Privatization is a possibility but one that may not succeed, given the lack of interest in acquiring small airlines.

> With the exception of Ethiopia and perhaps a few other countries, it is doubtful whether any national air carriers in LDCs come close to breaking even.

What is required is to re-evaluate air transport policy and to examine the economic costs of national self-reliance. Alternatives include regional alliances and agreements with international carriers that would undertake to provide a minimum level of service. Major tourism destinations are today offering to purchase a guaranteed number of seats for a finite period to motivate airlines to open new gateways. Such measures should be assessed for their suitability. In the end, the viability of international transport services and their cost will be determined by demand. In the long run, there are no substitutes for increasing the volume of exports and the number of visitor arrivals.

National transport networks

> National transport policy and networks are as important as international transport.

The national transport policy and networks are as important as international transport. Road is the major mode of transport in LDCs. Its development is essential for trade growth. Poor road networks add to the cost of operating road freight services and therefore to the cost of imported inputs and exported goods. In view of limited public-sector finances, the option of build-operate-transfer and other methods of private-sector financing of the road network have to be explored. The liberalization of road freight operations to allow foreign vehicles to operate may also help to bring down freight costs.

For commodities with high bulk (or weight) to price ratios, rail is the most economic form of transport. Railways have been neglected for many decades. Private participation may be the only real solution in many LDCs.

Telecommunications and e-commerce

Telecommunications provide the means of contact with distant export markets and help to mitigate another impact of 'natural' barriers. However, in general, LDCs trail far behind developed and the more advanced developing countries in their telecommunications infrastructure. In main telephone lines per 100 inhabitants, none of the East African LDCs exceed 0.5. South Africa, in contrast, has over 11.4.

This is a serious disadvantage for LDCs. Failure to obtain an adequate number of lines or poor reliability of international access can induce customers to look elsewhere.

The cost of making international calls to and from LDCs is several times the figure for communications between developed countries. Increasingly, the Internet is used for telecommunications as it is cheaper and often more reliable. But Internet services are also underdeveloped in LDCs.

The wait for a telephone line in LDCs can be inordinately long. In Ethiopia, it exceeds 10 years. The other LDCs have waiting times longer than a year, compared with the world average of 0.7 years, and these times are lengthening in many countries. This has fuelled the growth in the use of cellular services. While this has improved telecommunications, the cost of cellular services and problems of coverage make fixed lines the better alternative.

Cost is an important issue. The cost of making international calls to and from LDCs is several times the figure for communications between developed countries. Increasingly, the Internet is used for telecommunications as it is cheaper and often more reliable. But Internet services are also underdeveloped in LDCs.

In just the same way that access to transportation networks is necessary for lower trade policy barriers to lead to more trade, the liberalization of specific services will increase trade flows only if there is improved access to telecommunications services and the Internet. This will depend on the development of the telecommunications infrastructure and particularly on the availability of satellite or fibre optic connections to the rest of the world.

In many developing countries, the inadequacy of basic telecommunications services is the main constraint to e-commerce. Liberalization in the sector will allow the entry of more efficient services suppliers, which in turn will lead to freer trade in information technology products and services, as well as the trade in other services sectors (finance and distribution, to name two).

All countries (developed and developing) stand to gain from the trading opportunities offered by the Internet.

All countries (developed and developing) stand to gain from the trading opportunities offered by the Internet. Although the current stage of infrastructural and technological development in the richest countries indicates that the greater benefit from this trade today accrues to these countries, the distance of developing countries from the technological frontier may mean that they have the bigger potential to benefit from moving towards the frontier.

Export strategies

The national export strategy

There is a need for an explicit declaration by governments on the priorities for export development and the course of action they will take to establish an enabling environment for the export trade. Box 34 sets out the elements that such declarations (i.e. national export strategies) should address.

National export strategies should not be rigid or over-prescriptive.

However, it is important to bear in mind that these national export strategies should not be rigid or over-prescriptive. The identification of priority sectors, markets, and bases for competitiveness should form the basis for a vision that can be shared with the private sector. Such strategies should guide and, hopefully, inspire, not direct or command. While they are a means for prioritizing resource allocation, they should not attempt to influence market outcomes by resorting to policy instruments such as tax incentives and subsidies.

The use of product- and sector-specific export incentives has served mainly to concentrate the trade in particular sectors. Their track record in increasing exports overall is poor. It is obvious that no analysis, no matter how detailed or vigorous, could possibly hope to identify all the market opportunities that entrepreneurs could exploit. If a few sectors are given tax incentives and subsidies, it may divert entrepreneurs away from opportunities elsewhere.

Box 34

The national export strategy: elements to address

Priority markets and sectors

The choice of priority markets will need to be made on the basis of size and attractiveness, taking account of current patterns of trade, market access, distance and the degree of entrenched competition. The selection of sectors will be influenced by the share of exports, recent growth, market trends and opportunities, the degree of competitiveness and the underlying comparative advantage that can be turned into competitive advantage by the strategy.

Market positioning and competitiveness

In broad terms, the strategy should set out market share targets and how products are to be positioned (price, quality, service offer) in the market to attain those targets. In order to do this, strategy-makers need to evaluate the basis on which the country's exporters can succeed in the market against their main competitors.

Policies

The strategy should propose reforms in trade and private-sector development policies (PSD) to improve export incentives and hence to intensify the export orientation of the economy. It should also enunciate the policies required to improve market access for the priority sectors. Explicit and firm undertakings should be given on policy reform.

Trade-related business services

This should list programmes that the government will undertake to ease constraints to PSD and trade, focusing on trade-related business services. The programmes should be specific, describing the main projects to be implemented under them.

Assistance to priority sectors

For the priority sectors, specific programmes and projects to accelerate competitiveness and exploit market opportunities should be elaborated. These may address needs for specific business services (such as training and SQAM systems) and for particular types of infrastructure (for instance, cool chains and air links).

One example is red rice exported from Bhutan (see box 35). In the domestic market, consumption of red rice is giving way to cheaper white rice imported from India. Bhutan has little apparent competitive advantage in producing rice. Yet one entrepreneur has started to export red rice as an organic product to the United States at prices over twice that of the international price of white rice. It is highly unlikely that any planner would have spotted such an opportunity. Moreover, if tax incentives had favoured traditional exports such as fruit, the entrepreneur might not have bothered to exploit the opportunity.

Export strategies should be specific

It is vitally important for export strategies to be specific in their commitments on policies and programmes.

It is vitally important for export strategies to be specific in their commitments to policies and programmes. It is essential to determine the costs of implementation and to identify sources of funds so that government budgets can make explicit provisions for them.

National export strategies must be broad in their outlook and hence cannot address sectoral needs and constraints at the level of the firm in any detail. This must be left to the strategies for the priority sectors. There is a pressing need for such strategies in LDCs, as specified in the Joint Integrated Technical Assistance Programme (JITAP), which combines the expertise of WTO, UNCTAD and ITC to assist selected African countries, including several LDCs, in export development (see chapter 5 for a description of this programme).

> **Box 35**
>
> ***Bhutan: up the value chain with red rice***
>
> **Company:** *Chharu Tsongdrel, owned by former district administrator Dasho Tshewang Penjore, and located in Paro, Bhutan, specializes in the export of red rice. In 1992 the proprietor's son discovered in the files of a recently privatized firm that an American businessman had been seeking a way to import Bhutanese red rice for several years. A major problem was scepticism that it was possible to keep the bran intact while removing the husk. Dasho Tshewang Penjore believed this was possible and contacted the businessman, who spent two years finding potential buyers in the United States.*
>
> **Performance:** *Since the first trial order of 1 ton by an American distributor in 1994 and 4 tons the next year, orders have grown at the rate of 45% a year. The entrepreneur's son has been working for five years to promote Bhutanese red rice in the United Kingdom, and a trial order of 10 tons has been just been received. Importers supplied the rice to upmarket health food chains. Packaging in traditional Bhutanese handmade paper bags with traditional designs increased the appeal. An article in a major American newspaper noting the use of the rice in a top-level restaurant gave the product wide exposure, leading to several other reports on the introduction of Bhutanese red rice into American home cuisine.*
>
> *The attractive export price has enabled the entrepreneur to offer higher rates for the paddy than farmers can obtain on the local market, boosting their income and winning acceptance for the enterprise.*
>
> **Key success factors:**
>
> ❑ *The proprietor Dasho Tshewang Penjore, a district administrator until his retirement in the mid-1980s, is a risk-taker. He started with no experience of the rice business and a very basic knowledge of rice processing. But he was willing to go for the highly competitive American market with his product.*
>
> ❑ *The importer's advances financed the business in its early stages.*
>
> ❑ *The proprietor's son has played a crucial role in efforts to diversify the market for the business.*
>
> ❑ *The Bhutanese Government had a liberal export policy, making it easier for the entrepreneur to launch into the business.*
>
> **Constraints:** *Bhutanese farmers were at first reluctant to sell their rice, fearing they would not receive payment. The entrepreneur got round this by paying the farmers in cash immediately after purchase. Training of workers in cleaning and grading rice was both difficult and time-consuming. All operations other than milling are manual. Lengthy customs and shipping formalities at the port of Calcutta in India delayed the trial order for months.*
>
> *Bhutan has not much of an infrastructure for exporting. The absence of a dry port makes deliveries more expensive. The rice has to be packed into secure wooden boxes, reducing the volume that can be loaded into a container.*
>
> *The entrepreneur has invested in a larger-capacity milling machine but the intensive manual work required for the other operations is making it difficult to handle orders efficiently.*

Sectoral export strategies

Ideally, the policy environment should be addressed by the national export strategy. Where there are no national export strategies, however, bottom-up policy reform may be instigated by export strategies for priority sectors.

The main thrust of sectoral strategies, however, should be:

❑ *To identify priority markets.* This should be presented in geographic and product terms, taking account of market size and attractiveness as outlined in the national export strategy, focusing on markets in which the sector has the basic competitiveness to establish strong and sustainable market positions.

❑ *To define key factors for success.* Based on an assessment of market conditions and trends, sectoral strategies should set out the changes, in product specification and performance, quality, packaging and price, that are essential for success. They should also describe the marketing and sales initiatives required to exploit market opportunities, giving special attention to how the sector can move up the value chain and secure adequate exposure to end-users and consumers.

❑ *To identify the required trade-related business services.* Sector strategies should identify programmes and projects that need to be implemented to ease constraints. Some of the changes proposed may have policy implications for liberalizing the provision of services. These implications must be clearly set out for policy-makers.

❑ *To identify measures to overcome constraints within the firm.* These measures could include improving the structure of the industry by supporting SMEs, introducing know-how and best practice in operational management through FDI, and addressing vertical and horizontal linkages through cluster development. They could also provide for means of measuring competitiveness to identify weaknesses at the level of the firm and specify sectoral marketing and product adaptation programmes where there are synergies to be gained from sector-wide initiatives.

Sectoral strategies must also be specific in the course of action proposed and identify costs and sources of funding.

> Sectoral strategies should set out the changes that are essential for success on the basis of an assessment of market conditions and trends.

Trade strategies and the Integrated Framework for LDCs

An important development in the formulation of trade strategies in LDCs is the Integrated Framework for Trade-Related Technical Assistance. The Framework is the outcome of a commitment made by six multilateral agencies (IMF, ITC, UNCTAD, UNDP, the World Bank and WTO) to coordinate their assistance in trade and investment promotion in order to facilitate the integration of certain countries into the global economy. This commitment was made by the six core agencies among themselves and with other multilateral and bilateral donors as a result of the High-Level Meeting for LDCs organized by WTO in October 1997 in Geneva. The Meeting itself sought to fulfil a commitment made earlier by developed countries to deploy special efforts to help LDCs make better use of the opportunities for trade opened up by the institution of a rules-based multilateral trading system.

Pro-poor trade sector strategies

As a preliminary step to trade-related technical assistance, the Integrated Framework is promoting the formulation of a pro-poor trade sector strategy in each LDC. The strategy is to be an important part of each country's national poverty reduction strategy. The poverty strategies are presented in Poverty Reduction Strategy Papers (PRSP) under a process supported by the World Bank and IMF. The Papers will form the basis for the Banks' concessional assistance to low-income countries – including debt relief under the Heavily Indebted Poor Countries (HIPC) Debt Initiative.

> Pro-poor trade sector strategies will form the basis for concessional assistance from the World Bank and IMF to low-income countries.

Six components

A pro-poor trade sector strategy has six components involving both substance and process:

❑ It has proposals for reform in enabling policies (e.g. on the investment environment, the trade regime) and support institutions (especially in the areas of trade facilitation and trade promotion).

❑ It has action plans at the product-sector level, including project proposals to capitalize on the major opportunities identified in the strategy.

❑ It is based on, and is supported by, strong ownership by all trade-sector stakeholders. Efforts must be made to build that ownership into the strategy, which must be truly representative of the 'shared vision and commitment' of all stakeholders.

❑ The formulation and implementation of the strategy must be driven by the identification and monitoring of clear indicators of outcome in terms of poverty reduction. This is consistent with an underlying principle of the poverty reduction papers (monitoring of poverty reduction) and with the notion that trade development must deliberately and clearly improve the lot of the poor in LDCs.

❑ Finally, the strategy should clearly identify technical assistance and capacity-building priorities to support its implementation as well as recommend actions that high-income and regional partner countries could take to improve the access of LDC exporters to their markets.

The key principle of any poverty reduction strategy should be that it is country-driven, oriented to achieving concrete results, comprehensive in looking at poverty's cross-sectoral determinants, and providing a context for actions by various development partners.

Human resource capacity building is required at various levels. At the micro-level, subcontractors and exporters, producer groups and support institutions, including NGOs participating in a concrete project, need to strengthen their capacities. At the strategic level, national capacity-building including assistance to ministries and support institutions is required.

> *A pro-poor trade sector strategy has six critical components, dealing with both process and substance.*

Box 36

Cambodia: linking trade with poverty issues

Cambodia has made efforts to place trade in the mainstream of its overall development strategy, which was presented to the ITC Business Sector Round Table at the LDC III Conference in Brussels. Using the PSRP approach of the World Bank and IMF, the Cambodian Government has started a participatory process involving the Ministry of Commerce, an inter-ministerial steering group, the business sector, a donor group on trade and other stakeholders.

Because of its limited human, institutional, financial resources, Cambodia decided to focus its efforts on a few product sectors. Given widespread poverty in the country, the priority is to make exports work for the poor by developing rural markets, decentralizing the current export base and increasing national value-addition.

The strategic response to these challenges is to prioritize specific products (essential oils, edible oils, spices, fruits, rice, freshwater fish and handicrafts), all of special importance for the rural poor. Furthermore, to benefit poor regions, it was decided to set up export processing zones for garment and shoes in new regions and to develop tourism in economically weak regions with potential for attracting foreign visitors.

➡

➡

To spur value addition, agro-processing, wood processing (including furniture production) and value-added fish products are target sectors. These sectors have a market potential, a strong supply base, and the possibility for building strong backward linkages which could enable poor producers to benefit from international trade opportunities.

The strategy is cross-cutting: it links trade with poverty issues and addresses the general trade environment including WTO matters, investment, and trade facilitation services for exporters. Defining priority actions to be taken by the Government and trade-sector stakeholders as well as providing a framework for trade-related technical cooperation with donors, the strategy offers an encouraging example of how to mainstream a pro-poor trade strategy into a national development strategy.

Box 37

Samoa: poverty reduction efforts by an NGO

Company: *The Pure Coconut Oil Company was created as a distribution company by the Women in Business Foundation (WIBF) of Samoa, a non-governmental organization at the grassroots level set up by women to help micro- and small enterprises to generate income. The foundation sells coconut oil and handicraft products. Its main source of external support is currently a grant from the Government of New Zealand. WIBF is an active member of the Samoan Association of Manufacturers and Exporters.*

Performance: *Though created in 1990 and registered as a charitable organization in 1991, WIBF is the only major NGO involved in micro-financing in the country; it is active in 86 villages with UNDP help. Funding to buy the equipment for coconut oil production came from the Canadian Government.*

The company has been exporting a ton of coconut oil monthly to Australia. Because WIBF promotes organic farming, exports of this oil could rise to 3 tons a month, and sales to the United States have started.

WIBF has established sales outlets in New Zealand and the United States (Hawaii) for handicraft products. The main market for these has so far been the many Samoans living abroad. Its best income-generator has been fine mats. It also has bee-keeping projects (funded by FAO).

WIBF is helping similar organizations to get started, conducting training in Tuvalu and assisting NGO creation in Fiji, Kiribati and Tonga. It has recently been invited by OXFAM New Zealand and Trade Aid of New Zealand to be their Samoan partner.

Key success factors:

❑ *WIBF became aware early of the rising demand for organic products. It now has five organic certified farms. Among its products, traditional medicines and coconut oil have been certified organic.*

❑ *WIBF targets women and young people. Suppliers and producers are involved in projects at village level.*

❑ *The foundation is an active participant in local and overseas trade exhibitions. It is a leading organizer of market days associated with major events.*

Constraints:

❑ *Funding limitations, which means most marketing is by word of mouth*

❑ *WIBF members and customers, women in rural villages for the most part, have minimal knowledge of the cash economy, so that they need training in income management as well as in income-generating activities.*

The enterprise perspective

In formal terms, poverty reduction through trade principally takes place via increased participation of low-income producer groups in the trade-related production chain, i.e. through backward linkages such as subcontracts issued by large firms to a number of small producers down the chain. In several instances clusters of small production units in specific geographic regions facilitate such cooperation. This factor has helped minimize many of the manufacturing costs associated with transportation and information flows.

Poverty-focused social concern plays a major role in many of the success stories of LDC enterprises.

However, the social dimension plays a major role in many of the success stories of LDC enterprises. Some of this concern can be traced back to an NGO's experience with a number of the entrepreneurs or to the deep roots an enterprise has in its community (see box 38).

Box 38

Nepal: incubator with a social dimension

Company: *Lotus Holdings is an LDC investment management company, created in 1998 with funding from Sulo Shrestha-Shah, the entrepreneur behind the Nepalese rug manufacturer Formation Carpets. Company revenues are derived from fees for operations and management services as well as from investments of the assets of its individual investors and promoters. Its stated long-term goal is a 'self-reliant, socially and economically developed society through the growth of business enterprises'.*

Performance: *An entrepreneur who had been working for exporting companies for 10 years was approached and convinced to set up a company. Lotus supported the entrepreneur, taking care of many of the administrative details of running the business. This model – of spinning off new companies and providing them with managerial and administrative support– has proved highly successful.*

In three years, Lotus Holdings of Nepal has set up 12 thriving exporting companies. Among these are two carpet and rug producers, a manufacturer of handmade paper, a maker of pashmina and hand-woven products, and a trading company. Two more carpet factories are planned. Total exports from the five exporting companies more than doubled between 1998/99 and 1999/00, reaching US$ 281,428.

Key success factors:

❑ *From the beginning, Lotus brought ethical and social dimensions to its start-ups. A good example is Rugs for All, a successful recent start-up. It was born when Lotus first bought a rug design and made up samples for buyers – the reverse of the usual process by which a buyer selects a design and asks the manufacturer to produce it. Formation Carpets, Lotus's main investor, decided not to produce the design, but agreed to back the creation of a new company to fulfil the order.*

❑ *As part of its investment philosophy, Lotus insisted that Rugs for All should offer higher wages and institute social norms and a corporate philosophy. When the start-up reached the break-even point, it was required to contribute at least 1% of its turnover for the welfare of the employees (all companies within the group are required to do this). This fee goes to the education of the employees' children, health insurance and day care facilities. A Lotus subsidiary administers the services funded by the 1% fee.*

❑ *From its inception, Lotus sought to fill the needs of entrepreneurs who required managerial and technical support as they set up their businesses. Through its subsidiaries, it provides management and technical assistance, financing assistance, accounting help, as well as Internet and information technology services. It actively networks the managers of its holding companies and encourages cross-fertilization of ideas and contacts with the aim of spinning off new companies.* ➡

> ➡
>
> ❑ *In addition, it provided a framework for ethical business practices. This framework helps promote and sell products by assuring buyers in developed countries that employees work in satisfactory labour conditions. Such social measures have paid off for Rugs for All in importing countries, especially Germany, where press coverage was favourable to the enterprise.*
>
> ❑ *Lotus Holdings also strongly supports the creation of a 'networked' feeling in its associated companies. There are regular 'family' meetings to share information. Opportunities identified by one company are shared with the others. Often, Lotus reports, export openings have been passed on. And providing services to manage welfare provisions frees the companies from having to increase their administrative burden.*

'The private sector can play a crucial role in poverty eradication by contributing to economic growth and creating employment.'
– *United Nations Programme of Action for the Least Developed Countries for the Decade 2001-2010*

For others, however, this appears as just sound business sense. Workers have to be trained and kept within the organization for as long as possible once they are skilled. For employees, the priorities – particularly among women with families – may not be the highest wages but the most family-friendly work place. A number of LDC business leaders have deliberately fostered a sense of ownership among their employees. Sometimes this means giving them shares in the business.

Enterprise approaches, with and without assistance

Case studies presented at the ITC Business Round Table in Brussels offered several examples of an enterprise-driven approach to poverty reduction through trade. With its market niche in paprika powder, for instance, the enterprise Cheetah Paprika, Zambia, works with 30,000 growers and provides training (notably on harvest and post-harvest techniques) and information on group formation, crop finance, packaging materials and local delivery points.

Through training and capacity-building, as well as health and education programmes, entrepreneurs in LDCs have been implementing a business-driven approach to poverty reduction through trade.

Capacity-building has also been oriented to compliance with international market standards. Partnerships with NGOs and donor agencies have helped to provide technical assistance. Frager of Haiti produces vetiver essence, the ingredient of fine perfumes and industrial fragrances. For Frager, close contacts with planters of vetiver are important, and technical advice is part of their working arrangement with farmers. In Frager's case, no government or international donor support was provided.

Programing export-led poverty reduction programmes

Concern with poverty reduction in bilateral and international organizations, including the United Nations system, does not assume that the benefits of economic growth trickle down automatically to the poor. Instead, it is recognized that the benefits of growth must be explicitly redistributed to the poor or, even better, they must be brought deliberately into the growth process through direct employment and entrepreneurship. This vision of how to go about poverty reduction is squarely shared by ITC's approach to export-led poverty reduction (EPR).

Economies that are open to trade and investment tend to grow faster than closed ones. While economic growth alone cannot guarantee a substantial and sustained reduction in poverty and inequality, accelerated growth is a necessary condition for reducing poverty. Many of the poorest developing countries have been unable to integrate successfully into global markets or, as a result, to participate in the growth-inducing and potentially poverty-reducing benefits of integration. This holds true in particular for sub-Saharan African countries, with low levels of industrialization and heavy dependence on exports of primary commodities. The problem for many of them is not that trade is impoverishing them but that they are in danger of being largely excluded from it.

> The problem for many sub-Saharan African States is not that trade is impoverishing them but that they are in danger of being largely excluded from it.

The poor bear the brunt of adjustment costs

Although at the macroeconomic level, trade liberalization in a comprehensive development framework reduces the incidence of poverty, the poor are much more vulnerable to shifts in international prices, and this vulnerability is increased by a country's openness to trade. The process of shifting resources away from import-competing to newly competitive export industries takes time and creates adjustment costs in terms of unemployment. Again, the poor bear the bulk of the adjustment cost resulting from greater openness. In the long run, however, the adjustment costs are expected to be largely offset by the gains. In the longer term, the poor benefit from trade through economic growth that is more open, oriented outward and broad based, bringing higher value added and employment to larger groups of people.

The capacity challenge

Protection rarely helps the poor, and trade policy is not as effective as other measures in shielding vulnerable population groups. The challenge is to enable the poor to exploit opportunities in trade and inward investment. Crucial in this regard is capacity-building to empower small producers to adapt to new forms of work and acquire the new skills needed to respond to the opportunities of globalization and to enter into production for export. This presupposes an integrated view of trade and poverty and suggests that trade should be included in a country's comprehensive development and poverty reduction strategy.

Building blocks for sustainable export-led poverty reduction projects

There are 10 building blocks for viable and sustainable EPR projects. These are:

- Identify products and markets with export potential;

- Develop or adapt export products to meet the market's standards and quality requirements;

- Select and organize poor producers;

- Choose the right product market for the producer organization based on its supply potential;

- Organize linkages between producers and buyers;

- Arrange for financing and credit;

- Enhance human resource development;

- Strengthen support services;

- Include the gender dimension; and

- Take account of the environmental dimension.

Chapter 5 looks at the business development mechanisms and services a country can employ to help create an enabling environment for exporters.

Chapter 5

Support services for export development in LDCs

Exporters in LDCs have limited access to the trade-support services they need to compete with exporters in the more advanced countries. These services also have an important bearing on transaction costs, capacity and competitiveness. They include trade-related finance and financial services, trade facilitation, SQAM systems, counselling and export-skills training. They can go a long way towards helping to establish an enabling environment for trade.

Development programmes have focused on building capacity in the trade support institutions providing these services. International agencies have put in place innovative trade development mechanisms such as matchmaking and business partnering between developed and developing countries. This chapter discusses the needs of LDC exporters for trade support services and various programme responses.

Box 39
JITAP: developing trade capacity in Africa

For a number of developing countries, especially in Africa, playing a full part in the international trade community is impossible simply because they lack the capacity to deal with the technical issues at the level of detail required today. JITAP, the Joint ITC/UNCTAD/WTO Integrated Technical Assistance Programme in Selected Least-Developed and Other African Countries, was created as a four-year programme to tackle these shortcomings through a major capacity-building effort.

JITAP has been operational since mid-1998 and has eight participating African countries. The Programme takes a participating country through six stages designed to build national capacity to understand the evolving trade system and its implications, to adapt the national trading system to the obligations and disciplines of the multilateral trading system (MTS), and to seek maximum national advantage from the system by zeroing in on product-specific export opportunities and elaborating sectoral action plans to seize those opportunities.

Trade support institutions and networks

Trade support institutions (TSIs) include dedicated trade promotion organizations (TPOs), private business organizations, consultancy firms, training bodies, certification institutes, and even some banking services.

TPOs can claim to have long established their value as part of national trade development strategies, particularly in countries where the private sector is weakly networked, lacks the facilities to obtain information on foreign trade markets and buyers' needs, or does not have effective representation. However, the overall success rate of TPOs and the networks they have tried to create has been variable. Some commentators have blamed the strong public-sector identification of TPOs for the failings. Others have pointed out that TPOs are often scapegoats for shortcomings in the business environment.

A meeting of strategy-makers called by ITC in 1999, however, concluded that TPOs can be useful but that they need to change, along with national trade development strategies. More focus is needed on the onshore needs of exporters, e.g. trade finance, quality management and trade information, for example. And partnerships with the private sector are essential. Moreover, policy-makers and TPOs need to encourage networking of similar and complementary services to create a 'critical mass' of service capacity and synergies to produce better-quality service and higher levels of efficiency.

Successful countries, strong TPOs

'Traditional trade promotion services are no longer sufficient to promote international competitiveness. National export strategies which confine themselves to these operational programmes are unlikely to meet the challenges that we are now facing ... not to mention those that are just around the corner.'

– J. Denis Bélisle, Executive Director, ITC, Geneva, at the 1999 Executive Forum

Many, if not most, successful exporting countries have established a strong central or national TPO to coordinate implementation of a national export strategy. They include the Japan External Trade Organization (JETRO), the Korea Trade-Investment Promotion Agency (KOTRA), the Finland Trade Promotion Organization (FINPRO) and Trade New Zealand (TRADENZ). Many developing countries have established similar TPOs. In fact, encouraging this has been a major component of the ITC technical cooperation programme over the years. But the majority of these have not achieved equivalent success.

Causes of failure

A large part of the disparity in TPO performance can be attributed to the character of linkages between the organization and the private sector, and more specifically, to the level of direct private-sector involvement in the planning and management of TPO operations. TPOs with little or no direct private-sector involvement at the planning and management level have been seen to perform poorly. Their programmes tend to be static and insufficiently demand- or needs-based. They have also been generally judged as ineffective and bureaucratic.

TPOs work best when private-sector driven

It is now widely accepted that TPOs function best when they are private-sector driven. This means that the TPO is either directly controlled and run by the private sector, as is the case with FINPRO, or is closely oriented to business and commercial goals through private-sector representation on the governing board, as with Trade New Zealand and Enterprise Ireland.

Wrong focus: offshore not onshore networking

Another reason for the less than satisfactory performance of TPOs in developing and transition economies is that they have not developed the operational linkages with other trade support institutions (public- and private-sector) which are needed to ensure that the full range of export services are available to the private sector. In short, they have continued to concentrate on offshore market development and promotional activities, rather than on addressing the fundamental constraint to improved export performance – the inability to develop internationally competitive export capacities that are consistent with market requirements. In many developing countries, the TPO has remained too narrowly focused and has not established itself, from the technical standpoint at least, as a national trade support institution fully networked with other TSIs offering specialized technical services. Networking of trade support services can provide the critical mass of a needed service, as well as complementarity and synergy in the provision of services.

Only indirect influence

A third reason for the lack of success (and credibility) of many TPOs is that they have only indirect influence on a key promotional instrument (and one of the most, if not the most, resource intensive of such instruments) – commercial representation abroad.

Within the context of a broader definition of trade promotion, the challenge confronting the national TPO is to develop a new set – what might be called a second generation – of services, or to facilitate other, specialized trade support institutions providing such services (see box 40).

The challenge confronting the national trade promotion organization is to develop a new set – what might be called a second generation – of services.

Box 40
The ITC Executive Forum: an orientation for trade support services

What should a national export development strategy encompass, given the dynamics of today's international market? Should it focus on market development and on improving traditional promotional instruments – trade fair participation, trade missions and commercial representation services in foreign markets? Or should it concentrate on the delivery of services that address 'persistent market failings', such as the reluctance of the prospective exporter to purchase information, to cover initial market contact and exploration costs, or to invest in technological innovation? Should national export strategy combine promotional initiatives, organized on behalf of existing enterprises, with programmes designed to generate new export capacities?

These were the questions posed to strategy-makers at ITC's first Executive Forum on National Development Strategies, held in 1999. The answers that emerged from the three-day discussions made it clear that national strategies must be redefined, and trade support institutions have to embrace new roles to keep up with the rapidly changing environment.

The view was that to be effective, a national export strategy must be comprehensively integrated into the overall economic planning framework. It should not simply deal with offshore market development and promotion. It should also encompass the longer-term onshore challenges of establishing a national competitiveness framework, creating an export culture and national consensus, and developing new export industries.

The challenge confronting the national trade promotion organization is to develop a new set – what might be called a second generation – of services, or to facilitate specialized trade support institutions providing such services. The orientation of such programmes should be towards:

❑ *Developing the overall competitiveness of the enterprise, rather than increasing its immediate export sales.*

❑ *Supporting industry associations and clusters of firms, rather than concentrating on the individual enterprise.*

❑ *Providing long-term support, rather than one-off assistance.*

❑ *Developing capabilities, both production and managerial, rather than simply marketing competence.*

❑ *Promoting technology acquisition, investment and subcontracting, rather than focusing on just 'getting the goods out of the country'.*

The second Executive Forum looked at strategies for trade promotion in a digital economy, while the third, held in Montreux, Switzerland, at the end of September 2001, was called to look at ways to ensure that trade support networks are working.

Common elements in strengthening TPOs

Strengthening trade support institutions is a high priority for many businesses.

While the assistance required will vary from organization to organization, the common elements of the way in which they need to be strengthened are:

- Increase the participation of the private sector in their management and supervision to make them more responsive to the needs of exporters;

- Reduce their policy and administrative functions so that they can focus on promotional activities;

- Reduce the scope of their in-house capacity by providing matching grant assistance that enables exporters to use private-sector providers of promotional services;

- Make them focus on value for money in the services they provide by making them recover a proportion of their cost through user charges. This will also help them to focus on services for which there is greatest demand.

Box 41
The TSI Index: LDCs are stronger on commitment

The Trade Support Institution Index was developed by ITC to provide trade support organizations and similar bodies with a practical diagnostic tool to assess their performance according to 12 factors identified as critical to TSI success. The index enables the TSI to assess its strengths and weaknesses, identify areas for improvement, and assess its comparative position regionally, internationally or by group (for example, TSIs in LDCs).

The index includes a data-gathering instrument in electronic format consisting of questions relating to external and internal factors. To date, responses have been received from TSIs in 28 countries, including eight LDCs.

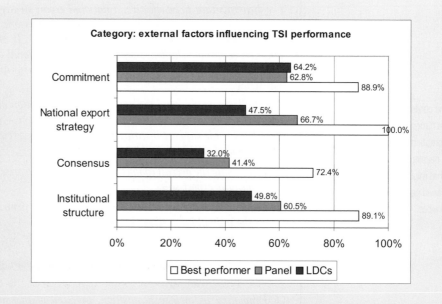

TSIs in LDCs scored highest in commitment (64.2 out of 100) and organizational strategy (68.5). On commitment, they even scored higher than the average (62.8). Their lowest scores were in consensus (32) and funding (19.2).

➡

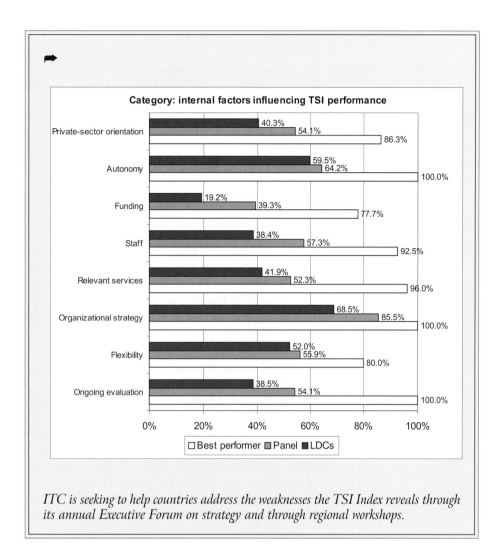

Category: internal factors influencing TSI performance

	Best performer	Panel	LDCs
Private-sector orientation	86.3%	54.1%	40.3%
Autonomy	100.0%	64.2%	59.5%
Funding	77.7%	39.3%	19.2%
Staff	92.5%	57.3%	38.4%
Relevant services	96.0%	52.3%	41.9%
Organizational strategy	100.0%	85.5%	68.5%
Flexibility	80.0%	55.9%	52.0%
Ongoing evaluation	100.0%	54.1%	38.5%

ITC is seeking to help countries address the weaknesses the TSI Index reveals through its annual Executive Forum on strategy and through regional workshops.

Business organizations

Trade associations, chambers of commerce and industry organizations can, and frequently do, play a vital role in providing support for exporters. They should have intimate knowledge of the constraints to exporting and should be able to organize sector-wide initiatives to address them.

In LDCs many business organizations have a meagre capacity to provide services to members.

The problem in LDCs is often the meagre capacity of these organizations to provide worthwhile services to their members. Their lack of resources stem from the low membership fees that businesses can afford. In turn, this constrains their capacity to provide commercially valuable services, which further limits their ability to attract members and to charge higher membership and user fees.

Support for these organizations can be very worthwhile, in economic as much as in political terms. They often function with little bureaucracy and some have wide reach in the private sector. What is required is technical assistance to upgrade their capability and financial resources for launching member services such as providing information on markets and technical issues specific to their members. They may also be assisted to promote exports, in conjunction with the TPO.

First-hand knowledge

Trade associations have a particularly valuable role to play in developing sectoral strategies and undertaking initiatives to address constraints within the firm. They often have first-hand knowledge of trends and prospects in export markets and can help analyse and address competition issues. A number of the successful entrepreneurs in LDCs – from a Bangladeshi garment manufacturer to a Nepalese employment agency director – have highlighted the importance of their trade associations in uniting industry colleagues and helping tackle administrative problems.

Networking trade-related stakeholders

National networks of trade-related stakeholders should include all the institutions addressing trade development issues, e.g. TPOs, business organizations, government ministries (such as ministries of trade, finance, agriculture and health), provincial governments, standards bodies, universities, business training institutes, banks, consulting and law firms, and citizens' groups). Donors represented in the country, active in trade development, may also be considered part of the network. Individual network members are active to the extent that they seek information or support from, or to influence, other network members. They are often constituted into a formal network, cooperating on a defined task.

The network needed to address export strategy issues, which may often be latent, requires the inclusion of a broad spectrum of institutions representative of all affected and contributing elements of government and society. This is to ensure that strategies are mainstreamed into national development priorities, owned by relevant private- and public-sector actors, and understood and supported by the public. This contrasts with the more continuously active sub-networks cooperating on specific, day-to-day tasks. One example is a trade training programme, normally anchored in a business training institute, which might incorporate expertise from banks (for trade finance issues), from standards boards (for quality management issues), and from product organizations or TPOs (for market development issues).

An important advantage of networking in resource-scarce countries is that it can bring together a critical mass of expertise to provide effective services. For example, WTO-related information and capacities to deal with issues of the multilateral trading system have been particularly scarce in LDCs.

One response has been the creation of national networks of trainers and experts in WTO matters, encouraged (to give two examples) by JITAP, the joint ITC/UNCTAD/WTO capacity-building programme in Africa, and by ITC's World Tr@de Net. National inter-institutional committees (composed of key ministries and private-sector organizations) have been created to handle the issues and challenges of upcoming WTO negotiations.

Networking can produce complementarities and encourage specialization. These can lead to synergetic service provision, resulting in a broader information exchange, the introduction of professional standards and the identification of service gaps. Networking among relevant institutions can be especially important in capacity-building programmes, preventing excessive dependence on one organization. By including all key players, these programmes bring to bear their different perspectives and produce the critical mass and efficiencies which make the difference between effectiveness and failure.

> **Box 42**
> **World Tr@de Net**
>
> *Since the establishment of the World Trade Organization in 1995, considerable expertise on the business implications of the WTO Agreements has been built up in many countries. But key players are often not aware of each other's activities and need support for their country initiatives.*
>
> *The ITC approach to finding the most cost-effective way of bringing together a critical mass of core WTO expertise at the national level with the minimum delay is to establish interactive networks of multiplier agents and to provide catalytic support to these networks. Typically, they include WTO focal points in ministries, business and trade associations, Trade Points, trade support institutions, academia, specialized consultants and the press.*
>
> *Bangladesh's network, for example, includes the country's main chambers of commerce and industry, the International Jute Organization, the Bangladesh Association of Software and Information Services, the Institute of Business Administration of the University of Dhaka, the Bangladesh Standards and Testing Institute, the Daily Independent and the Daily Star, as well as other commerce and industry organizations.*
>
> *More than 30 local networks have been created in African, Asian and Latin American developing countries as well as in eastern and central Europe since 1998. Six to nine countries join the ITC World Tr@de Net every year; members reached 33 by mid-2001, including eight LDCs.*
>
> *World Tr@de Net programmes are designed to ensure wide impact, to be cost-effective, and to address country-specific priorities. Each national network is assisted in preparing and implementing a national action plan addressing globalization and WTO issues deemed crucial by the business community. ITC then provides support in the form of information and training to each network.*

Trade finance and financial services

Lack of access to trade finance is cited by businesses and business associations as the main constraint to export development. In the main, this reflects the problems of accessing credit and equity finance experienced by all but the largest enterprises. But there are also major shortcomings in the provision of finance specifically for trade and in financial services for trade such as insurance.

SMEs left out of schemes

Credit lines are often unable to offer enough support to agricultural exporters, particularly SMEs.

Where credit is not available for export-oriented investment, because of the perceived risk in lending to exporters or because medium- to long-term loans are not available, the solution that has been used by governments and international financial institutions is to provide credit lines. These credit lines are often revolved, providing an incentive to minimize default.

Credit lines typically provide windows for working capital and/or medium- to long-term investment. The problems associated with accessing the former is that short-term credit requirements for exporters that need to purchase large volumes of stock can be very high. Exporters of agricultural commodities or agricultural inputs for processing may need to buy the year's stock over a short period. Their working capital requirements shoot up seasonally and their balance sheets are unlikely to be able to support them, particularly in the case of SMEs.

> ### Box 43
> ### Trade financing services: going all the way to the bank
>
> *A key issue for exporters in LDCs is access to finance at reasonable cost. Exporters are frequently unable to fulfil the complex requirements of banks. Because of their limited knowledge of trade financing issues, small businesses are often unable to negotiate adequately with finance institutions.*
>
> *To help simplify and standardize the screening and evaluation of credit requests, ITC has issued a handbook explaining the general process of credit analysis and providing all the elements for developing a credit scoring system adapted to banks in individual countries. While the cost of using this tool is extremely low, its impact on exports by small businesses can be substantial.*
>
> *A practical guide to obtaining export credits, How To Approach Banks, designed specifically for SMEs, has been customized in 28 countries, putting the tool in the hands of at least 5,000 entrepreneurs.*
>
> *ITC has held seminars and courses and developed interactive self-learning tools in cooperation with a network of national organizations. Topics include trade in the euro and export financing.*

Lack of longer-term credit leaves exporters without funds to improve technology and products.

Credit restrictions a constraint in many LDCs

The low availability of medium- to long-term credit is an impediment in many LDCs. The lack of development of term deposits and other instruments for longer-term savings places a supply constraint on the banks. Without access to medium- and long-term borrowing, exporters are likely to be unable to make strategic investments to improve technology and products. Some process industries and the tourism industry find this a major problem.

Why financial institutions should bear the risk

Lending through credit lines to such borrowers requires the use of financial institutions that have intimate knowledge of the borrower and can monitor the deployment of capital effectively. The financial institution should bear the risk: otherwise there is a danger that it may not appraise loans diligently and monitor them closely to lessen the risk of default. Though default rates have been high on some schemes, many other schemes have produced low rates of default and shown good returns in terms of increased exports.

The range of instruments

A paper presented by export finance consultant Andrew Singer at the ITC Business Sector Round Table, from which this section has been drawn, examined the range of financial instruments, their use and their drawbacks:

Irrevocable letters of credit are popular in advanced banking nations because of the attractive interest rates and low risk.

Post-shipment financing of exports can play a major role in speeding through payments for an LDC producer. Hardly any LDC exporters require credit terms of more than a couple of months, which simplifies procedures, and there are well-established financial instruments. For example, an irrevocable letter of credit from an international bank enables the exporter's bank to discount the credit, paying the exporter immediately (less a modest discount to cover the interest due for the period of the advance), knowing that the international bank will make the payment. This business is popular in advanced banking nations because it offers attractive interest rates and low risk.

Credit insurance against payment default by the customer has proved to be a powerful tool for trade promotion. Many countries operate best practice systems: the Czech Republic, Sri Lanka and Tunisia, for example. Until recently, credit insurance has been less important for LDCs. But the World Bank, which had earlier reservations about such schemes, has now introduced a regional system for southern Africa.

Preshipment financing poses a difficult challenge in LDCs, since this depends on the exporter meeting the conditions: goods have to be up to standard, delivered on time and in the quantities ordered (without breakage or pilferage). If authorities hold the goods up at the embarkation or delivery port, the transaction may not go through.

Even experienced bankers in a highly competitive financial sector – a rare situation in LDCs – would evaluate a risk very carefully in these circumstances before extending credit. Finding competence at the bank level for evaluating the credit risks of export-related transactions is a major problem, as several case studies of successful entrepreneurs make clear. A number of these business leaders have urged public-sector institutions to take a more active role in introducing this competency into the financial system.

Finding competence at the bank level for evaluating the credit risks of export-related transactions is a major problem.

Export credit guarantees, for example, have been successful in Lesotho, Swaziland and Zambia. However, the pooling of non-performance risks between banks, though believed to work quite well in some countries, has been criticized for its potential to lead to corruption through politically motivated loans to borrowers who are unlikely ever to repay the loans.

Back-up credit for banks, often housed in the central bank as a revolving fund, can be used if there is a shortage of funds due either to the lack of savings to fund fast export expansion or to the paucity of foreign currency. Financial experts currently do not favour special designation of funds within the banking system, preferring competition for the available funds to meet different purposes because this is more likely to promote efficient allocation of scarce resources.

Central banks in LDCs, by issuing high-interest Treasury bills, are drawing funds from the banking sector.

However, there are additional difficulties that make this viewpoint debatable. The cost of credit is a major problem in LDCs. Central banks in LDCs, by issuing high-interest Treasury bills, are drawing funds from the banking sector, and thus deterring commercial banks from riskier lending to local enterprises.

Are there *better forms of collateral* available? The simplest solution that does not involve credit is *leasing*. For this to work, however, the leasing company would need to be confident, as a result of regulations and enforcement arrangements, that it could remove its machines from the exporter's factory, if need be.

Another source may be *counter-guarantees* from the exporter's customer or a *long-term credit* organized by the client. These are rare, but sometimes bilateral donors set up lines of credit tied to exports of machinery from the donor country, and a number of success stories achieved their breakthroughs because of supportive customers.

Matching grants and challenge funds

Matching grant schemes are now firmly established on the export scene. They have been widely used by the European Union under the Lomé Convention with developing countries. One reason for its popularity with exporters is that the entrepreneur stays in control of the transaction, receiving usually half of any costs of buying services to improve competitiveness on the basis of a plan which the exporters themselves submit.

Challenge funds are a newer form of grant finance. The British Government has a Business Linkage Challenge Fund for firms in southern Africa, as yet the only scheme known for LDCs. Under this system firms compete with others for the money available. The approach tends to be more flexible than matching grant schemes, which usually have tightly set criteria.

Country risk guarantees

Credit guarantee agencies are used mainly in connection with large capital projects. LDCs, with a few exceptions, are not major participants in this market.

Most developed and major exporting developing countries have established credit guarantee agencies or export-import banks which provide guarantees against default on foreign debt on the part of importers. These guarantees are useful in the provision of project finance, channelled through banking intermediaries, which enables the buyer to finance the import. This facility is used mainly for large capital projects.

LDC experiences

LDCs, with a few exceptions, are not major participants in the market for large construction or capital equipment projects. For them, the more useful form of guarantee is against default on letters of credit (L/Cs) and to provide cover against non-payment of debt when no L/Cs are involved.

Default on L/Cs, irrevocable or otherwise, is not as uncommon as it should be. Many LDC exporters face difficulties because their customers, usually from other developing countries, fail to honour L/Cs, often attempting to make claims that the terms of the L/C were violated. This adds to the risk of exporting and can cause serious financial problems for exporters.

In some product sectors the customer's purchasing power has resulted in the exporter giving the importer substantial credit.

There are product sectors (such as the artisanal product sector) where the customer's purchasing power has resulted in trade being conducted without L/Cs. Here the exporter often gives the importer substantial credit (90 days and over). The track record of developed country importers operating on these terms is not unblemished. There can be genuine disputes over the quality and timeliness of supply, the specification of products, packaging and so on. Or, these reasons can be cited simply to delay payment.

For LDC exporters, the failure of their customers to honour L/Cs or to make the required payment without L/Cs can have serious consequences. Many LDCs operate retention schemes which oblige exporters to deposit foreign exchange shortly after the transaction is due to be completed. Officials insist on the deposit of foreign currency irrespective of whether the exporter has been paid.

Thus, exporters with bad debts are likely not only to make a loss on the transaction, but are obliged to find the foreign exchange required to deposit with the central bank. Most developed countries and many exporting developing countries have therefor introduced small guarantee schemes. Many LDCs, however, do not have such schemes.

The discounting of L/Cs, noted above as attractive to many financial institutions in developed countries, is an important source of working capital for exporters in LDCs. However, the charges for such discounting can become prohibitive unless there is sufficient competition for this service.

The high cost of financial services for exporters, especially insurance, can also be a significant factor in total transaction costs. Amjadi and Yeats (1996) reported that sub-Saharan Africa's net freight and insurance payments in 1991 were about 15% of the total value of the region's exports – nearly three times the corresponding indicator of export transaction costs for all developing countries.[18] For specific countries the divergence was even more marked, with net freight and insurance payments for the 10 landlocked countries in the region at 42% of the total value of exports. With the deregulation of financial sectors in reforming economies, one would anticipate a decline in the cost of financial services.

Trade facilitation

There has been progress in many developing countries in matching efforts at liberalizing traded and non-traded sectors with the streamlining of administrative procedures. Many of these countries have had highly regulated regimes, which created opportunities for bureaucratic inefficiencies, corruption and rent-seeking activity. Changing the ethos and restoring the integrity of domestic institutions and administrative systems is often a slow process, and it would appear that there is a need for further effort to reduce delays, for example, in customs and licensing procedures. It is difficult to assess quantitatively the impact of such 'environmental' factors on the costs of doing business, but these factors are invariably perceived by business persons and investors as important.

Bureaucracy in customs

An ITC survey of businesses in East Africa found bureaucracy and related services to be important constraints. The reason is clearly seen when analysing customs clearing times. The *Africa Competitiveness Report* published by the World Economic Forum shows that these range from five weeks in Ethiopia to two weeks in Madagascar. Customs procedures in terms of documentation requirements, inspection by national standards officers and poor data management systems are the main problems.

Customs clearing times can be as much as five weeks, and preshipment inspection can delay exports even longer.

Preshipment inspection

Many LDCs now operate preshipment inspection schemes. Importers have to pay for the cost of inspection by private firms and the charges can add 2%-5% to the price. Countries that operate the system do not provide lower customs clearing times to compensate, which in the case of one African LDC that is seeking to reform its administration average is just under four weeks.

Customs: essential instruments of national policy

As observed by the World Customs Organization in its 1997 *Survey of Customs Reform and Modernization Trends and Best Practices,* governments expect customs, as essential instruments of national policy, to maintain the right balance between control and facilitation by reforming and modernizing their management and operational methods. The Kyoto International Convention on the Simplification and Harmonization of Customs Procedures, as amended in 1999, sets out recommendations on how the balance can be struck. The detailed recommendations should provide guidelines for governments.

The recommendations include standard and simplified procedures that should be well publicized, a partnership between trade and customs authorities, coordinated interventions with other agencies, and the use of pre-arrival information and risk management techniques. The convention also recommends the use of systems such as the Automated System for Customs Data (ASYCUDA), developed by UNCTAD.

---

18   A. Amjadi and A.J. Yeats, 'Have transport costs contributed to the relative decline of African exports?', working paper (Washington, World Bank, 1996).

Box 44

Automated System for Customs Data (ASYCUDA)

ASYCUDA (UNCTAD's Automated System for Customs Data) is a computerized customs management system which covers most foreign trade procedures. The system handles manifests and customs declarations, accounting procedures, and warehousing manifest and suspense procedures. It generates detailed information about foreign trade transactions which can be used for economic analysis and planning.

With 32 active projects and expenditures exceeding US$ 6 million, ASYCUDA is the single largest technical cooperation programme in UNCTAD. More than 70 countries worldwide have adopted the ASYCUDA programme, and 60 are utilizing it on a regular basis. Among LDCs, Chad, Nepal, Samoa and Vanuatu have adopted ASYCUDA.

The cost of nomenclature problems

The lack of a separate identification for craft items in statistical nomenclatures, for example, has been a major drawback in recognizing the contribution of artisanal products to international trade and in developing such exports. ITC and UNESCO organized a symposium on customs codification for crafts in the international market in 1997. On the basis of its recommendations, adopted by 44 countries, ITC submitted a proposal to the World Customs Organization that was accepted as a starting point for future work to provide statistical visibility for crafts.

Business law

At the close of the twentieth century, 15 mostly West African States adopted a common set of business laws and regulations to facilitate intraregional trade. This provides some indication of the importance which policy-makers now

---

Box 45

Juris International: information on the law of trade

Juris International is a legal service providing information and training on international trade law in English, French and Spanish. It offers databases, diagnostic tools and training materials. Designed for business lawyers and small and medium-sized enterprises, it also serves governments and State institutions. The information is provided free of charge through ITC's databases and CD-ROMs.

The aim is to help companies and business lawyers in developing countries to find appropriate legal information in full text format and in their own working languages for drawing up international contracts and resolving international trade disputes. Model contracts can be used as a generic tool by companies and adapted to specific products.

For institutions developing new arbitration or mediation programmes, early training is given in dispute resolution. Juris International also offers training in contract negotiation and drafting, the legal impact of multilateral instruments (including the WTO Agreements) on private business, and how governments should adapt their international legal frameworks for international trade.

attach to the legal framework within which exporters have to operate. As ITC's experience with buyers-sellers meetings shows, enterprises in LDCs often have difficulty obtaining up-to-date information about regulations in other countries, even in the same region, and harmonization of standards is rare. The Organisation for the Harmonisation of the Business Law in Africa (OHADA), adopting a common set of regulations, asked ITC to help place these laws in the hands of legal advisers by publishing the full OHADA texts and regulations in several languages on CD-ROMs and on the Internet – putting information about these new standards in the hands of a group wider than the regional core community.

SQAM systems

The need for accreditation

Since the international trade agreements overseen by WTO went into force and in view of the globalization of commerce, accreditation has become an important part of quality assurance. Accreditation underpins the mutual recognition agreements entered into by countries and certification bodies to facilitate trade. As accreditation must now be built into the quality infrastructure, there has been a shift from an emphasis on MSTQ (metrology or measurement traceability, standards, testing and quality assurance) to SQAM (standards, quality assurance, *accreditation* and metrology).

Accreditation of conformity assessment procedures is needed to ensure a level playing field among competitors.

Formerly, the national standards bodies in developing countries, where they existed, provided services in all areas of MSTQ and had no competitors. The emphasis was on import control and consumer protection. Now conformity assessment activities (testing, calibration, certification and inspection) have been liberalized. These need to be accredited to ensure a level playing field among competitors.

Countries need an adequate quality infrastructure

In addition, to benefit from the WTO Agreements on Technical Barriers to Trade (TBT) and on the Application of Sanitary and Phytosanitary Measures (SPS), countries must have an adequate SQAM infrastructure so that they can:

- Take an active part in preparing international standards;

- Provide information to importers and exporters on technical regulations, standards and conformity assessment procedures;

- Have accredited conformity assessment bodies; and

- Enter into mutual recognition agreements with trading partners.

In this new situation, the government's role in SQAM is in the following

- Standardization: the establishment of national standards, membership of international standards bodies and participation in international standardization work;

- Metrology: maintenance of national physical standards which are traceable to international standards;

- Legal metrology: consumer protection to ensure that weights and measures used in trade are accurate;

- Accreditation: ensuring that conformity assessment bodies are competent, impartial and work with integrity; and

- Information on standards, technical regulations and conformity assessment procedures: setting up national enquiry points under the TBT and SPS Agreements to provide information to exporters *from* the country and exporters *to* the country.

Few enquiry services

In general LDCs are not members of the standards-setting organizations.

However, of the 30 LDCs that are Members of WTO, fewer than half have TBT and SPS enquiry points. Though 16 LDCs are members of the International Organization for Standardization (ISO), only two are full members and can vote on ISO standards.

The situation is better with regard to the standards-setting organizations mentioned in the WTO SPS Agreement. Some 39 LDCs are members of the Codex Alimentarius Commission (which deals with food products), for example, but no LDC is a member of the international bodies concerned with measurement traceability and accreditation.

In general, LDCs are not members of these international organizations because they do not have the national infrastructure to enable them to participate effectively. Some simply do not have the financial and/or human resources for membership.

Major problems for LDCs

The private sector in many developing countries is being given an increasing role in conformity assessment.

As a result, LDCs face major problems in:

- Playing an effective part in the international standardization process;

- Meeting international standards and technical regulations in export markets;

- Having an adequate national conformity assessment and accreditation infrastructure, because of limited physical and technical resources; and

- Concluding mutual recognition agreements for conformity assessment procedures.

Models in other developing countries

Despite this, LDCs can look to other developing countries for models of successful SQAM infrastructures. The private sector is being called on to play an increasing role in conformity assessment. For example, Mauritius has a national standards body which provides MSTQ services and has been accredited for ISO 9000 certification. Private bodies compete with the national standards body in providing testing and certification services. The national accreditation body was at the pre-operational stage at the start of 2001. Malaysia provides the secretariat for the ISO Technical Committee on rubber and rubber products. A separate Malaysian body offering MSTQ services has been accredited for ISO 9000 and ISO 14000 certification and for quality in three-quarters of its laboratories.

> **Box 46**
>
> **Export quality management**
>
> *Export quality management (EQM) is becoming indispensable for exporters, including those in LDCs. Health and safety regulations, whether for human beings, animals or plants, and environmental protection standards, are constantly changing at the international and national level. It is difficult for export-oriented small businesses in developing and transition economies to keep up with the changes. The results can be lost contracts, rejected shipments and costly repairs.*
>
> *ITC's Export Quality Management Service provides training, information and advice. It has held many seminars on the business implications of the TBT and SPS Agreements since the establishment of WTO in 1995. It handles about 500 inquiries a year. It has implemented major projects of technical cooperation on export quality management issues in several countries.*
>
> *The EQM Service publishes guides and technical notes on key quality-related subjects: standards, technical regulations, conformity assessment and quality management (including the ISO 9000:2000 family of standards). Its inquiry service and publications are free of charge for institutions and firms in developing countries and economies in transition.*
>
> *The EQM Service works closely with standardization and quality-monitoring institutions at the international, regional and national level. As a result, trade support institutions are increasingly adapting their facilities and services to the requirements of the WTO Agreements concerned.*

Promoting foreign direct investment

There are numerous LDC exporters benefiting from foreign alliances and joint ventures.

Weaknesses in the capacity and competitiveness of individual firms often stem from deficiencies in the structure of the industry in which the firms participate. The issues for strategy-makers to examine are the degree of concentration of ownership and output, the involvement of foreign investors, the backward linkages with suppliers and the degree of horizontal linkages between firms.

A proportion of foreign ownership is important for competitiveness. Many LDCs consider foreign direct investment (FDI) a source of jobs and competitiveness, and recognize the role that export-orientated FDI can play in export growth. However, perhaps the largest gains from FDI are to be had through its demonstration effect on the rest of the industry, in marketing strategies and skills, product development and innovation, the organization of production and in introducing best practice in the disciplines of management.

Where FDI is low in LDCs, the reason may well be the overall incentive in the economy. Sectoral strategy can play a role in attracting foreign investment by setting out the opportunities and profiling likely investors. These could prove valuable tools for the FDI promotion agency to use in targeting possible investors. The sector's enterprises can also use their own resources to seek joint ventures and alliances with foreign firms with the expertise and market presence they desire. There are numerous LDC exporters benefiting from alliances and joint ventures.

Procurement and supply management

Linkages with suppliers are recognized sources of competitive advantage and practical examples have been set by Japanese and, increasingly, other multinationals. Linkages are a strength of Italian industry in sectors such as textiles and machine tools; these have allowed it to withstand competition from lower-cost competitors.

The formation of vertical clusters, where mutual interest and self-supporting ties bind suppliers to their customers, is a potentially useful device for increasing competitiveness. Horizontal clusters can share marketing costs, economies in purchasing inputs, and information on market and product trends. There are examples of firms sharing costly or infrequently used equipment.

Trade associations can play an important role in cluster development.

Trade associations can play an important role in cluster development, both vertical and horizontal. It should be noted, however, that the track record of cluster development programmes is not one of universal success. They tend to work best when they are 'natural' in that there is already some collaboration taking place. Further, caution needs to be exercised about the pace at which collaboration develops and the activities it encompasses. Firms are reluctant to share commercial information. Nevertheless, where conditions are favourable, they can be a valuable tool in improving competitiveness.

Within individual companies, business practices can be revised to make SMEs more competitive by reducing procurement costs (or making the firm more attractive to customers by adopting 'green purchasing' methods), by training staff in up-to-date management procedures, and by ensuring that packaging meets the standards of the market. A number of LDC successes placed a major emphasis on ensuring that their products were attractively packaged for their markets, even paying design firms in developed countries to ensure acceptability in a sophisticated consumer market.

Management procurement, costing and marketing practices need not be expensive to obtain results, however. The life-cycle approach to purchasing is often economically justifiable without considering the need to be competitive in the future. Ground-truth costing of production can be a first step towards moving into profitability. Marketing to establish a niche market can mean nothing more than ensuring that products have an ethnic design on the package, as a successful Bhutan exporter of red rice has found (see box 35).

Trade information

One of the essential requirements is up-to-date information. Sometimes trade support institutions can answer questions asked by exporters, but SMEs in LDCs may find themselves having to go further afield. Among export success stories, the importance of information is stressed repeatedly, whether obtained through study trips abroad, connections with people who know the market, regular attendance at trade fairs, or frequent contacts with clients.

An ITC survey in 1997 showed the importance that exporters place on receiving up-to-date information on international markets. In the East African LDCs, the proportion that ranked information as a high priority for trade-related technical assistance was not less than 69% in any country. In Ethiopia and Mozambique the proportion was 100%. As businesses are only too aware of their limited resources (in relation to need), the vast majority ranked strengthening TSIs as a high priority for obtaining such assistance; the proportion in Uganda and Ethiopia was 100%.

> **Box 47**
> **Trade Secrets: The Export Answer Book**
>
> *Though some exporters' information needs are highly specific, many are common either internationally or locally. The difficulty is in finding the information in a handy form. ITC's Trade Secrets series answers common questions on exporting in a question-and-answer format, and provides related references to publications, websites, organizations and services.*
>
> *The first book in the series is entitled Trade Secrets: The Export Answer Book. Partner organizations use ITC's guidelines for national adaptation to tailor the generic version of this book to local needs. During the one-year process usually needed to adapt the publication, partner organizations consult with ITC at every stage. Contents vary widely among countries to reflect the unique aspects of their trade environments, infrastructure, availability of resources, legal system and precedents, distance and location of target markets. The first customized version, for India, released in November 1998, was described in the press as 'a ready-to-use comprehensive reference guide for those in international trade, targeted at first-time and infrequent exporters and consultants [and covering] the whole gamut of export-related issues'. Uganda is among the latest of LDCs to produce a national version.*
>
> *Training has been provided in over 60 countries on how to adapt and publish the answer book. Among the LDCs are Bangladesh, Burkina Faso, Côte d'Ivoire, Guinea, Mauritania, Nepal and the United Republic of Tanzania.*
>
> *ITC has also put together the following question-and-answer books: Secrets of Electronic Commerce: A Guide for Small and Medium-sized Exporters; and International Trade Rules: An Answer Book on the WTO Agreements for Small and Medium-sized Exporters. A book on export quality management is under preparation.*

Benchmarking

Benchmarking is a useful tool for measuring competitiveness, both of industries against their international competitors, and individual firms against the industry average. Taken a step further, it is a valuable tool for transmitting best practice, because firms that are strong in some disciplines are put in contact with and assist weaker firms, benefiting, in turn, from the strengths of others. By undertaking benchmarking at an international level, SMEs learn what it takes to be competitive in a global economy and to access information on how to attain international standards.

Fully fledged systems

Fully fledged benchmarking systems exist in the United States and some European countries. The ITC Competitiveness Gauge for manufacturers of automotive parts is of one the rare examples of a benchmarking system created for companies in developing countries. Like some other systems, it allows firms to compare themselves against the sector average. The basic data requirements, in terms of forms that must be filled in, and their analysis, are not complex.

For many SMEs, improvement starts when they begin to collect information.

As with all benchmarking systems, it is difficult to obtain the commitment of firms to take the trouble to fill in forms on time, diligently and regularly (see box 48). But Gauge reports reveal a number of enterprises whose competitiveness matches or exceeds that of the best performers. For many

SMEs improvement starts when they begin to collect information. Some find themselves seeking out for the first time information on basic aspects such as defect ratios, customer return rates, critical financial ratios and analyses of suppliers and clients.

Box 48

ITC's International Competitiveness Gauge: benchmarking performance

'How competitive is my enterprise on the international scale?' This is probably the first question a small entrepreneur will ask when an export prospect opens. And one the smart business executive will continue to ask. 'It is absolutely vital that the companies know where they are in relation to international competition,' says Clive B. Williams, Executive Director of the National Association of Automotive Component and Allied Manufacturers of South Africa. 'But benchmarking is out of the reach of most small enterprises, largely because of the huge expense and resources needed.'

ITC's International Competitiveness Gauge helps small manufacturers of automotive components in developing countries to establish benchmarks by comparing themselves with national and international enterprises, and to identify best practices, prepare a profile and make an analysis with the assistance of industry associations. The Gauge uses specially developed benchmarking software and its application is accompanied by counselling services. Industry associations in partner countries operate the Gauge, training their staff in benchmarking and adapting the training manual to local needs. So far the Gauge has not been used in any LDC, but benchmarking for the processed fish, leatherware and cut-flower industries has been initiated; these industries are of particular interest to LDCs.

Establishing benchmarks for industries consisting of firms with differing competitive strengths will take time. In general, firms do not like to share information on their competitive strengths with competitors. Nevertheless, benchmarking is a useful tool for diagnosing competitiveness at the level of the individual firm.

Benchmarking tools complement standard TSI support for enterprises. TSIs often make their services available to all types of SME. Benchmarking makes it possible to identify the companies that are most likely to succeed with support services. It also identifies what kind of support services should be targeted at which firms.

E-facilitation

In the new economy of computers, e-communications, the Internet, the Web, e-business and electronic business-to-business facilities, international competitiveness is being redefined at the level not only of the individual firm, but also of the nation. Research conducted for ITC's Executive Forum 2000 on Export Development in the Digital Economy, and the consultations held in conjunction with it, suggest that e-trade capability within the business community has become a de facto determinant of export performance for developing and transition economies. According to an analysis which compared business-to-business e-commerce in 17 industry sectors with traditional business methods, such as the use of paper, telephones and fax machines, the estimated savings were in the range of 2% to 40%.

For many SMEs, improvement starts when they begin to collect information.

Rubens Ricupero, Secretary-General of UNCTAD, declared: 'E-competency is of vital strategic importance. The problem is not so much one of acquiring equipment or technology. It is a problem of a change in mentality, a change in policies. I would say even a cultural change. It is not something that you can import. It involves many different elements in the way not only the private sector but also the public sector does business.'

The Forum discussions among public and private strategy-makers indicated that national strategy-makers should take immediate and targeted action to create an environment conducive to the rapid growth of e-trade capability and to promote the development of e-competency at the level of both the individual firm and the various organizations, public or private, that are involved in supporting the national export effort.

On the basis of the debate in Executive Forum 2000, there was wide consensus among strategy-makers that:

- Direct participation in the digital economy is imperative to maintaining and building on the export performance of the country as a whole, as well as that of the individual enterprise.

- Developing e-competency within the business community and reinforcing this competency through suitable public-sector e-support programmes and public-private-sector partnerships are essential to success.

Who should lead this public-private-sector partnership, or at least be responsible for its initiation and coordination? The consensus at Executive Forum 2000 was that circumstances in the majority of developing and transition economies demand public-sector leadership. Many of the challenges of the digital economy require strategic decisions taken at the national level. Only government can provide the enabling environment for the development of e-competency and e-trade capability. Only government can tackle the various issues as a national priority. Daniel Mpolokoso, Managing Director, ZAMNET Communications Systems, Lusaka, Zambia, for example, argued: 'Government is the key. Only government can do anything about incentives, facilitating venture capital, reducing tariffs and regulations, and creating an environment conducive to this business.'

The Forum participants identified three issues for strategy-makers to tackle in the short term to increase e-competency within their economies:

- Awareness-building and needs appreciation: businesses are not all at the same level of e-competency, and therefore have different needs;

- Developing e-trade capability at the level of the individual firm – involving the provision of financial and skills development support;

- A targeted approach: availability of training and mentoring programmes and access to concessionary finance should be key elements of a strategic response to export development in the digital economy.

Assistance in firm-level export strategies

Export strategies need to address the two critical issues of which markets and market segments to target and how to compete in international markets to secure strong and sustainable positions.

In LDCs, many firms require assistance in preparing such strategies. The greatest area of need is likely to be market research on international markets. Product-specific strategies should provide some of the information needed but firms will also require in-depth research into the markets and market segments served by their products and services.

What market research should do

Support agencies may need to draw up an agenda of actions required to compete successfully in target markets.

Taking account of the firm's own core competence, market research should provide answers to the question of which markets and market segments to target. In turn, this should provide an agenda of actions required to compete successfully in target markets. These could range from marketing, organizing sales and distribution channels, adapting products, product diversification and innovation, measures to improve efficiency, training and improving the quality and packaging of the product. In addition, there may be a need to introduce quality assurance and certification programmes.

Box 49

Business training

Training and capacity-building are described by successful exporters as major needs of firms in LDCs. Several achievements in the exporting business have been built on the attention entrepreneurs gave from the beginning to this aspect of running a business. They saw the shortage of skilled personnel as a major challenge for a fledgling firm to overcome. ITC has developed tools to close the demand and supply training gap in developing countries. These include:

❑ *Business Management System (BMS): a comprehensive business management series of training modules.*

❑ *PLANSME: software for strategic management planning, based on BMS.*

❑ *NEEDSME: diagnostic decision support software for needs assessment, aimed at diagnosing areas of weakness in the overall management of an enterprise.*

❑ *DEMANDME: software for questionnaire design, an important tool for trade support institutions.*

❑ *Two handbooks for consultants and researchers on needs and capacity assessment.*

❑ *A training the trainer and counsellors programme for training institutions, and*

❑ *A training the master trainers progamme to build national capabilities for training.*

What help may be needed

Firms are also likely to require assistance in implementing the export strategy. Some activities, particularly marketing and training, can be carried out with other firms at the sectoral level. Thus missions abroad, inward missions of buyers and participation in international fairs can be organized at the sectoral level. Others, such as product adaptation, increasing efficiency and improving quality can be effected only within the firm.

Assistance in developing and implementing export strategies could be provided through business support organizations. The method of delivering assistance would preferably be through a matching grant scheme using specialist private-sector suppliers.

Public-private partnerships

The private sector as well as the public sector must be committed to an export strategy.

The establishment of an enabling environment, and the development of export strategies in particular, must be a joint undertaking of the public and private sector. The private sector is the principal agent for export development. It must be committed to the course of action proposed, sharing in the vision elaborated. The role of the public sector is to enable export development, through effective policies and programmes addressing needs for trade-related business services. The two must work hand in hand.

JITAP (see box 39) has elaborated a methodology for developing export strategies in the countries covered which gives concrete form to such partnerships. The strategies are being formulated by joint teams drawn from the public and private sectors, the latter represented by trade associations and experts from within the sector. In this way, the two sectors can inform each other of their objectives and needs, and consensus can be built on the vision and way forward.

International matchmaking and business partnering

The hurdles for LDC companies are often just too high to secure access to industrial markets.

It is not enough for a government to create an enabling environment for business nationally. Countries such as Uganda or Ghana have continuously met the structural adjustment criteria set by the World Bank and IMF for more than a decade but both are still struggling to establish themselves as attractive to world markets and entrepreneurs for more than primary commodities. The hurdles are often just too high for indigenous private companies in LDCs to compete with large, modern and financially strong companies from the developed countries or to secure access to markets of the North.

Reasons for disappointment with enabling policies

In the past, too, it was often thought that if donor countries concentrated on securing enabling environments internationally as well as nationally, the private sector would seize the opportunities made available. The persistent low performance of LDCs in attracting substantial and sustainable foreign direct investment shows that this assumption was optimistic. This is due not only to the difficulty of actually improving the enabling environment but also to the fact that the provision of enabling environments is considered not enough in LDCs, the markets being too small or the return on investment being too low.

The case for FDI

FDI provides new capital, employment, economic growth and export revenues.

The case for direct promotion of private-sector investments in LDCs is clear. FDI contributes to the strengthening of the private sector in LDCs and helps expand the small economic base in these countries. Moreover, it provides new capital, employment, economic growth and export revenues. Developing countries gain access to new technology, know-how and management skills for further development. Contacts between companies in the North and South create an expanding network, enhancing the entrance of LDCs in the global economic arena.

Encouraging the North to link with the South

In recent decades, governments in industrialized countries have developed a number of direct instruments to help their national companies become active in the developing world. These include feasibility studies, support for pilot projects, financial assistance and credit insurance. However, until a few years ago few provided the means for a structural linkage between firms in the developed world and developing countries.

Addressing shortcomings

These shortcomings have been addressed by matchmaking and similar business-partnering programmes run by various aid and development organizations. These help to create linkages by bringing together potential business partners from industrial and least-developed economies. The sponsoring organization generally also provides technical or financial assistance to the private-sector partners in order to foster their mutual cooperation and help them develop a profitable relationship.

What kind of matchmaking?

Many of the linkage programmes directly stimulate European companies to invest in developing countries, including some LDCs such as Bangladesh, Mozambique, Uganda and the United Republic of Tanzania. The investment is usually some form of business cooperation or joint venture with a developing country partner. This support and the linkage with a company in Europe allows the indigenous company in an LDC to acquaint itself with the international market, understand the complexities of international competitiveness and adjust its production process. It may even lead to a complete restructuring of the company.

SMEs are attractive partners for matchmaking because they have the potential to make a substantial impact on development.

Most of the matchmaking and partnering programmes are aimed at SMEs in both industrialized and developing countries. Multinational enterprises do not need public-sector support for their investment projects. Investments in SMEs frequently lead to higher employment, successful expansion of production and spin-offs than do investments in micro-enterprises which often cannot meet the challenges of the market and have a very limited capacity to hire workers and pay them a decent salary. SMEs are also able to attract additional capital much more easily than micro-enterprises.

The basics of matchmaking programmes

Current matchmaking programmes have their own specific characteristics. A few steps are common to most:

- *Identification of target countries.* This depends on the donor countries' foreign and aid policies, as well as the economic policies and institutional preparedness of the possible recipient.

- *Establishment of country-specific parameters.* These define the sectors or industries that are eligible for support, the interaction with the local government, operating procedures and, in some cases, the local operating and implementing agent.

- *Call for project proposals.* SMEs in the donor country are invited to make proposals for investment on the basis of given parameters. An announcement is also made in the recipient country, generally through the local embassy of the donor country. The call for proposals specifies such aspects as maximum assistance budget, partner contribution requirements, and the minimum scope of activities.

Usually matchmaking takes place with the help of the local embassy or implementing agency in the LDC.

- *Matchmaking.* This is brought about in various ways, for example:

  - A donor country enterprise identifies a potential partner in a developing country on its own.

  - An enterprise in the recipient country with a concrete idea actively seeks a partner in the donor country.

  More often than not, the sponsoring institution arranges for matchmaking with the help of the local embassy or implementing agent in the LDC and its own contacts with the business community in the donor country.

- *Project submission, evaluation and selection.* The various projects are submitted to the sponsoring agency and then evaluated by country and sectoral experts. A contract is signed with partners, stipulating the various responsibilities and setting time frames for implementation.

- *Project implementation and performance reviews.* The sponsoring agency supervises the implementation of the project and periodically reviews its performance.

Matchmaking: some examples

Some of the matchmaking programmes sponsored by European countries are listed below:

- Cooperation Programme with Emerging Markets (PSOM), run by Senter International, an autonomous agency of the Netherlands Ministry of Economic Affairs (see box 50).

- Public-Private Partnership (PPP) projects run by the German Agency for Technical Cooperation (GTZ);

- Matchmaking Programme of the Norwegian Agency for Development Cooperation (NORAD);

Though relatively new, all matchmaking programmes are developing fast.

- Private Sector Development Programme of the Danish International Development Agency (DANIDA).

These programmes are relatively new. PSOM started in 1997 in China, Egypt, India and South Africa and initiated activities in LDCs in 1999. PPP began in 1999, though it has expanded rapidly, having matched more than 100 projects to date. The NORAD Matchmaking Programme, which started in 1995, has focused on only two countries so far, Sri Lanka and South Africa, though NORAD is considering expanding to others soon. The DANIDA programme has existed since 1995 and currently supports cooperation between Danish companies and companies in 11 countries, including Bangladesh, Mozambique, Nepal, Uganda and the United Republic of Tanzania.

Netherlands: PSOM (Cooperation Programme with Emerging Markets)

Under PSOM, an eligible project:

- Offers a real prospect for investment or a sustainable trade relation with a company in a PSOM country.

- Provides for installation of equipment (hardware), transfer of knowledge from the Netherlands company to the local company, technical assistance, training, market research, demonstration of project results and institutional reinforcement.

- Has a positive impact on local employment in the selected sector.

- Has a genuine, visible spin-off for Netherlands firms.

- Is tailored to local circumstances and local skills levels, and uses proven technology.

- Should not be disadvantageous to the poor and to women or have a negative impact on the environment.

Box 50

Netherlands: a PSOM project in Mozambique

This PSOM project aims to produce coconut substrate from the outer shell of the coconut for use in the horticultural sector in southern Africa and Europe. It will help start production of this substrate and support the logistic chain for export and marketing.

The Mozambican partner has 10 copra factories in operation. Coconut fibre is currently a waste product from the copra process. This fibre can be ground to a growing substrate for plants, for which there is a demand. The project is sited near one of the copra factories in Quelimane.

A joint venture has been established by three project partners – Comos BV and Braaks Ltd from the Netherlands and Grupo Madal SARL in Mozambique.

The production capacity of the factory is four tons of substrate per day. The new company will create 80 to 90 jobs to handle coconut fibre processing, substrate packaging, marketing and transport, and employee training.

The first phase of the project has been scheduled to run from August 2001 to August 2002 and will receive financial support in the amount of EUR 626,000 (US$ 500,000).

– Based on information provided by André Dellevoet, PSOM project officer.

PSOM contributes two-thirds of the total project budget, up to a maximum of 5 million Netherlands guilders. However, the average size of projects is expected to be around 1 million to 1.5 million guilders. The participants provide for the balance of the project budget. The hardware to be exported should have a Netherlands content of at least 60% in terms of production and components and comply with the country's environmental and safety standards.

Norway's NORAD – a focused approach

Norwegian companies which want to have a developing country partner submit a profile to the coordinating centre in Norway, which reviews it and sends it to a corresponding centre in the host country. When a match is found, NORAD can back the Norwegian company with up to 20,000 Norwegian kroner (just over US$ 2,000) to help finance the first exploratory trip to the country concerned. If the parties agree to develop their relationship further, they can apply to NORAD for support. Developing country companies can also initiate the process.

As regards Sri Lanka, the matchmaking programme has received 120 profiles from Norwegian companies since 1995. Of these, 104 matches have been found, 78 companies have visited Sri Lanka and 22 have carried out preliminary studies. In all, 16 companies have signed cooperative agreements and 12 joint ventures have been formed. In addition, 96 companies from Sri Lanka have contacted the programme. Collaboration under the programme covers diverse activities from boat building to furniture and mattress production, fishing, data processing and environmental inspection.

Germany's GTZ – helping companies to expand abroad

The Public-Private Partnership (PPP) projects are aimed at *Mittelstand* companies[19] which would not, on their own, have the resources to find appropriate partners abroad. PPP steps in with support when the projects are considered to be worthwhile from a development perspective and when the financial assistance is likely to ensure the sustainability of the ventures.

PPP projects are planned, financed and implemented jointly. There are no pre-qualifications by country or sector. The companies submit their proposals direct to GTZ and go through a six-step feedback and approval process.

More than 100 PPP projects have been implemented in many countries, including Bangladesh, the Congo, Ethiopia, Mali, Senegal, Uganda and the United Republic of Tanzania. One example is cooperation with the Association of German Flower Traders. Increasingly German consumers want assurances that production follows international environmental and social norms. Flower farms are certified and receive the 'Flower-Label'. LDC producers who join the Flower-Label partnership commit themselves to respecting ecological standards, eliminating child labour, protecting mothers and implementing minimum wages. Producers in five African countries and 36 German importers have joined the programme.

Box 51

Germany: PPP – principal criteria for support

There are four principal criteria to qualify for PPP support:

❑ *The venture has to have a clear impact on development, fit the overall policies of the German Government, and have a positive environmental and social impact.*

❑ *The project should be an activity which the German enterprise would have had to undertake anyway.*

❑ *The enterprises make a significant financial commitment to the project, in the order of 50% of costs.*

❑ *Public and private contributions must ensure rapid and efficient project implementation.*

Denmark's concept of business linkages

The DANIDA approach is similar to that of GTZ, under which Danish companies are invited to submit proposals for cooperation with a partner in one of 11 target countries. These include Bangladesh, Mozambique, Nepal, Uganda and the United Republic of Tanzania. The LDC company can also submit a proposal and ask for help in finding a suitable Danish partner.

---

19 Mid-size highly specialized companies, generally producing intermediate goods, considered the real engine of the German economy.

The PSD programme provides a combination of advisory services, grants and loans to the partners. It has two phases:

- *Preparatory phase.* DANIDA offers advisory services to assist in the identification of partners, a full grant to cover the costs of the first visit and subsidies of up to 90% of the costs of studies and surveys.

- *Project phase.* DANIDA provides a grant of up to 90% for the costs of set-up, training, technical assistance, export promotion and environmental provisions. It also offers limited loans to pay for imported production equipment if finance cannot be obtained from other sources.

Box 52

Danish-Bangladeshi business-to-business cooperation

Babylon Garments Ltd in Dhaka and Men's Fashion A/S in Kolding, Denmark began cooperating in 1995. Five years later they established a joint venture, Aboni Textiles, and received a grant from the PSD programme in the amount of Danish kroner 4.4 million (US$ 550,000). The objective of the joint venture was to establish a T-shirt factory and to produce and dye cotton fabric.

The total investment for this project is DKr 56 million (US$ 7 million), which will be financed by Denmark's Industrialization Fund for Developing Countries (25%), Men's Fashion (25%) and Babylon Garments (50%).

The new factory of Aboni Textiles has now been built. Machinery from Denmark arrived in early 2001. Production of dyed cotton fabric for the domestic market began in April 2001 and the manufacture of T-shirts for export was expected to begin in September 2001.

    – Based on information provided by Helle Johansen, PSD officer, Danish Ministry of Foreign Affairs

---

United States

The US Chamber of Commerce has begun a matchmaking operation with the support of the United States Agency for International Development. Initially oriented towards South-East Asia, the Chamber is considering expanding its activities to other regions. Its Strategic International Assistance and Matchmaking (SIAM) programme, as an example, is oriented exclusively to Thai-American partnerships. Its objective is to provide assistance in finding potential trade and investment partners for long-term relationships and laying out the institutional and financial framework so that the programme can be sustained independently.

The issue of capital supply

One of the issues on which the programmes differ is the need for inclusion of a capital component. Most of the bilateral programmes such as DANIDA's PSD Programme or the German PPPs concentrate on the 'software', i.e. technical assistance and training, market and feasibility studies or project management. These elements are wholly or partially financed on a grant basis.

Some schemes provide capital for machinery or a loan. Others concentrate on the 'software'.

The Netherlands PSOM provides a capital component for machinery, buildings and materials on a grant basis (up to two-thirds of the cost).The other programmes leave this to financial sector institutions. DANIDA has also realized that an investment project may need a capital component and can provide loans within the framework of the PSD Programme, but the interest charged is close to market rates.

The experience of PSOM shows that the combination of a capital and technical component within the same programme through a partial grant appeals to many companies. Even in an LDC like Mozambique the threshold has proved low enough for companies to embark on an investment with local partners on a pilot basis.

Matchmaking can overcome the problems of collateral for SMEs in developing countries.

Private companies willing to invest in developing countries where the market is considered highly volatile are looking for maximum support for the total investment. For small and medium-sized companies that need only modest investment capital (between US$ 500,000 and US$ 2 million, there are few alternatives. Financial institutions such as the International Finance Corporation or the European Investment Bank work at higher thresholds, i.e. normally a minimum of US$ 5 million. They also usually charge market rates and sometimes require payment of administrative fees in addition.

Few SMEs can offer the collateral that these financial institutions demand. The result is that their portfolio is hardly accessible to SMEs that wish to initiate a risky investment in an LDC. Private-sector development schemes such as matchmaking fill that gap.

Looking ahead

This book has showcased several successful LDC exporters, truly a new generation of modern business leaders, exploiting opportunities through innovation, hard work, progressive management and an understanding of a fast-changing and increasingly demanding international business environment. It has described in some detail export opportunities open to LDCs and how attention to the national enabling environment can help many more LDC exporters succeed, eventually making successful exporters more the rule than the exception in these countries. Their important contribution, as exporters, to national poverty reduction has also been highlighted.

ITC and the Government of Norway hope that this book will broaden the dialogue among stakeholders on how to convert LDC export opportunities into business. The dialogue, initiated at Business Sector Round Table, will continue through regular updating of the ITC BSRT web page (*www.intracen.org/bsrt*).

As new opportunities arise, exporters will innovate and adapt to new challenges, and new champions will emerge. To succeed broadly in the highly competitive and changing international markets, LDCs and their exporters will need access to state-of-the-art technologies, a national enabling environment underpinned by good trade policies and strategies, top-notch trade support services and physical infrastructure to facilitate production and marketing, as well as partners to help fulfil these needs.

Against this backdrop, it would perhaps be useful in a few years to revisit the issues presented at BSRT, to gauge the evolution of successful LDC exporters and the realization of opportunities identified, to assess progress in development of policies, strategies and other export-enabling factors, and to analyse new opportunities and identify the new paths that should be mapped out for discussion in the continuing dialogue among the stakeholders dedicated to the LDCs' export success. Meanwhile, readers are invited to contribute their thoughts and share in the information available on the BSRT web page.

Appendix I

LDC business success stories

Twenty LDC exporters took part in the ITC Business Sector Round Table held in Brussels on 16 May 2001 to tell their success stories, describe what for them constitutes an enabling environment, and indicate which support services would have helped them when they were starting out. Many others supplied case studies of achievement in LDCs. This appendix summarizes some of these stories.

Bangladesh

Conexpo

Seven times a National Export Trophy winner, Conexpo is Bangladesh's biggest handicraft exporting firm, selling to 25 countries and specializing in basketry. Managing Director and Chief Executive Officer (CEO) Abu Alam Chowdhury, who created Conexpo as sole proprietor in 1976 to produce cane furniture for the domestic market, says the turning point was participation in a Milan trade fair as a nominee of the Export Promotion Bureau (EPB). This exposure to the overseas market changed his views, after several disappointing experiences, on the potential for selling abroad, particularly to Europe.

Conexpo now has 20 steady buyers in Europe. In 1994 it diversified from basketry and gift items to a new hand-stitched product: patchwork quilts. EPB introduced Conexpo to the first buyer of this product, a firm in the United States, which operates a quota-free market for quilts.

A founder member and two-time president of the Bangladesh Handicraft Exports Association, Mr Chowdhury notes that the Association's lobbying persuaded the Bangladesh Government to drop two major obstacles to exporting: the high customs duties on imported raw materials and advance income tax on export earnings. A duty drawback scheme has been operating for handicrafts since 1995 and income-tax exemption since 1998.

The firm has 11,000 designs and adds at least 50-60 designs each year. For Mr Chowdhury, who produces many designs himself using traditional motifs, the lack of a national design centre is a serious barrier to competitiveness.

> Conexpo
> 36 DIT Extension Road
> Naya Paltan (2nd floor)
> Dhaka-1000, Bangladesh
> Tel: +880 (2) 8316606
> Mobile tel: +880 (11) 857162
> Fax: +880 (2) 8312826
> Email: conexpo@bdcom.com
> Contact person: Mr Abu Alam Chowdhury, Managing Director and
>   Chief Executive Officer

Fortuna Apparels Ltd

See box 16, chapter 3.

> Fortuna Apparels Ltd
> Fortuna Bhaban, Kunia
> K. B. Bazar
> Gazipur, Bangladesh
> Tel: +880 (2) 9801702-4
> Mobile tel: +880 (17) 532325
> Fax: +880 (2) 9803134
> Email: fortuna@vasdigital.com; fortunag@bol-online.com;
>   rlil@bol-online.com
> Contact person: Engineer M. Abu Taher, Managing Director

SAR & Co. Ltd

Under its Chairman and Managing Director Musa Meah, SAR took the risky step in the second half of the 1990s of making a large investment in modern machinery and equipment to process ready-packed shrimp products instead of simply dealing in block-frozen shrimp. Within four years, the once-sick firm became a National Export Trophy winner. Its capacity utilization is 80%, compared with 30% on average for other firms exporting only block-frozen products. The company's Dolphin brand has become popular in export markets, and annual exports amount to US$ 19 million FOB.

SAR notes that government support, including tax breaks for exporters and a soft loan for factory renovation and for installing refrigeration facilities meeting international standards, was essential at key moments in its growth. SAR also pays tribute to the Export Promotion Bureau and the Bangladesh Frozen Food Exporters' Association for their support, and notes that many of the government policies in place today are the result of lobbying by the Association.

> SAR & Co. Ltd
> Dilkusha Centre (6th Floor), Suite No. 601 & 602
> 28, Dilkusha C/A
> Dhaka-1000, Bangladesh
> Tel: +880 (2)9567479
> Fax: +880 (2) 9564065
> Email: kcgrp@bdonline.com
> Contact person: Mr Musa Meah, Chairman & Managing Director

Benin

Fusion et galvanisation béninoise (FGB)

Established in 1985, FGB produces publicity articles such as key-chains, badges and bottle openers in the capital Porto-Novo. The only known enterprise of its kind in West Africa, its export business is worth over CFAF 100 million a year. Working first regionally, and gaining a word-of-mouth reputation, FGB works with an Italian partner, which helps train its 50 staff. It gained an International Gold Star for Quality from an exhibition in Geneva, Switzerland in 2000. The shortage of qualified personnel for maintaining its machines, forcing the company to bring in European specialists, has made operations difficult at times, but the major constraint has been the import tax on its raw materials.

> Fusion et galvanisation béninoise (FGB)
> BP 638, Porto-Novo, Benin
> Tel: +229 (2) 24181
> Fax: +229 (2) 24232
> Contact person: Mr Mamah Moobi

SEPT SA

See box 13, chapter 2.

> SEPT SA
> 03 BP 2816, Cotonou, Benin
> Tel: +229 (3) 04940
> Fax: +229 (3) 04493
> Contact person: Mr Loukman Sani Agatha

Bhutan

Chharu Tsongdrel

See box 35, chapter 4.

Choki Handicrafts

When Kunzang D. Thinley established Choki Handicrafts in 1993, Bhutanese handicraft production was largely geared toward textile items. Mr Thinley, an art school graduate, believed there was a market niche for crafts such as decorative items, masks, and other indigenous artisanal products. His hunch was right. In 1997, he was awarded the Best Entrepreneurship Award by the Ministry of Trade & Industry of the Government of Bhutan.

The firm has now grown to 15 full-time artisans in the handicraft section and numerous freelance workers in the arts section. In 1999, it expanded by creating an art and crafts school where students, mostly from poor families, receive free education and free board and lodging. In addition to arts, the five-year course covers mathematics, English and the Bhutanese language. Fourth-year students produce handicrafts that are sold to meet a part of their school expenditures.

Choki's steady growth is credited to advice from the entrepreneur's father, the founder of a major art school, and a comprehensive six-week entrepreneurship course offered by the Entrepreneurship Promotion Centre of the Ministry of Trade & Industry. Financing was secured under the special Entrepreneur Development Programme loan scheme. In addition, Mr Thinley notes help from a productivity management course in Japan, UNDP sponsorship for participation in further training, and the benefits resulting from privatization of the sector.

> Choki Handicrafts
> Thimphu, Bhutan
> Tel: +975 (2) 324 728
> Fax: +975 (2) 323 731
> Email: chokihan@druknet.net.bt
> Contact person: Mr Kunzang D. Thinley

Etho Metho Tours & Treks Ltd

See box 17, chapter 3.

> Etho Metho Tours & Treks Ltd
> Thimphu, Bhutan
> Tel: +975 (2) 323162/323693/326112/326113/326114
> Fax: +975 (2) 322884/323883
> Email: ethometo@druknet.net.bt
> Internet: *www.visitbhutan.com*
> Contact person: Mrs Dago Bida

RSA Private Ltd

Once an exporter of oranges and apples, RSA, set up in 1994, switched to mineral products. Rinchen Dorji, the Managing Director, who graduated with a Bachelor of Commerce degree from Calcutta in 1970, had served the Bhutan Government for over 20 years and was a seasoned management expert. His guiding principle is not to export products that are already covered by others. RSA specializes in identifying new product lines. Mr Dorji made RSA the pioneer exporter of coal and minerals from Bhutan, with markets in Nepal and Bangladesh. Starting with coal for cement production, RSA moved on to gypsum, and then to limestone powder when Nepal began importing cheaper gypsum from India.

> RSA Private Ltd
> Phuentsholing, Bhutan
> Tel: +975 (5) 252120
> Fax: +975 (5) 252248
> Email: mdbpcl@druknet.net.bt
> Contact person: Mr Rinchen Dorji

Burkina Faso

Association pour la promotion des groupements féminins (APGF)

As its name indicates, APGF is a mixture of NGO and private enterprise. It works exclusively with women in rural areas and the poor quarters of Ouagadougou, producing scarves, coverlets and wrap-around skirts during the nine-month dry season. Founded in 1990, APGF today has 125 associates working in 25 production centres. Since 1996 its annual output has been rising about 14% yearly; a third of this output is exported.

APGF's members started with little experience or understanding of international trade. Training has been provided through the Burkina Faso foreign trade office (ONAC – Office national du commerce extérieur) in the techniques of international commerce. Germany's GTZ and the European Union offered on-the-spot training in design.

APGF has taken part in numerous international fairs in West Africa, Europe and Canada, enabling it to build up a network of trading partners. It won a second prize in 1998 at a biennial buyers-sellers fair in Burkina Faso.

APGF has established a feedback system with its customers to ensure that producers know what clients want in terms of colours and textures. The sales department also keeps in contact with buyers to ensure they are satisfied with the quality of the products. However, the shortage of financial resources available to a small producer in an LDC has made it impossible for the Association to respond to large orders or to take part in a number of promising exhibitions.

> Association pour la promotion des groupements féminins (APGF)
> 01 BP 4855, Ouagadougou 01, Burkina Faso
> Tel: +226 (3) 70525
> Fax: +226 (3) 11469
> Email: kabrer@hotmail.com
> Contact person: Ms Rasmata Kabre

Station MAYA/AFRUICA

In 1983 André Roch Mayabouti, just leaving secondary school, decided to establish himself as a farmer on the family plot of 25 hectares. Growing mangoes and cereals and raising rabbits, he quickly realized that to conserve the mango, he needed to process it. He contacted the Burkina Faso energy institute (Institut burkinabé d'énergie) to learn about conservation methods, and a Swiss NGO (Centre écologique Albert Schweitzer, CEAS) to learn about support for peasant farmers. CEAS admitted him into the organization as an individual farmer and sent on examples of dried mangoes to Switzerland for testing and certification. He then received an order for five tons of dried mangoes from a fair trade shop in Geneva in 1989 and decided to concentrate on dried fruit as his main revenue earner.

Today Station MAYA has some 30 staff and exports mangoes, coconut, hibiscus, citronelle (lemon grass) and sesame to the value of CFAF 55 million annually. It works closely with 63 village groups based within 50 km of the farm at Bobo-Dioulasso. MAYA credits its take-off particularly to a loan from CEAS to buy equipment and rolling credit for its start-up. A senior member of the Cercle des sécheurs (dryers' association), MAYA says it has also received important assistance from this association in management and quality assurance.

> Station MAYA/AFRUICA
> 01 BP 2460
> Bobo-Dioulasso 01, Burkina Faso
> Tel: +226 (9) 72640
> Fax: +226 (9) 70802
> Email: afruica@fasonet.bf
> Contact person: Mr André Roch Mayabouti

Société PROMEXPORT

PROMEXPORT, created in 1992 as a company owned wholly by citizens of Burkina Faso, was a national pioneer in the agro-sector, starting at a time when business was just being freed from State control. Today the company is the country's major exporter of fruits and vegetables in the private sector. Its exports reach about US$ 750,000 yearly.

PROMEXPORT credits support from local bankers and foreign importers as a major element in its success, enabling it to gain recognition as a producer of fruits and vegetables. As it specializes in out-of-season produce for a French client, PROMEXPORT's market is limited to four months a year. This narrow window of opportunity required an awareness campaign among local peasants, used to growing round-the-year cereals, to convince them of the importance of giving attention to their export produce. It also meant struggling with the vagaries and high costs of air transport, until the company struck a deal with some local air carriers five years ago. PROMEXPORT currently has 10 staff and 150 seasonal workers. To fill the gap in seasonal activity, it has branched into exporting nuts and seeds. From 120 producers for the predecessor company in 1980, direct suppliers have grown to 500.

> Société PROMEXPORT
> 01 BP 3118
> Ouagadougou 01, Burkina Faso
> Tel: +226 (3) 10078
> Fax: +226 (3) 33362/10078
> Email: promexport@hotmail.com
> Contact person: Mr Cyprien Faho

Burundi

COMEBU

See box 12, chapter 2.

COMEBU
23-24 avenue de France
BP 1801, Bujumbura, Burundi
Tel: +257 (2) 25241
Fax: +257 (2) 23786
Contact person: Mr Stanislas Habonimana

COTRIEX

See box 27, chapter 3.

COTRIEX
BP 2251, Burundi
Tel: +257 (2) 24917/22798
Mobile tel: +257 (9) 10345
Fax: +257 (2) 21852
Contact person: Mr Adrien Sibomana

Chad

Société commerciale du Chari et du Logone (SCCL)

Chad is the world's second largest producer of gum arabic (after the Sudan). SCCL, one of six major Chadian exporters, accounts for 35% of the country's gum arabic sales abroad. Founded in 1983, it has 21 permanent staff and 150-200 seasonal workers.

Between 1995 and 1997 the price at which suppliers could sell gum arabic dropped by more than half, because users had large stocks from previous purchases. Nevertheless, SCCL achieved good results in 1996 and its exports rose between 1996 and 1998 from 1,800 tons to 2,468 tons.

Part of the reason was SCCL's marketing strategy. The international market is largely in the hands of a small number of multinationals. SCCL opted to deal with a single partner – Colloïdes naturels international, based in France, which has taken a 38% stake in the company. Colloïdes gives priority to buying its gum from SCCL. In return, SCCL sells its products only to the French-based firm, which works the gum arabic for re-export to other markets. SCCL has thus been able to concentrate on meeting the standards of its customer: in selecting the gum, treating it, checking the weight of orders and ensuring delivery on time.

SCCL buys its gum arabic from Chadian peasants, often organized into production groups, which generally take responsibility for transport to N'Djamena, the capital. The deals are usually concluded orally, without any written agreement, and are therefore based on mutual trust, built up over the years. The firm has also acted as a school for the Chadian gum sector – most of the directors of companies in the same sector in Chad have worked with SCCL before creating their own businesses.

Société commerciale du Chari et du Logone (SCCL)
BP 1110, N'Djamena, Chad
Tel/Fax: +235 517961
Email: sccl@intnet.td
Internet: *www.tchadrepertoire.com*
Contact person: Mr Abdoulaye Djounouma

CotonTchad

See box 24, chapter 3.

CotonTchad
BP 151, Moundou, Chad
Tel: +235 691210/691062/691026/691193
Fax: +235 691332
Contact person: Mr Tedji Mbainaissem

Ethiopia

Meskel Flowers, Inc.

See box 31, chapter 3.

Meskel Flowers, Inc.
PO Box 2917, Addis Ababa
Ethiopia
Tel/Fax: +251 (1) 614161
Contact person: Mr Eskinder Joseph

Gambia

The Coconut Residence

See box 18, chapter 3.

The Coconut Residence
P.O. Box 3160
Serrekunda, The Gambia
Tel: +220 463377/463399
Fax: +220 461835
Email: coconut@qanet.gm
Contact persons: Messrs. Farid Bensouda-Nettlau and Walter Lohn

Gambia Horticultural Enterprises Ltd (GHE)

GHE, established in 1990 as a sole proprietorship, now has 17 full-time staff, supplying off-season fruits and vegetables to Europe. From a small office in the proprietor's home, the company has grown in 10 years to a large site on the main Banjul/Serrekunda Highway. It has also acquired farmland near the international airport.

The company ascribes its success largely to backing from two of Gambia's leading commercial banks and its consistently impressive cash flow and liquidity situation. Managing Director Momodou A. Ceesay recognized the potential while running a lime-juice business exporting to Europe. But he was also aware of the realities of horticulture exporting: small-scale producers are particularly vulnerable because the large exporters give priority to their own produce over those from out-growers in meeting demand. He set about finding buyers in Europe through personal contact. From US$ 20,000 in the first year of operation, the annual turnover has grown to US$ 150,000. About 60% comes from export of fresh fruits and vegetables: mangoes, chillies, aubergines, limes and Asian vegetables.

To meet the marketing imperative, GHE has a corps of highly trained staff with several years of experience in the production and export marketing of horticultural products. The British partners finance part of the enterprise's production and marketing costs. For nine small-scale fruit and vegetable out-growers, GHE has found outlets abroad and provides seed for free and fertilizer at cost. It has also established itself as by far the largest Gambian dealer and distributor of vegetable seeds, fertilizers, pesticides, farm and garden tools, and equipment.

Gambia Horticultural Enterprises Ltd (GHE)
P O Box 2425
Serrekunda, The Gambia
Tel: +220 394819
Fax: +220 3948 20
Email: gamhort@qanet.gm
Contact person: Mr Momodou A. Ceesay

National Partnership Enterprises Ltd (NPE)

National Partnership Enterprises Ltd (NPE), created in 1977, rose from a small cottage industry to become the Gambia's largest and most consistent supplier of premium-quality seafood to Europe. It has been able to meet EU quality standards despite relying on artisanal as well as commercial fishing.

Managing Director Ousman B. Conateh started with a staff of three to buy artisanal catches from a small shed in Banjul, transporting the seafood by truck to Senegal for re-sale to buyers in Dakar about three times a week. Within a few years, NPE had grown to providing 10 artisanal fishermen with free nets and dug-out canoes with outboard motors to meet demand. Through its Senegalese marketing partners, NPE came into contact with a Brussels-based seafood importer in 1982. The company guaranteed a market outlet for all NPE's seafood that met specifications. As a result, NPE was able to get assistance from the World Bank to install freezers, ice-making machines, cold stores and a processing floor. Between 1985 and 1992 NPE also procured three fishing trawlers, and in 1992 the Danish assistance agency DANIDA helped it expand its freezing and storage facilities.

NPE now has about 300 fishermen supplying seafood. Trained to maintain the plant under an EU trade development project, NPE staff ensure that European HAACP standards are met. NPE's European buyer pre-finances the design and production of packaging materials. But the absence of a fishing port affects the speed at which trawlers can discharge their catch. The establishment of a port is to the financed by the African Development Bank but work had not yet begun in 2001.

National Partnership Enterprises Ltd (NPE)
Halfdie, Banjul
The Gambia
Tel: +220 228771
Fax: +220 227956
Email: npe@gamtel.gm
Contact person: Mr Ousman B. Conateh

Guinea

Distribution internationale des produits agricoles de Guinée (DIPAG)

Labil Oliva Bama was awarded a FF 50,000 prize for the best project for a new entreprise (the future DIPAG) when he studied at the Marseilles Institut de développement, a centre specializing in supporting African students in France who want to set up their own business. The prize helped Mr Bama – a graduate in agronomy from the Université de Conakry and the Montpellier Tropical Agriculture Centre – to set up DIPAG in 1987. During his training in Marseilles, he had made contact with French importers and drew up a plan to supply them with tropical fruits and vegetables targeted particularly at African expatriates living in France. By 1990 Mr Bama was also supplying the United States (particularly New York), Morocco, Ukraine and Senegal.

One key to success has been the quality of the products, embodied in the slogan 'Natural Products, Naturally Good', and energetically marketed as such.

DIPAG has launched a series of brands, ranging from Solea for African food products, Bamia for tropical honey, Sarma for tropical herbal teas, and Gerto for fruit juices. Exporting 100 tons in 2000, up from 75 tons of fresh produce in 1997, DIPAG has 70 part-time workers and five permanent staff. Financing has been a major problem: French importers were willing to give DIPAG a revolving credit line for its exports if a local bank would put up a guarantee. No local institution was willing to back an agricultural project, and DIPAG could not go ahead with its export expansion.

> Distribution internationale des produits agricoles de Guinée (DIPAG)
> BP 4310, Conakry, Guinea
> Tel: +224 12 679475
> Fax: +224 413990
> Contact person: Mr Labil Oliva Bama

Nabekam Bio

See box 7, chapter 2.

> Nabekam Bio
> BP 2769, Quartier Almamya, Commune de Kaloum
> Conakry, Guinea
> Tel: +224 451990
> Mobile tel: +224 112 12113
> Fax: +224 430714
> Email: nabekam.bio@mirinet.net.gn
> Contact person: Mr Ismaêl N'falla Nabe, President

Haiti

Barbancourt SA

Barbancourt SA is the oldest distiller of rhum in Haiti. Started in 1862, it has 250 employees. It buys its sugar cane from more than 200 small planters on the Plaine du Cul-de-Sac near the capital Port-au-Prince. Producing practically the only Haitian rum that has a good name on the local as well as the international market, the company aimed for quality from the start. The founder Mr Barbancourt Dupré would not accept the cane products used to manufacture the local rhum and dealt only with suppliers who could provide him with the best quality. The rum has to age 4-15 years, so producers are conservative about increasing production unless there is a secure market for the final product.

Employees make their career in the company, serving an average of 10 years. Departures are rare. Barbancourt offers a pension plan as an essential element in keeping personnel.

At first selling mainly to the United States, it turned in the 1970s to Canada and to Europe.

The company faces tax disadvantages – the cane by-product used for cheap local rum is not dutiable while rum is taxed as a luxury item. It is also an international business, despite the importance of local sourcing for its raw material: the bottles are imported from Guatemala, Costa Rica and Italy. The seals come from Argentina, the labels from Germany and France. But the firm has never received any support from public authorities or from organizations, private or international. It receives no export incentives and access to credit is limited. Interest rates on loans for agricultural production are not an incentive. Nevertheless, the firm's Managing Director Thierry Gardère thinks that improvements in the country's infrastructure would have a positive impact on the cost of operations at all levels.

Barbancourt SA
#16 rue Bonne Foi
Port-au-Prince, Haiti
Tel: +509 5107110
Internet: *www.barbancourt.com*
Contact person: Mr Thierry Gardère

Frager

See box 5, chapter 2.

JMB Export SA

Created in 1983 by biologist Jean-Maurice Buteau, JMB is now the major exporter of Haitian mangoes. With its own distribution chain in Miami, Florida, it is an international business worth US$ 20 million-US$ 24 million a year. Within four years of its establishment, JMB became the first Haitian enterprise to meet United States phytosanitary standards, thanks to its pre-clearance programme which uses a system of washing mangoes with warm water instead of a carcinogenic gas. Based in the main mango-growing region of Plaine du Cul-de-Sac, JMB has emphasized quality for a product without defined standards (which increases the risk factor for suppliers). Processing has to take no longer than three days for the mangoes to be fresh. JMB put itself on the international market by attending trade fairs, targeting distributors to large hotels, restaurants and supermarkets as well as Haitians abroad. Mr Buteau also believes that good working conditions form a key factor in productivity and rotates personnel to keep up motivation.

JMB Export SA
Route nationale #1, Impasse Cazeau
Port-au-Prince, Haiti
Tel: +509 2505385/2505995
Contact person: Mr Jean-Maurice Buteau

Madagascar

ID Art Mony

ID Art Mony, created in 1991, produces household linens and embroidery. Today it employs 60 full-time workers. Obtaining its raw material from a Malagasy company, it exports mainly to France and Switzerland. It sees Canada and the United States as possible markets. It sells to wholesalers who pass on the articles to specialized retailers. Business has been expanding steadily, reaching French francs 275,000 in 2000 and a profit margin of 15%.

Madagascar's textile industry has become very attractive to foreign buyers in the past 15 years, particularly in competition with Mauritius. ID Art Mony is small, but it has been able to hold its own and prosper because of its attention to quality. It was created by Mme Claudine Randriambololona Rabenja, who trained in France as a hairdresser in 1972, then returned to set up her own business in Antananarivo. Largely because of the economic situation, hairdressing was not profitable. She had learned embroidery from her mother. So she shut down the hairdressing salon and turned to clothing manufacture. From 1991-1992 she helped teach embroidery and clothing manufacture in a training centre for young mothers who needed a skill to get employment. She became president of the embroidery crafts trade union Syndicat des métiers d'arts (SYMA), then took management training courses in Rotterdam and at home. After four years in business, Mme Randriambololona Rabenja decided to go into exporting when she saw how tourists enthused about Malagasy embroidery products. She had the company featured in a crafts catalogue that had wide international distribution. The EU artisan promotion project ADEVA gave her a loan in 1996 to expand her operations. However, the business also lost FF 100,000 when a client absconded with an order, and the company had to take out a loan to keep going. The size of workplace available also limits ID Art Mony's scope for expansion.

> ID Art Mony
> BP 3510, Isoraka
> 2, rue de Russie
> Antananarivo, Madagascar
> Tel/Fax: +261 (20) 2267675
> Email: smarty@dts.mg
> Contact person: Mrs Claudine Randriambololona Rabenja

Manda

See box 19, chapter 3.

> Manda
> IVM 104 MK, 67 Ha Sud
> 101 Antananarivo, Madagascar
> Tel: +261 (20) 2264329
> F: +261 (20) 2224324
> Email: manda@dts.mg
> Contact person: Mme Razakanavalona Bakoly

Ramanandraibe-Exportation Ltd

The Ramanandraibe family started their Madagascar export business in 1972, taking over the activities of a colonial enterprise exporting various food products. With a FF 100 million turnover and 350 agents around the island, Ramanandraibe-Exportation is the country's principal exporter of coffee, vanilla and essential oils, its second largest exporter of cocoa, and its third biggest exporter of cloves.

Unlike its local rivals, the company – part of the large Joseph Ramanandraibe group, founded in 1927 – made it a point to cover all of the island's productive zones with agents to buy from suppliers. This system has enabled the company to gain a reputation for quality, leading to an exclusive supply contract with the United States for Malagasy vanilla. Its membership of a respected group has eased its relations with banks.

> Ramanandraibe-Exportation Ltd
> Toamasina, 5, rue Lieutenant Hubert
> Madagascar
> Tel: +261 (20) 2222044
> Fax: +261 (20) 2234753
> Email: ramex@dts.mg
> Contact person: Mr Marcel Ramanandraibe

Malawi

Nali Limited

See box 6, chapter 2.

Packaging Industries Malawi Ltd (PIM)

See box 4, chapter 2.

Mali

Galerie Indigo

The Galerie Indigo in Bamako, Mali, is the outlet for a network of 100 craft associations, cooperatives and individuals from Côte d'Ivoire, Burkina Faso and Mali. Products selected for export include traditional textiles, Tuareg boxes, leather pouches, silver jewellery, knives, pillows, wrought iron, wood utensils and statues, and traditional jewellery from the three countries.

The Galerie's founder, Mamadou Léo Keita, was the commercial director of Mali's International Company for Trading, Marketing and Export. He had participated in a USAID programme called Entrepreneur International. At the time he was trying export gum arabic.

In 1992, when he had just started the Galerie, Mr Keita was invited with three compatriots to take part in a course in exporting craft work to the United States. This made him aware of the potential in the business. His products were so well received and sold so well that he was invited to send exhibits to an African Market Place in Los Angeles, California. That year brought him his first exports of crafts and offers of partnership. In 1999, Galerie Indigo generated CFA 33 million in revenues (of which CFA 20 million from exports), five times more than its original capital investment.

From selling only Malian products, the Galerie now also sells artefacts from Burkina Faso and Côte d'Ivoire to Latin America (Chile and Peru), Europe and the United States. It has eight full-time staff and a workshop in another part of the capital which employs six persons during periods of greatest demand.

> Galerie Indigo
> Place de l'OMVS
> BP 757, Bamako, Mali
> Tel: +223 220893
> Fax: +223 233339/339450
> Email: indigo@spider.toolnet.org

SOMAPIL

See box 14, chapter 2.

Société des produits tropicaux (SPT)

SPT, created in Bamako in 1998, is the biggest exporter of gum arabic in Mali. Though the country can produce 10,000 tons of this product, it exported only 688 tons in 1999, of which 175 tons from SPT. State control of gum arabic collection until the early 1970s and drought in the years thereafter left the industry in a disorganized state from which it has not yet recovered.

The future promoter of SPT became aware of the industry's potential while still at school. He started collecting gum arabic at markets in his home town of Ségou to sell to big traders in Bamako. One of these took him into the business. The trader then went bust, but not before introducing the promoter to a French buyer who gave him his first independent order. France remains SPT's major client.

In 2000 the entrepreneur added to his storage facilities and expected to export 255 tons yearly in 2000-2001, an increase of 31.4% on 1998 and 1999. He attributes his success to care in keeping up quality levels (which had led to the problems of his Mali partner). He also plans to create a processing plant in Bamako with European partners to increase the product's value added.

Société des produits tropicaux (SPT)
BP 1546, Bamako, Mali
Tel: +223 210120
Mobil tel: +223 777086
Fax: +223 210120
Contact person: Mr Mamadou Gueye

Mauritania

MIP-FRIGO

MIP-FRIGO is unique in Africa – a company specializing in exporting vacuum-packed, computer-controlled fish dinners using the local catch and meeting international standards of product quality and hygiene. Today its market is Europe (mainly France), but after one year of operation, talks with potential clients in the United States and Japan are already at an advanced stage.

The promoters put up 35% of the capital, the rest came from official loans. A French assistance agency is helping finance training and technology transfer. Established on 28 November 1999, MIP-FRIGO found a partner in a French group which owns a large restaurant chain covering all of France. It installed high-tech equipment (all operated by Mauritanians) capable of handling 5,800 tons of fish a year, equivalent to 6 million individual portions. It obtained the necessary recognition from the European Union that it meets EU standards. In 2000 it exported 5,000 tons of product. It employs 80 persons, including three senior executives and eight middle-level staff, and provides work for another 100.

To prevent unavoidable variations in supply from jeopardizing its ability to maintain deliveries, MIP-FRIGO has established a fishing village 70 km from the capital Nouakchott, housing 60 fishermen and running 20 boats. This fishing community supplies exclusively to the company. To encourage artisanal fishermen, MIP-FRIGO offers them contracts guaranteeing payment for the fish at market prices (25% - 35% more than the prices offered by other buyers). It provides outboard motors, nets and fuel to be given first choice of any catch.

MIP-FRIGO
BP 712, Nouakchott, Mauritania
Tel: +222 256847
Fax: +222 293849
Contact person: Mr Mohamed Abdallahi Ould Yaha

Tiviski

See box 9, chapter 2.

Tiviski
BP 2069, Nouakchott, Mauritania
Tel: +222 2251756
Fax: +222 2257192
Contact person: Mrs Nancy Abeiderrahmane

Mozambique

Magin Confecções Lda

See box 10, chapter 2.

> Magin Confecções Lda
> Av. Karl Marx No. 1744/52
> PO Box 2554
> Maputo, Mozambique
> Tel: +258 (1) 422421/303694
> Fax: +258 (1) 421469
> Email: magin@virconn.com

Nepal

Formation Carpets

See box 8, chapter 2.

> Formation Carpets
> GPO Box 3459
> Kathmandu, Nepal
> Tel: +977 (1) 538273
> Fax: +977 (1) 538473
> Email: formation@lotusholdings.com.np; sulo@fc.wlink.com.np
> Internet: *www.formationcarpets.com*

Lotus Holdings Pvt. Ltd

See box 38, chapter 4.

> Lotus Holdings Pvt. Ltd
> GPO Box 3459
> Lalitpur, Nepal
> Tel: +977 (1) 538273/530313
> Fax: +977 (1) 532013
> Email: info@lotusholdings.com.np
> Internet: *www.lotusholdings.com*

Around the World Services P. Ltd (AWS)

See box 14, chapter 2.

> Around the World Services P. Ltd (AWS)
> GPO 8975 EPC 7260
> Kathmandu, Nepal
> Tel: +977 (1) 272080/272348
> Fax: +977 (1) 278266
> Email: aws@around.wlink.com.np
> Contact person: Dan B. Tamang, Managing Director

Samoa

Hellaby Samoa Ltd

Despite its European origins, corned beef (*pisupo* as it is more commonly known in Samoa) has become an integral part of Samoan life. In family gatherings, *pisupo* is a must on the menu, and boxes of the corned beef are a common gift.

Hellaby was established in 1983 as a joint venture between Hellaby New Zealand, the Government of Samoa and a number of local private investors. Its main activity was to produce corned beef. Other than the local butchers, it is the country's sole producer of this product. All raw materials other than labels are imported from New Zealand. Hellaby New Zealand sold out to local shareholders in 1986, by which time the company had expanded to other meat products.

Today the company has gone back to its core product and the Samoan Government has approved the sale of its 9% shareholding as part of its privatization strategy. Hellaby exports 10% its output, mainly to the Cook Islands and recently to Tonga. It has also accessed a new market in Wallis and Futuna. Hellaby received Samoa's first Exporter of the Year Award and Manufacturer of the Year Award in the new millennium.

Hellaby ascribes part of its success to its focus on quality. The locals consider its product to be of better quality than the cheaper imports. Hellaby has obtained technical assistance from the Samoan Centre for the Development of Enterprises to improve quality control procedures and set up a testing laboratory.

> Hellaby Samoa Ltd
> Contact person: Mr Konrad von Reiche

Nonu Samoa Enterprises Ltd

See: box 32, chapter 3.

> Nonu Samoa Enterprises Ltd
> PO Box 1099 Apia, Samoa
> Tel/Fax: +685 23010
> Contact persons: George and Tia Tinielu

Women in Business Foundation

See box 37, chapter 4.

> Women in Business Foundation
> Contact person: Mrs Adimaimalaga Tafunai

Togo

Petit Prince

Finding a niche market, shortening the distribution chain, concentrating on value-added, overcoming commercial barriers – Petit Prince, a Togo handicrafts producer, has used all these to carve out a position in international trade. But its success has also depended on the dynamism and creativity of the director of the family business, Nadim Michel Kalife, Dean of the Faculty of Economic Sciences and Business at the University of Bénin. 'I wanted to translate economic theory into practice,' he says.

Kalife's father established Petit Prince in 1929 as an importer of luxury articles to be sold as birthday and New Year's day presents. When Kalife took over the family business as a young man in 1983, he decided to find local substitutes for these items. To widen its market, the business participates in two annual professional shows in France and distributes a catalogue of its products. This publicity effort costs Petit Prince at least US$ 20,000 a year. But Kalife reckons that at least 2% - 3% of the company's contacts with visitors result in a sale.

Today Petit Prince estimates its export trade at CFAF 50 million - CFAF 80 million (US$ 70,000 - US$ 114,000) a year, peaking at US$ 150,000 in 1999 after a big dip in 1998. Kalife says that his export business has created up to 100 jobs in addition to work for his suppliers.

Though Kalife reports regular attempts by French crafts workers to copy the Togo designs, the Petit Prince goods survive because their professional finish sets them apart from imitations. Kalife notes with gratitude aid from the United

Nations Industrial Development Organization in 1990 and 1992 which covered six months of training for his workers and three months of running his workshops.

> Petit Prince
> BP 22, Lomé, Togo
> Tel: +228 216905
> Fax: +228 216884

Or:

> Créations d'Art du Petit Prince (CAPP)
> 5, ave. Daniel Lesueur
> F-75007 Paris, France
> Tel: +33 (1)40560983
> Fax: +33 (1) 47344893
> Contact person: Mr Nadim-Michel Khalife

Société industrielle de coton (SICOT SA)

SICOT is the country's second biggest spinner of cotton, working in partnership with the State-run Société togolaise de coton (SOTOCO). It receives one-third of the national output of cotton, with SOTOCO taking care of the rest. It sells mainly to the Aiglon SA in Geneva, to which the company belongs, while marketing is handled by Aiglon out of Brussels. Before 1995, SICOT was concerned only with buying and selling cotton fibre. It took advantage of the liberalization of the Togolese economy to launch into exporting, at first to help SOTOCO dispose of its surplus production. Despite its links to Aiglon, however, SICOT can also sell to clients who buy directly on the Togolese market. Another company has just entered the market, competing for the cotton, but the continuing role of the State restricts the expansion of the industry: both private companies are operating under capacity.

> Société industrielle de coton (SICOT SA)
> BP 12465, Togo
> Tel: +228 304207
> Fax: +228 304214
> Contact person: Mr Anselme Gouthon

Togo métal et bois (TMB)

Togo métal et bois started as a family firm 30 years ago. Its turnover today is CFA 1,110 million. It has 110 employees, including 70 carpenters and woodworkers. It has become Togo's biggest exporter of teak furniture. Its opportunity in the export market came 10 years ago when South-east Asian teak became too high-priced to be competitive. Now that the price of Indonesian wood has plummeted, again, making Europe a tough market to retain, TMB has shown its flexibility: it has switched to the West African region, cut prices in half for local deliveries, and kept up earnings. One reason for its strong position in regional and international markets is the attention TMB gives to design and promotion. One of the company's three units is concerned solely with exhibitions and fairs. Design piracy is a continual problem, particularly because of the limited protection given to original creations, and the company is careful about the products it presents at fairs before manufacture. TMB also prides itself on its relations with its staff, pointing to the fact that it has never suffered a strike.

> Togo métal et bois
> BP 149, Lomé, Togo
> Tel: +228 210677
> Fax: +228 211196
> Contact person: Mr Boustani Eli

Uganda

Begumisa Enterprises Ltd (BEL)

Fish maws, bladders and air sacs are delicacies in Asia. In Uganda, they are traditionally considered waste. Begumisa Enterprises, established by George Begumisa and three friends, has transformed them into a US$ 4.6 million business.

'When the company started in 1987, only the vultures were our competitors,' Mr Begumisa recalls. It began as an importer of items such as fishnets, but frustration with the bureaucracy and taxation policies led the company to turn to exporting. Mr Begumisa noted that fish parts, the waste by-products of fish-processing companies which started operations in the 1990s, were polluting the lakes; he had heard that these parts were considered delicacies by some Asians. He determined to try to export them. The first trial sales to the United Kingdom and Hong Kong (China) were rejected for low quality, but on the third trial he succeeded in showing that the company could supply products of the right quality.

The company now has 300 staff and another 300 associates, selling mainly to China but also to Malaysia, Singapore, Taiwan Province (China) and the United Kingdom. It has received an award from the Ugandan President as best exporter of the year. It prides itself on the working environment and the facilities it offers employees. BEL acknowledges the help it has received from the Government in the form of investment incentives. It has also benefited from training, assistance in participation in trade fairs and exhibitions, and market information from the Uganda Export Promotion Board. It plans to take part in the country's Export Credit Guarantee Scheme. BEL says it has also profited from membership of the Uganda Manufacturers Association, the Uganda Chamber of Commerce and Industry, and the Uganda Fish Processors and Exporters Association, whose members supply it with fish parts.

> Begumisa Enterprises Ltd
> P.O. Box 10702
> Kampala, Uganda
> Tel: +256 (41) 254984
> Fax: +256 (41) 233829
> Email: begumisa@infocom.co.ug
> Contact person: Mr. George Begumisa

Greenfields (U) Ltd

See box 11, chapter 2.

> Greenfields (U) Ltd
> P.O. Box 1931
> Kampala, Uganda
> Tel: +256 (41) 321141
> Fax: +256 (41) 231856
> Email: gullo@calva.com
> Contact person: Mr Philip Borel

Mairye Estates Ltd

See box 28, chapter 3.

United Republic of Tanzania

Afro-Cooling Systems Ltd

See box 14, chapter 2.

> Afro Cooling Systems Ltd
> PO Box 901, Mandela Express Way
> Tabata, Dar es Salaam
> United Republic of Tanzania
> Tel: +255 (22) 2400393, +255 (22) 2400128
> Fax: +255 (22) 2443351, +255 (22) 2400322
> Email: comafric@aml.udsm.ac.tz
> Internet: *www.comafric.com*
> Contact person: Mr Ramesh Patel

Arusha Cuttings Ltd

Within three years, Arusha Cuttings increased its sales from TSh 200,000 to TSh 860,000. It is now a well-established supplier of chrysanthemum cuttings to the Netherlands, working with one customer in that country. Co-director Tjerk Scheltema from the Netherlands had been working in the horticulture industry, producing flower seeds in West Kilimanjaro. He noticed that flower production was moving from Europe to equatorial regions where production could take place most, if not all, of the year. He identified the Arusha climate as more favourable than the climate in some parts of Kenya and Uganda where production had already started. He therefore felt confident about the potential of the Arusha venture.

Nevertheless, Arusha Cuttings faced a number of difficulties. Skilled labour was in short supply, and the company needed to put in enormous effort into staff selection and training. Responding to the need for strict management control, the company introduced management-by-audit techniques. As the use of agro-chemicals is strictly controlled, the company spent time in finding the right chemicals and winning over the authorities to their use. The shortage of air freight facilities at Kilimanjaro Airport led it to export by truck to Nairobi. It has had to struggle with administrative repayment and energy problems.

Mother plants for Arusha originate from the Chrysanthemum Breeding Association, a company in the Netherlands which specializes in producing new varieties. They arrive in the United Republic of Tanzania as cuttings or in-vitro plants. Cuttings are picked daily and exported three times a week. A specialized team of quality controllers judge the leaf area, thickness of the stem and weight of the cutting. The system reflects Mr Scheltema's experience with quality control and his organizational skills.

> Arusha Cuttings Ltd
> Njiro Industrial Area, Plot 51-54
> Arusha, United Republic of Tanzania
> Tel: +255 (27) 501990
> Email: tjerk@arushacutting.com
> Contact person: Mr Tjerk Scheltema

Glitter Gems Ltd

See box 3, chapter 2.

> Glitter Gems Ltd
> PO Box 253, Arusha
> United Republic of Tanzania
> Tel: +255 (27) 2548830/1, +255 (27) 2548560

Fax: +255 (27) 2548239/8948
Email: glitter@raha.com
Contact person: Mr Abdulhakim Mula

MIKONO/Handicraft Marketing Company, Ltd

Unlike most of its competitors, Handicraft Marketing Company (MIKONO, meaning hands) seeks primarily to generate income for marginalized artisans. The successor to the Tanzania Handicraft Marketing Corporation (HANDICO), it was created in 1997 under the Government's privatization programme.

The change in management and the introduction of a professional approach to business under general manager Deo Kafwa, who had 15 years of experience in handicraft marketing, enabled MIKONO to re-establish itself in the export market. Mr Kafwa recommended the change of name because HANDICO had become associated with delayed or unfulfilled orders, poor quality, bad design and poor response to inquiries. Company products were positioned as cultural items or given functional values, for example as salad bowls. Management engaged in market research, took part in trade fairs, joined the International Federation for Alternative Trade, which supplies marketing information, and became a member of a fair trade organization in the Netherlands. With UNDP sponsorship, the company obtained support from the Board of External Trade to undertake a market survey in the United States. From US$ 10,000 in 1997, exports have grown to US$ 100,000 in 2000 and were expected to rise by another 50% in 2001.

During the first three years of its existence, MIKONO purchased artisanal products from 400 groups, giving employment to 8,000 artisans. It developed a website to speed up communication with overseas centres and started a systematic staff training scheme. It has re-established its old outlets in Europe, Japan and the United States and has secured new markets in Australia, Belgium, France, Germany, Italy, the Netherlands and the United Kingdom. In March 2001 MIKONO opened a gallery in the city centre to display its artisanal products and credit the artisans and their groups.

MIKONO/Handicraft Marketing Company, Ltd
PO Box 9363
Changombe/Nyerere Rd., Dar es Salaam
United Republic of Tanzania
Tel: +255 (51) 2863011
Fax: +255 (51) 114261
Email: mikono@africaonline.co.tz; amka-tz@maf.org
Internet: *www.peoplink.org/mikono*
Contact person: Mr Deo Kafwa

Zambia

Cheetah Paprika

See: box 29, chapter 3.

Cheetah Paprika
10101 Lusaka, Zambia
Tel: +260-(1)-287 661
Fax: +260-(1)-286 665
Email: cheetah@zamnet.zm
Contact person: Mr Mark Terken

Terra Nova Farm

Long-term finance from the World Bank and funds for supplies and technical expertise from a European Union project enabled Terra Nova Farm in the Mazabuka District of Zambia's Southern Province to switch in 12 years from being an exclusive supplier to the domestic market to an exporter of the bulk of its output. Today it exports 560 tons of coffee.

Terra Nova, the family-owned business of Joseph Taguma, originally produced Irish potatoes, maize and wheat. The difficult economic situation of the 1980s gave little hope for traditional farming. The switch to flowers and vegetables, the company's first venture into export crops, did not have a long-term foundation for survival: these were notoriously difficult to grow and the export trade depended heavily on efficient (and expensive) air cargo facilities. Coffee seemed an attractive option, but it requires substantial investment (with irrigation a must, given Zambia's single rainy season), takes at least three years to earn revenues, and the international market is subject to considerable price swings.

However, the Zambian Coffee Growers Association (ZCGA) offered the support of an industry infrastructure, and World Bank and EU finance were available under a development initiative. 'The provision of long-term finance enabled the plantation to be established, but it was the timely provision of inputs and regularly available expert advice that ensured its success,' Terra Nova reports. The Terra Nova management and ZCGA staff also benefited from ITC-sponsored seminars on marketing and risk management, and in-service training stints abroad in coffee-producing and consuming countries.

> Terra Nova Farm
> Mazabuka District, Zambia
> Tel: +260 (1) 286447
> Fax: +260 (1) 287654
> Email: zcga@zamnet.zm
> Contact person: Mr Joseph Taguma

Appendix II

Business Sector Round Table

Converting LDC Export Opportunities into Business: A Strategic Response
Brussels, 16 May 2001

Programme

13.00 – 14.00   Registration

INAUGURAL SESSION

14.00 – 14.20   Welcome statement: Jean-Denis Bélisle, Executive Director, ITC

Opening statements

Rubens Ricupero, Secretary-General, UNCTAD
Ablasse Ouedraogo, Deputy Director-General, WTO
Jorgen Estrup, Chief Economist and Special Adviser to the Director-General, UNIDO

SESSION 1: PRODUCTS AND MARKETS FOR LDC EXPORTS: OPPORTUNITIES AND SUCCESS STORIES

14.20 – 16.00

Moderator: Mpho Malie, Minister for Trade, Marketing and Industry, Lesotho

Products and markets for LDC exports: Opportunities and success stories

Speaker: Friedrich von Kirchbach, Chief, Market Analysis Section, Division of Product and Market Development, International Trade Centre

Converting export opportunities into business: Issue-based presentations by entrepreneurs from LDCs

Animator: Peter Walters, Director, Division of Product and Market Development, International Trade Centre

Issue 1: Moving up the value chain

Speakers: Monica Khoromana, Managing Director, Nali Ltd
Pierre Léger, Directeur-Gérant, Frager, Haiti

Issue 2: Niche marketing and product innovation

Speaker: Ismaêl N'falla Nabe, Co-proprietaire, Nabekam Bio, Guinea

Issue 3: The services revolution

> Speaker: Nim Gyaltshen, Managing Director, Etho Metho Tours
>   & Treks Ltd, Bhutan

Issue 4: Moving from comparative to competitive advantage

> Speakers: Eskinder Joseph, Managing Director, Meskel Flowers, Inc., Ethiopia
>   Esmail Hassan Dassat, Managing Director, Magin Confecções Lda,
>   Mozambique
>   Mark Terken, Managing Director, Cheetah Paprika, Zambia

Issue 5: Overcoming technical and other barriers

> Speakers: Georges B. Mwase, Operations Manager, Greenfields Ltd, Uganda
>   Nancy Abeiderrahmane, Directrice générale, Tiviski, Mauritania

16.00 – 16.10

Overview of success factors and constraints for export development in LDCs: The young entrepreneur perspective

> Speaker: Sujit Chowdhury, Secretary-General, 8th World Summit
>   of Young Entrepreneurs and Executive Director, Institute for
>   Leadership Development

16.10 – 16.50   Discussions

16.50 – 17.10   Coffee break

SESSION 2: CREATING AN ENABLING ENVIRONMENT FOR EXPORT COMPETITIVENESS IN LDCs

17.10 – 19.00

> Moderator: Musa Sillah, Minister for Trade, Industry and Employment,
>   Gambia

Introduction to enabling environment: Policies, strategies and mainstreaming; Integrated Framework for Trade-Related Technical Assistance to Least Developed Countries

> Speaker/Moderator: Musa Sillah

Trade strategy formulation and mainstreaming in Guinea

> Speaker: Mamadou Saliou Sow, Conseiller du Ministre Coordonnateur
>   National du PCSDSP (Programme Cadre pour le Soutien et
>   le Développement du Secteur Privé), Ministère du Commerce,
>   de l'Industrie et des Petites et Moyennes Entreprises

Trade policies and mainstreaming trade in national poverty reduction strategy through the PRSP

> Speaker: Uri Dadush, Director, Economic Policy and Development
>   Prospects Group, World Bank

Foundations for a shared vision: Process, partnership and essential elements for trade sector strategy formulation and implementation in Cambodia

>Speaker: Sok Siphana, Secretary of State, Ministry of Commerce, Cambodia

Trade strategy formulation: The private sector perspective

>Speaker: Adrien Sibomana, Président, GEXHOBU, Burundi.

Introduction to enabling environment: Trade support services and business partnering

>Speaker/Moderator: Musa Sillah

The importance of quality and standards for the export competitiveness of LDCs

>Speaker: Shyam Kumar Gujadhur, Senior Adviser on Export Quality Management, Division of Trade Support Services, International Trade Centre

Export finance mechanisms for LDCs

>Speaker: Andrew Singer, International Consultant on Trade Finance, International Trade Centre

Business partnering: The Netherlands Programme for Cooperation with Emerging Markets (PSOM)

>Speakers: Bas C.M. Pulles, Manager, Emerging Markets, Senter International
>Andr Dellevoet, Senior Adviser, PSOM and Africa Coordinator, Senter International

Business partnering: The Case of Lotus Holdings, Nepal

>Speaker: Rajiv Pradhan, Chief Executive Officer, Lotus Holdings

19.00 – 19.45 Discussion

19.45 – 20.00 **CONCLUSIONS AND CLOSING REMARKS**

>J.D. Bélisle, Executive Director, International Trade Centre
>M.V. Dagata, Director, Division of Technical Cooperation Coordination, International Trade Centre

Concluding statement

Mr Bélisle, in opening this Round Table, asked us to focus on three questions.

He asked what realistic export opportunities there were for LDCs and laid out an analytical framework for identifying opportunities. Perhaps the most important conclusion is that many of these new export opportunities have little to do with the past. They concern niche marketing of organic, fresh and dried fruits and vegetables for European customers, and fresh cut flowers for the French and German markets; moving up the export value chain with vacuum-packed fish dinners for the European market and garments from Mozambique to South Africa; surmounting technical barriers to the export of fish from Uganda to Europe.

It has been said that we may be seeing a new generation of LDC exporter and the beginnings of the rebuilding of the export base in several LDCs. This generation is characterized by: first, a new vision and the entrepreneurial daring to venture into new fields; second, a commitment to social goals and a desire to establish links with the rest of the economy to create employment; third, a belief in the workers, attention being given to building their skills and sharing the fruits of success with them; fourth, a long-term commitment and dedication to the business, motivated by a desire to make it sustainable rather than a search for short-term profit; and fifth, a resolve to trade in quality products that customers really want.

The analytical framework in which the presentations in the Round Table were made can be considered useful and ITC will work to improve it. While export opportunities can be identified systematically, most would conclude that nothing can replace the entrepreneur with the vision to see the opportunity and the capacity to convert it into business.

Secondly, Mr Bélisle asked how successful exporters could become less the exception and more the rule in LDCs. This was discussed at length during Session Two. The key is largely, though not exclusively, in the exporting LDC itself. There is an evolving consensus on the nature of a national enabling environment, on what it takes to produce successful exporters. The new generation of exporters we have seen here today is evidence that changes are under way in many LDCs and are taking root. The Uganda reform effort was given as an example. Exporters have also told us that a great deal has been done and that much more needs to be done in improving governance and reforming policies. For example, heavy import taxes on processing machinery are still prevalent in some countries. Our Chairman added that hard infrastructure, i.e. roads, airports, seaports, energy, telecommunications, needed urgent attention. Trade finance, trade information, quality management and other business services and trade facilitation (including customs inspection and clearance) all require continued attention. Other speakers agreed. We are confident that a critical mass of change based on what we have seen today will produce successful LDC exporters, the new rule, no longer the exception.

Mr Bélisle's final question was how exports could make the difference in reducing poverty. We have seen how 30,000 contract farmers in Zambia are raising their incomes and skills while supplying the paprika market. Likewise, hundreds of farmers in Guinea are exporting organic fruits and vegetables, thousands of farmers in Haiti are producing vetiver for the perfume market, and artisans in several product areas are learning to upgrade their products for export markets. To make this happen generally, policies must promote broad-based, export-led growth. Pro-poor strategies are needed which link sectors, and allocate resources for sectoral export plans as well as for sustainable export-led poverty reduction programmes. We have heard about the experience of various countries (Guinea, Burundi and Cambodia, to mention a few) with strategies and particularly with the mainstreaming of trade. The World Bank described how trade strategies should be integrated into PRSPs. A public-private sector partnership is needed with exporters-entrepreneurs at the centre, driving the process.

Advance copy

A

**UNITED
NATIONS**

General Assembly

Distr.
LIMITED

A/CONF.191/L.9
17 May 2001

Original: ENGLISH

Third United Nations Conference on the
  Least Developed Countries
Brussels, Belgium, 14-20 May 2001

Parallel event

BUSINESS SECTOR ROUND TABLE

**CONVERTING LDC EXPORT OPPORTUNITIES INTO BUSINESS:
A STRATEGIC RESPONSE**

Summary prepared by the Conference secretariat

1. The Business Sector Round Table, held on 16 May 2001, was organized by the International Trade Centre (ITC). It centred on the positive theme of identifying ways to enhance the role of exports in a development and poverty reduction strategy. More than 50 per cent of the participants were from the LDC private sector. The Round Table was an effort to identify appropriate policies from success stories at both the firm and the national level so that other firms and other countries can replicate them.

Products and markets for LDC exports: opportunities and success stories

2. In discussing the opportunities and success stories in exports from LDCs, it was emphasized that, although global trends appear negative, there is reason for optimism. For example, in spite of the long-term decrease in the share of LDCs' non-petroleum exports in world trade, there have been significant increases in the export of manufactures for some countries. For LDCs as a whole, including oil producers, exports cover up to 80 per cent of imports. Intra-regional trade in Africa is also increasing, especially in SADC. Also, several LDCs derive more than half of their export earnings from services. In spite of the generally low competitiveness of LDCs, there are a large number of cases of highly competitive industries, built up by successful entrepreneurs.

3. A framework for identifying opportunities was developed which profiled five themes: (i) moving up the value chain; (ii) niche marketing; (iii) converting comparative into competitive advantage; (iv) the services revolution; and (v) overcoming technical and structural barriers. The key factor in identifying market opportunities and converting them into business is the vision and entrepreneurial drive of individual exporters. What the framework allows policy makers and businesses to do is to take a strategic approach that helps them identify target markets and ways to build strong and sustainable market positions.

4. Several sectors were identified as presenting potentially high export opportunities. Those sectors include cotton and cotton fabric, tourism and other services, fish industry, coffee, wood and wooden products, oil seeds, vegetables, fruits, nuts, spices, cut flowers and medicinal plants. Other areas of interest include leather products, handicrafts, back office services, and software.

5. While each business succeeds for unique reasons, there are common factors that contribute to their success. Many businesses have little to do with the past focus on selling commodities. They deal with niche products for niche markets, moving up the value chain through processing and design, responding to the ever-rising demand from consumers for higher quality standards, entering brand new markets like services, or shortening the distribution chain to capture a greater share of the value. Examples of this include niche marketing of: organic fruits and vegetables from Guinea for the European market; paprika powder from Zambia for the North American market; hot-sauce exports from Malawi to South Africa; essential oils from Haiti for the growing global cosmetics industry; garments from Mozambique for the South African market; fresh-cut flowers from Ethiopia for the German and French markets; gourmet fish dinners from Mauritania for sophisticated world markets; culturally sensitive tourism services from Bhutan to visitors from all over the world; and Internet video streaming software technology from Nepal for North American customers.

6. The presentation of success stories by entrepreneurs from LDCs highlighted the following as critical factors for building such competitive advantage:

- Increasing the range of products and identifying market demands;

- Putting the emphasis on the quality of the product, and exercising strong control on the trackability of products, especially on the quality of food-products;

- Introducing the use of new technologies;

- Promoting involvement and loyalty of staff, as well as integration into the life of the local community;

- Building cooperation with suppliers, providing them with necessary inputs, training, and access to better technologies;

- Pursuing integration with clients, in order to obtain necessary pre-financing, technologies or packaging;

- Reducing the number of middlemen.

7. Conditions that contribute positively to the overall business-operating framework included:

- Political stability and security;

- A favourable legal framework,

- Foreign technical assistance.

8. The success stories are all the more remarkable in that they often happened in adverse conditions. The panelists identified the following bottlenecks:

- Lack of necessary capital to finance investments;

- Lack of information on possible opportunities in terms of external assistance, markets, technologies, and market access conditions;

- Barriers to entry, such as technical barriers to trade;

- Lack of necessary infrastructures in terms of transport, telecommunications, etc.;

- Weak national administrations.

Creating an enabling environment for export competitiveness in LDCs

9. Export success depends critically on an enabling environment across the micro- meso- and macro-levels. In spite of highlighted success stories and the new market opportunities that have been created, there are still many constraints facing export entrepreneurs in LDCs. Three principal cornerstones for an effective enabling environment for fostering rapid development of competitive export firms in LDCs are required to overcome them:

- An effective macro-policy framework, including macroeconomic stability and stable and competitive exchange rate regimes, positive trade policy and market access conditions;

- An effective infrastructure of trade support services that encompass both "hard" infrastructures like roads, airports, telecommunications, electrical power, or water resources and "soft" infrastructures like trade finance services, trade information and trade promotion services, export quality management services, trade facilitation services and investment promotion services;

- An effective entrepreneurship and investment climate in the export business sector.

10. LDCs have limited financial, human and institutional resources. They therefore need to focus their efforts and prioritize their actions if they are to succeed. This could include targeting key sectors for export development, but not necessarily "picking winners". It is better to identify sectors where there are already clear winners and focus efforts and priorities to allow current winning businesses, as well as new ones, to expand, grow, and multiply rapidly in those sectors. The sectors should also include labour-intensive and rural-based activities, since the vast majority of the poor live in rural areas. Policies should also be implemented to ensure that exports raise the value added created by the poor and hence raise their income. This can be done in a number of ways. For example, production can be shifted from subsistence farming to non- traditional export crops that fetch far better prices on the market.

11. Countries have made great strides in improving the macro environment for business. Taxes that used to discourage exports have been reduced, if not eliminated altogether. Inflation has been brought under control, and overvalued exchange rates are mostly gone. So investment returns are becoming more predictable and exports made easier. Investment frameworks have become much more understanding of the needs of businesses and exporters. However, more remains to be done, including often on the legal and good governance front. Enforcement of the rule of law, including enforcement of contracts and elimination of corruption, often remain problem areas for business.

12. Export success at the firm level may not always translate into a reduction of poverty. In order for that to happen, a country must have a vision as to how trade policy fits into coherent development and poverty reduction.

13. One international effort to achieve this involves the Integrated Framework for Trade-Related Assistance. Through this programme trade policies will be mainstreamed into poverty reduction strategies. However, in order for these policies to be effective, trade must be seen in relation to other priorities, such as education, health and governance. Trade should not be overemphasized, but it should not be ignored.

14. If trade is going to have a substantial impact on poverty reduction, trade development strategies must be mainstreamed through national development agendas, particularly poverty reduction strategy papers. There is a need for poverty reduction strategies to encompass trade and for trade development strategies to prioritize sectors that will impact poverty. Successful examples include Zambia, where 30,000 contract farmers are producing paprika, Haiti, where 27,000 families are growing vetiver (an ingredient for essential oil), and Nepal, where there are hundreds of home carpet and pashmina weavers.

15. The enabling environment should also focus on firm-level initiatives that are vitally important for export success. The Round Table discussed three such issues: management of export quality, trade finance and business partnering. In the area of product quality, LDC exporters must strive to meet not only the market requirements for their products, but also the technical requirements to access these markets. However, even if appropriate markets have been targeted and a product development plan is established, many LDC exporters have a difficult time accessing trade finance to ensure that their products finally enter the market. Another problem is that in many cases LDC exporters require a business partner in the importing country. However, due to their small size, it is difficult for them to incur the expense of identifying appropriate partners.

16. The overriding theme of the Round Table was that exports can play an important role in poverty reduction. However, in order for this to be an effective strategy there must be strong private and public sector linkages.

- - - - -